Citizenship Regimes, Law, and Belonging

Citizenship Regimes, Law, and Belonging

The CAA and the NRC

ANUPAMA ROY

Great Clarendon Street, Oxford, OX2 6DP,
United Kingdom

Oxford University Press is a department of the University of Oxford.
It furthers the University's objective of excellence in research, scholarship,
and education by publishing worldwide. Oxford is a registered trade mark of
Oxford University Press in the UK and in certain other countries

© Oxford University Press 2022

The moral rights of the author have been asserted

First Edition published in 2022

All rights reserved. No part of this publication may be reproduced, stored in
a retrieval system, or transmitted, in any form or by any means, without the
prior permission in writing of Oxford University Press, or as expressly permitted
by law, by licence or under terms agreed with the appropriate reprographics
rights organization. Enquiries concerning reproduction outside the scope of the
above should be sent to the Rights Department, Oxford University Press, at the
address above

You must not circulate this work in any other form
and you must impose this same condition on any acquirer

Published in the United States of America by Oxford University Press
198 Madison Avenue, New York, NY 10016, United States of America

British Library Cataloguing in Publication Data

Data available

Library of Congress Control Number: 2022931364

ISBN 978–0–19–285908–2

DOI: 10.1093/oso/9780192859082.001.0001

Links to third party websites are provided by Oxford in good faith and
for information only. Oxford disclaims any responsibility for the materials
contained in any third party website referenced in this work.

Acknowledgements

All books are outcomes of not only the efforts of the author but a host of people who contribute in different ways to make their writing possible. In writing this book and preparing it for publication, I was supported by friends, family, colleagues, and institutions. I am grateful to all of them for being with me in this journey and making me believe that it was worthwhile. My engagement with citizenship debates, especially in India, has been an enduring one. The ever-changing and contested field that citizenship represents has kept me vigilant—especially towards the ramifications of these changes in the lives of people and for Indian democracy. I am indebted to those who helped me with my research on the NRC in Assam, especially to Akhil Ranjan Datta for our conversations on the NRC, and to Banasmita Bora for helping me negotiate the field in Guwahati. My fieldwork in Cooch Behar was made possible by Abdul Matin and Shreya Ghosh. Shreya accompanied me into the field, helping me understand the conversations which were in most cases in Bangla, and transcribing the interviews. I also acknowledge the field visit grant under the UPOE-II scheme of Jawaharlal Nehru University, which funded the research.

I presented my research in universities, colleges, and other independent forums and received important feedback for which I am deeply thankful. The Political Science Department of Gauhati University, the Kerala Council for Historical Research (KCHR), Trivandrum, the Department of Political Science, NEHU, the Krantijyoti Savitribai Phule Women's Studies Centre of Savitribai Phule University, Pune, the Department of Political Science, Lady Sri Ram College, University of Delhi, the Jamia Teachers Association, Jamia Millia Islamia, the School of Law, Governance, and Citizenship, Ambedkar University Delhi, the Institute of Political and Sociological Studies, in Julius Maximillian University of Wurzburg, Germany, the College Students Welfare Committee and the Centre for South East Asian Studies, Gauhati University which hosted the Golap Borbora annual lecture, the Department of Political Science,

Sikkim Central University and Rajeev Gandhi National Institute for Youth and Development, in Gangtok, Sikkim, Deshbandhu College, Delhi University, Kirori Mal College, Delhi University, the Department of Humanities and Social Sciences, IIT Madras, the Department of Political Science, Himachal Pradesh University, Department of Political Science, Ramanujan College, Parivartan—the Gender Forum at Kirori Mal College, the Department of Humanities and Social Sciences, IIT Guwahati, and the Centre for Law and Humanities, O. P. Jindal University, Sonipat—hosted my seminars and lectures—giving me the space to obtain responses from a diverse audience.

With deep affection and gratitude, I acknowledge those whose friendship has been a constant source of strength. I also remember the loss I suffered while writing this book. My mother-in-law, bedridden throughout the pandemic lockdown, passed away a month after I finalized the manuscript. I dedicate this book to her and to my mother, who left me ten years back. I also dedicate it to the enduring love of my family and most particularly to Ujjwal, Anatya, and Suchismita, and my sisters Anamika and Aparna.

Contents

	Introduction: Citizenship, Law, and Belonging	1
1.	Hyphenated Citizenship: The National Register of Citizens	33
2.	Bounded Citizenship: The Citizenship Amendment Act 2019	83
3.	Liminal Citizenship: The 'Returnees' and 'New' Citizens	163
4.	Recalling Citizenship: The Constitutional Ethic	203
	Conclusion	243
Bibliography		251
Index		261

Introduction

Citizenship, Law, and Belonging

Amidst the violence that accompanied partition, the governments of India and Pakistan, which disagreed with each other on most things, agreed to exchange their 'lunatics'. In a powerful story about how this exchange unsettled the lives of 'lunatics' living in asylums, Saadat Hasan Manto wrote of Toba Tek Singh—a 'place name' which became synonymous with a person—and eventually became a trope for forced movement across the freshly crafted borders. The refusal of Bishan Singh or Toba Tek Singh—the man who stood on his feet for fifteen years—to be transported to India, was not taken seriously by officials on the Wagah border. No one could unequivocally tell him where his village was—in India or Pakistan. He was a harmless old man and confused in mind, they thought. Bishan Singh died an anguished death in the no-man's-land between the two countries. Another inmate of the same asylum climbed atop a tree, completely clear in his mind that he did not want to live in either country. He was going to make the tree his home. Yet another inmate, a person with an engineering degree—an otherwise pensive man in the habit of taking long walks by himself—was so perturbed by the prospect of being allotted one or the other country that he took off all his clothes and shorn of all identifying accoutrements, ran into the garden.[1]

In another August, about forty-one years before Manto's Toba Tek Singh refused to be transported to a country not his home—Indians in another colony—fully conscious of the consequences of their action, refused to submit to a law that they considered immoral. The law in question—Registration Act of Transvaal 1906—required all 'Asiatics',

---

[1] There are several English translations of 'TobaTek Singh', a short story written by Saadat Hasan Manto in 1955. Among them is one available on www.sacw.net, February 1998 (accessed on 21 February 2020).

Citizenship Regimes, Law, and Belonging. Anupama Roy, Oxford University Press. © Oxford University Press 2022.
DOI: 10.1093/oso/9780192859082.003.0001

including Indians, to register before a designated registrar, submit their fingerprints, and acquire a registration certificate. This certificate was to be carried on their person all the time. Failure to do so would have consequences—a fine, imprisonment, and even deportation. The Indians in Transvaal considered it humiliating to submit to a discriminatory law that compelled them to undergo a physical examination for enumeration. In a public meeting in Johannesburg on 11 September 1906, they resolved not to comply with this law and passed what became popular as the 'jail going resolution'. Resolution IV, as the jail going resolution was called, declared that the Indians gathered in the meeting would prefer to disobey the law and go to jail, and would continue to do so till the British government withdrew the 'tyrannical' law.[2] On 1 July 1907, when the certificates were being issued, the Indians decided not to cooperate with the authorities. The few that registered felt ashamed to have capitulated, and several tore up their certificates of registration. Mohandas Karamchand Gandhi, a lawyer who would transform civil disobedience into an art, and make it an integral part of the war of positions in the struggle for national liberation in India, tried out and perfected its subtle skills and strategies in South Africa. Writing about the jail going resolution in the *Indian Opinion* as a 'game of chess', Gandhi countered a cartoon that had appeared in the newspaper *Star*. The cartoon in *Star* depicted the Registration Act of Transvaal as a chess move initiated by the 'white knight' against the 'black king', to push it into a vulnerable position. Gandhi reproduced the *Star* cartoon in the *Indian Opinion* along with his own response to it, in the form of another cartoon. In Gandhi's cartoon, a black pawn—representing the jail going resolution—was stationed strategically in a square guarding against any possible move by the white knight to checkmate the black king.[3]

Defying the commonly held belief that a 'lunatic' asylum is not a place where an action is determined by 'reason', the responses of its inhabitants in Manto's story open up powerful moments of interruption of the custodial power of the state. They also tell us, as do the dissidents in Johannesburg, of the blurred zones that exist between law's distance and

---

[2] 'Johannesburg Letter', 11 September 1907, *Collected Works of Mahatma Gandhi (CWMG)*, Vol. v, 426.
[3] 'Game of Chess', 18 May 1907, *CWMG*, Vol. vi, 483. See for a discussion, Singh (1999, 73–74).

proximity, important for understanding the relationship between legal rationality and the *force* of law. In these zones, citizenship becomes entangled with law's capacity to destabilize and recode ideas of belonging, by simultaneously *enforcing* and *masking* the power of the state to elicit obedience from citizens. It is, however, in these zones that the constituent power of the people is also expressed—in 'creative insurgencies' (Kraidy 2016) and 'dissident' (Spark 1997) and 'iterative' (Benhabib 2007) citizenship practices—that accumulate and become *critical* for unfettering the emancipatory potential of citizenship.

More than seventy years after the termination of ties with the colonial regime and the inscription of '*We the People*' as the 'source' of the authority of the Constitution, citizenship in India has become deeply contested.[4] While there were contests over citizenship in the past, the contemporary period is distinctive for the unprecedented display of a 'heightened consciousness' (Faulks 2000, Heater 1999) about citizenship, which spans the breadth of the country. This 'citizenship consciousness' has become manifest in the deep fault-lines caused by changes in the citizenship law, which has produced a *citizenship regime* inconsistent with the constitutional imaginary. In the summer of 2016, the Bharatiya Janata Party (BJP) led National Democratic Alliance (NDA) introduced the Citizenship Amendment Bill (CAB) in the Parliament which was entrusted to a Joint Parliamentary Committee (JPC) for scrutiny. The CAB was eventually passed in December 2019 when the NDA returned to power in May 2019 with an overwhelming majority in the Lok Sabha. In enacting the Citizenship Amendment Act (CAA) 2019, the ruling NDA invoked the constitutionally mandated power of the Parliament to legislate on all matters pertaining to citizenship. The CAA 2019 was brought with the objective of offering citizenship to those Hindus, Sikhs, Christians, Buddhists, Jains, and Parsis who had fled Pakistan, Bangladesh, and Afghanistan to escape religious persecution and had sought refuge in India before 31 December 2014. BJP leaders asserted that the amendment was essential to correct historical injustices caused by the partition of the country on the basis of religion, and the failure of

---

[4] This was achieved through Article 395 of the Constitution. Article 395 repealed the Indian Independence Act of 1947, which required that the Constitution of India be submitted to the British Crown in Parliament for validation.

Pakistan to protect its minorities—to which both India and Pakistan had committed themselves in 1950.[5] Through this articulation, the CAA 2019 recognized the right of specified religious communities to *return* 'home', in the fulfilment of a moral claim to obtain the legal protection of citizenship, whose denial would perpetuate a historical wrong.

The CAA was met with unprecedented opposition across the country by large numbers of Indians who were of the view that it was morally and legally indefensible. Quite like the protests by Indians in South Africa in 1907 who defied what they considered an immoral law, and the inmates in the asylum for whom the world of law was incommensurate with their familiar world and was, therefore, not just unintelligible but also unreasonable, the CAA was received with calls for civil disobedience. The government responded by declaring that the protests were illegal and anti-national: they were *illegal* for opposing a law that suffered from no procedural infirmities and was in conformity with the Parliament's 'legislative competence' drawn from the Constitution; and *anti-national* because those who opposed the law were part of a group that wanted to destabilize the country. The group in question has almost always been addressed by the present political regime as the 'tukde tukde gang' or a gang that aspires to fragment the country. The epithet *tukde tukde* gang is used ubiquitously by ministers in the NDA government and by BJP supporters to cast suspicion on left-liberal critics of the NDA government and those who protest against the policies of the government to justify bringing them under the purview of sedition and anti-terror laws.

In this work, I would attempt to bring the CAA to an anthropological scrutiny, locating the contemporary form and content of the citizenship law in a 'matrix ... of historical experience' (Guha 1982, 140–141). The law of citizenship in India may be seen as located within a realm of contestation over ideas of *who* belongs and *how*. The history of this contest and its resolution show distinct *logics* through which grounds of membership and terms of belonging were laid down in law, entrenching successive citizenship regimes. The association of the term *regime* with citizenship is crucial for making the argument that law must be seen not

---

[5] 'Citizenship Amendment Bill Atonement for Partition: Modi Vows to Pass law in Assam Rally Despite Opposition from Allies in State', *Firstpost*, 5 January 2019; 'CAA to Fulfill Old Promises to Religious Minorities in Neighbouring Countries: Modi', *Times of India*, 28 January 2020.

only in terms of its bare provisions but also examined for its political and ideological embeddedness. The 'bare act' of citizenship which comes to us as an accumulation of successive amendments represents the law's coalescent 'present'. The different temporalities of law are compressed in the bare act, occluding the historical layers, and flows that have marked the changes that occurred through successive amendments. In keeping with the arguments made in my earlier works (Roy 2010; 2016), I propose that the amendments in the Citizenship Act of 1955 do not follow a linear trajectory, whereby each amendment constitutes a moment of transition along a course of universalization. It rather sees successive amendments in the citizenship law as representing constitutive sites for citizenship practices that produce the structural effects of the state. These practices make the state appear as a tangible apparatus that stands apart from society, 'represented and reproduced' through the modality of law (Mitchell 1991). On the other hand, these practices, which are embodied in a law that determines membership in the political community, produce specific power effects, representing a distinctive political rationality in which 'power is organized as an activity designed to produce effects of rule' (Scott 1995, 193). Through the exercise of the legal power of identifying citizens, the state marks both the *objects* and the *field* of its power by delineating the zone in which its functionality can be operational (Scott 1995).

Earlier in 1950, T. H. Marshall had located the historical development of citizenship in the process of structuration of the state through functional differentiation between the branches of government, making them distinct instead of fused in a single entity (Marshall 1950). In his comparative study of the 'divergent' cases of citizenship in Europe—in France and Germany—Rogers Brubaker described the 'origins', 'functions', and 'effects' of national citizenship (Bockenforde 2016) as a 'specifically modern institution through which every state constitutes and continually reconstitutes itself as an association of citizens' (Brubaker 1992). As an instrument of 'closure', citizenship excludes those from other states, and as one of 'inclusion', it determines the membership of those who belong internally. In the exercise of its power of determining citizens and outsiders, the state 'territorializes' its authority. In the process of the 'standardization' and 'intensification' of its authority over a territory, membership in the state becomes the *only* status of 'politically relevant affiliation' and citizenship becomes associated with the 'formation of the state as a union of persons' (Bockenford 2016, 320).

Following from the above, I argue that the Citizenship Act of India may be seen as unfolding through specific amendments in the form of three *successive* regimes, distinguished by an underlying *logic* that makes each regime discrete: The enactment of the Citizenship Act of 1955 constituted a regime held together by the logic of 'transformative' (Baxi 2013, Bhatia 2019, Vilhena, Baxi, and Frans Viljoen 2013) that characterized the transition to constitutional democracy and republican citizenship; the amendment in the Citizenship Act in 1985 inserted the logic of 'exception' in the citizenship law for the state of Assam to install a regime of 'differentiated-universal' and simultaneously a system of *graded* citizenship; the amendment in 2003 put in place a provision empowering the Central government to prepare a National Register of Indian Citizens (NRIC) based on the 'distinguishability assumption' (Sadiq 2009) to establish a regime of 'documentary citizenship' (Sadiq 2009). The contemporary regime of citizenship, I argue, has emerged from the 2003 amendment, which provided the hinge point from which two discrete trajectories emerged—*leading* to the NRC in Assam (2015 onwards) and the CAA in 2016/2019. These two trajectories, I argue, have become conjoined in the contemporary landscape of citizenship in India to entrench a regime of *bounded citizenship* with claims to universalism *marked* by the majoritarian order of Hindutva.

While successive citizenship regimes displayed distinct political and ideological configurations, each regime also carried within it a *tendency* that sustained *across* regimes so that cumulatively the regimes appear to be a *system* gravitating from *jus sanguinis* to *jus soli* (Jayal 2013, Roy 2010, Rodrigues 2008). Each amendment in the citizenship law and the rules that accompanied it can, however, also be seen as constituting a space of 'assemblage'. Borrowing from Aihwa Ong and Stephen Collier (2005), assemblage is being used here as a heuristic device for an anthropological exploration (Collier and Ong 2005) of citizenship regimes. Such an exploration would allow the examination of law as a *subject* of anthropological enquiry (Nader 2002)[6] and also its scrutiny for the production

---

[6] Laura Nader refers to *law as an anthropological subject* suggesting the possibility of a range or connections while 'studying law in context'. Nader's notion of law's life was informed by the project of studying law in the terrain of the anthropologist—that is, non-western cultures. She

of anthropological *effect* (Supiot 2007).[7] Stephen Collier and Aihwa Ong argue that a range of phenomena that are otherwise referred to as global, assume form through articulation in *specific situations*. They call these situated articulations 'territorialised assemblages'. Assemblages are sites of mutations in citizenship, which emerge as a consequence of the convergence of diverse regimes of contemporary lives across a spectrum of both 'mobile and excluded populations' (Ong 2006) where new relationships are continually being reformulated through 'technological, political and ethical reflections and interventions' (Ong and Collier 2005, 4). These aggregates of relationships, which are gathered together due to a convergence of exchanges and flows of population, values, images, and technologies, open up new landscapes of citizenship, replete with what Ong calls 'entangled possibilities' (Ong 2006, 499). Rather than the territory of the nation-state, it is the space of the assemblage, which becomes the site for new political mobilizations and rights claims, made by a range of actors, not all of whom are citizens in the sense of membership in the nation-state (Ong 2006). This work deploys 'assemblage' as the lens to explore the specific sites of citizenship that get articulated through changes in the citizenship law. Examining the contemporary regime of citizenship, this work looks at the sites that get generated as a consequence of the amendments as an 'aggregate' of relationships, seeking anthropological insights into law's life (Nader 2002) as well as the lives that law impacts as an effect of its anthropological function (Supiot 2007). Following Alain Supiot, it evaluates *effect* in terms of the 'transformations' that law brings—on the one hand, creating 'legal subjects' as a bulwark against erasures by totalitarian regimes which establish domination by 'killing' the 'juridical person' (Supiot 2007, x), and on the other hand, the creation of sovereign individuals competing with each other in a 'dense web of

---

addresses the problem of translation and transference of legal categories, as well as the study of processes of social engineering through law that have continued from the period of industrialization and expansion of European colonialism, interrogating interlocking issues pertaining to power, control, autonomy, colonialism, industrialization and the imposition of Western Law (Nader 2002, 6–7, 9).

[7] Alain Supiot refers to the *anthropological function* of law, which he argues transforms 'each of us into a homo juridicus': 'The law connects our infinite mental universe with our finite physical existence and in so doing fulfils the anthropological function of instituting us as rational beings' (Supiot 2007, ix). He argues that this transformation is significant if one recalls one of the lessons from the experience of totalitarianism, wherein the first essential step 'on the road of total domination was to kill the juridical person' (Supiot 2007, x).

contracts' they are all part of. In this work, the effect of law in constituting specific sites of assemblage is enquired in terms of processes of inclusion and closures which come in various forms and structure people's relationship with the citizenship law.

Inherent to this inquiry/scrutiny is an examination of the 'iterations' of law (Singh 2020)—the manner in which law reproduces itself—in 'authoritative' spaces of interpretation such as the courts (Baxi 2008), in institutionalized spaces of 'democratic iterations' such as the Parliament (Benhabib 2007),[8] and in non-ritualized spaces such as the 'urban street' (Sassen 2011) through art and media (Kraidy 2017). These iterations reflect contending questions of national and territorial belonging (Chowdhory 2018) and the terms on which belonging would be recognized and affirmed—sutured to categories of birth and descent that structure the citizenship law. These questions are also imbricated in the field of contestation and conflict which is produced by the categories themselves. In the section that follows I would examine the three regimes of citizenship in India, explaining their distinctive logics. I would also draw attention to the enduring tendency towards *jus sanguinis* through successive amendments, which have culminated in the contemporary moment into a clearly identifiable association of citizenship with descent and blood ties. This section will end with a discussion of the contemporary landscape of citizenship, which I argue is characterized by the dominant logic of *jus sanguinis*, marked by 'blood and belonging' (Ignatieff 1993). Blood ties are transposed onto the unity of the people as a nation, making it the most definitive ground of belonging. Yet, this unity is also polyrhythmous (Barkley-Brown 1991),[9] so that one can see it expressed

---

[8] Benhabib defines democratic iterations as 'complex processes of public argument, deliberation, and exchange through which universalist rights claims and principles are contested and contextualized, invoked and revoked, posited and positioned throughout legal and political institutions, as well as in the associations of civil society' (2007, 14). The sites at which democratic iterations can take place are the entrenched and structured political and representative public institutions like the legislatures, decision making bodies like the executive and the judiciary, as well as in what she calls the 'informal' and 'weak' publics of civil society associations and the media.

[9] History, says Elsa Barkley-Brown, is like everybody talking at once, with multiple rhythms being played simultaneously (1991, 85). Events and people that get written about, she argues, '[did] not occur in isolation but in dialogue with a myriad of other people and events', so that at 'any given moment millions of people are all talking at once' (Barkley-Brown 1991) The historian isolates one conversation to explore but puts it in a context to make evident its dialogue with several other related conversations. The idea is to make the isolated lyric standalone, but at the same time be in connection with all the other lyrics being sung. The task of studying citizenship

in different forms of belonging—as 'hyphenated citizenship' through the NRC, 'bounded citizenship' through the CAA, and 'liminal citizenship' through the LBAT (Land Border Agreement Treaty). The last section will signpost these different rhythms of citizenship as they play out in the contemporary context, within the larger frameworks of law, state practices of rule, and the politics of belonging.

Regimes of Citizenship

A citizenship regime embodies the ways in which a law is enforced, the source of its validation, and the mystification/masking of law. The violence of law or conversely its founding in notions of justice configure and produce fields of contest around citizenship. The idea of a regime goes beyond the bare provisions of law, to identify the field of power that surrounds it, the debates on what is considered authoritative, the legitimation practices that justify the authorial power of the state over law-making, the interface of law with the lives that it intersects, and the notions of belonging that it puts in place. It is significant that all the three 'historical' regimes discussed in this section address the problem of 'mobility' of people in contexts of state and nation-making and the cartographic anxieties that accompany the making and enforcing of national borders. Integral to each regime is the notion of crisis that immigration and 'the awkward and threatening presence of aliens' and outsiders present to the 'settled' notions of membership and belonging (Roy 2010). The 'alien' or 'stranger' produces a 'crisis in citizenship' which is sought to be resolved through a 'tightening' of citizenship laws by all countries to reinforce the 'model' of citizenship espoused by them, for example, the centrality of 'social solidarity' in the republican models achieved through active participation in public life, and social integration and equality through freely chosen individual contracts in liberal models. The immigrant is considered a disruptive figure in both these models, interrupting both social solidarity and integration owing to his/her ambivalent location as a

---

as polyrhythmous involves a similar craft of extricating the different strands in plural lyrics of citizenship being sung simultaneously, and at the same time steering them back into their polyrhythmous location.

resident alien, and his/her inadequacy in entering into freely chosen relationships with other individuals. The 'crisis in citizenship' is expressed in both models as weakening the bonds of belonging that emerge from commonality. The articulation of crisis and the modes of its resolution produce 'zones of disturbed citizenship', which become the sites of contestation over appropriate norms, conditions, and terms of belonging (Roy 2010). These contests become exacerbated when illegality is ascribed to immigration, and the figure of the migrant, when inscribed as illegal, becomes also a threat to 'national security'. The question of belonging from the perspective of the state is one of assertion of jurisdiction, which has gravitated from its earlier meaning as a relationship of 'ligeance' and 'true and faithful obedience' elicited by the sovereign from its subjects, to a political relationship which recognizes claims to rights and entitlements by citizens from their governments (Shachar 2012). In addressing the problem of those who move by 'crossing borders', the state reasserts its jurisdiction by reinforcing 'cultural and political borders' against 'transgression', by buttressing its 'capacity' to 'control the status of the border' (Chowdhory 2018, 17). While for the state, this involves the 'function' of making citizens legible, for citizens it is a 'sense' of belonging and identity, expressed through 'bonds', 'ties', and 'attachments'—to something tangible such as land—or intangible, such as ties to people and the nation, which constitutes belonging.

Transformative Citizenship

The *legal* affirmation of citizenship happened with the enactment of the Constitution on 26 November 1949, when the Constitution of India was adopted by the Constituent Assembly. Citizenship provisions, along with those concerning elections, the provisional parliament and temporary, and transitional features, became operational on this date; the rest of the Constitution came into effect on 26 January 1950. The provisions in Part II of the Constitution addressed the complicated question of who would be considered Indian citizens in the immediate context of Partition and the creation of the new nation-state. If the debates around the CAA are at present embedded in the politics of Hindutva which serves as an ideological apparatus to cast citizenship into assertions of territorial sovereignty and totalizing power over people, at the inaugural moment of republican citizenship in 1949, citizenship was less about territorializing state power, and more about creating 'the people' as the source of state authority. In his speech to the nation on the eve of independence, Nehru declared that independence was the redemption of a promise made long ago by the Indian people. Indeed, independence to Nehru was a 'rare moment' in history, when 'we step out of the old to the new, when an age ends, and the soul of a nation, long suppressed finds utterance'. The 'tryst with destiny speech', as this speech is popularly called, was replete with references to the future that 'beckoned' the Indian people—for which they would have to strive hard. This future would be one without fear— a future of peace, freedom, and democracy—towards which India, 'our much loved motherland, the *ancient*, the *eternal* and the *ever-new*', and all Indians would march *collectively* to meet their intended destiny as a nation (Nehru 1947, emphasis added).

The 'transformative' as the logic which anchored citizenship at the commencement of the Republic has been invoked in this work to explain citizenship's inaugural moment from a cognate framework—that of transformative *constitutionalism*. The idea of constitutionalism as transformative has been put forward by scholars to elaborate on the different ways in which countries making the transition from colonial rule and authoritarian regimes understood their journeys towards the 'magnificent goal of democracy' (Baxi 2013). This goal became part of the somatic experience of people, alongside but also separate from what constituent assemblies were doing in their closed chambers. By holding out a powerful affective appeal of individual and collective transition to the camaraderie of equal membership in the political community, citizenship was positioned on a temporal register of the present which held out the promise of a future unburdened and unfettered from the humiliation of the colonial past. Largely associated with the South African experience, transformative constitutionalism has come to have a broader usage to encompass constitutions in the Global South—as a model in which the constitution was conceived as an emancipatory project. The 'metaphor of a bridge' (Langa 2006, 353) in the Preamble of the interim constitution of South Africa suggests that the journey to a democratic future is a continuous process and always unfinished. The 'passage' opened up by the bridge is a space 'between an unstable past and an uncertain future'. The value of the bridge 'lies in remaining on it, crossing it over and over to remember, change and imagine new and better ways of being' (Langa 2006, 354). In this perspective, transformation is a 'permanent ideal':

> as a way of looking at the world that creates a space in which dialogue and contestation are truly possible, in which new ways of being are constantly explored and created, accepted and rejected and in which change is unpredictable but the idea of change is constant. (Langa 2006, 354)

As a deliberative body that was entrusted with the task of making the higher-order law from which governments would draw their authority and legitimacy, the Constituent Assembly represented a space, where questions concerning the future polity, democracy, and citizenship were debated and 'resolved'. Upendra Baxi sees this process as one of locating the legal sovereign amidst 'prior [and continuing] histories of power and struggle' (Baxi 2008, 93). These struggles shaped the project of writing the constitution, the 'specific modes of governance and production of juridical norms', and also the relationship between the constitution, law, and the ongoing state formative practices (Baxi 2008).

The partition ushered in a period of deep uncertainties about belonging. The legal procedures to resolve them ranged from devising *ad hoc* rules to deal with contingencies and reciprocal arrangements and agreements between India and Pakistan for the exchange of people and property to the considerable buttressing of the police force and the bureaucratic apparatus of the state. The minutes of a meeting of the Standing Advisory Committee held in Delhi on 14 November 1949 under the chairpersonship of the Minister for Home Affairs Vallabhbhai Patel, give an insight into the augmentation of the policing activities of the state and the expenditure incurred on it: the passport check posts on the newly installed borders, the employment of extra police officers for the security of the sessions of the Constituent Assembly and additional police for the eviction of persons occupying evacuee property, the recovery of abducted persons,[10] and the 'sudden expansion of Delhi and the increase in

---

[10] Letter dated 29 May 1948 from the Home Secretary to the Chief Commissioner of Delhi to the Secretary, Ministry of Home Affairs. File no. 16/44/48 Police (I), National Archives of India (NAI).

its population' (due to the migration from Pakistan), to mention a few.[11] Writing about 'passions' in the Constituent Assembly, which met in the Parliament House 'a few miles from the refugee camp' for those displaced due to the Partition, with Nehru's official house too serving as a refugee shelter, Vatsal Naresh, points towards the sense of 'foreboding' that violence produced even among the members of the Assembly (Naresh 2018).

Indeed, the questions of citizenship were being addressed in a variety of situations, in a context, where people were moving across the newly created borders, displaced under conditions of extreme violence. In the periods of legal hiatus before the constitutional provisions pertaining to citizenship commenced (26 November 1949), and then again between the commencement of the constitutional provisions and the passage of the Citizenship Act of India (1955), conditions of indeterminate citizenship prevailed for those crossing borders without documents or on different kinds of travel documents and permits. The files in the Indian Citizenship Section of the Home Ministry in the 1950s reveal how executive decision-making and court decisions became crucial in the absence of precise laws. The movement of these files across different Departments and Ministries, including the Ministry of Law and the Ministry of Rehabilitation, and the Election Commission, depict conversations among institutions, where issues of relative powers over matters of citizenship were discussed and resolved.

While admitting the difficulties of framing 'legal' provisions for citizenship, the Constituent Assembly discussed the *principles* that would govern legal citizenship. The debates in the Constituent Assembly from 10 to 12 August 1949, when the final provisions of citizenship were deliberated upon and approved, show deep 'ideational' (Lerner 2016) and 'ideological' disagreement among the members. These disagreements reflected anxieties around the implications the constitutional framing of citizenship would have on the idea of *Indian* citizenship. Distributed along the familiar fault-line of whether 'birth' (the territoriality principle; *jus soli*) *or* 'descent' (the parentage principle; *jus sanguinis*) should be the foundational principle of citizenship, they were concerned with questions of both the *source* of citizenship and its expression as an

---

[11] Minutes of the Standing Advisory Committee, Ministry of Home Affairs, Government of India. File no. 16/31/49, NAI.

identity—attached to ideas of home and belonging. A close reading of the Constituent Assembly Debates shows, however, that the fault lines were unevenly drawn, and no position was absolute. Those who argued for *descent* as the source of citizenship also sought to make citizenship conditional for 'returnees' from Pakistan and were apprehensive of the 'dual ties' citizenship would generate when extended to the Diaspora community. Similarly, apologists for the principle of *birth* sought to make it conditional on domicile and combine it with 'inheritance' or lineage from Indian parentage. The need to specify the *uniqueness* of Indian citizenship among countries that subscribed to one or the other forms of citizenship was asserted amidst concerns that the inscription of 'birth' as a definitive condition of citizenship would make it 'cheap'. Anxieties were also expressed that indiscriminate absorption of people migrating across borders would make Indian citizenship precariously flexible and embarrassingly indecisive.

The discussions which ensued show that the Constituent Assembly constituted itself into a discursive body in which contestations over the provisions unfolded in a deliberative mode. Among its many strands—some of which reverberated in the debates on the CAB in December 2019 in the Parliament—what prevailed was a prior consensus among the members of the Constituent Assembly, regardless of their own positions on specific issues, on their collective commitment to the *objectives* of the Constitution. Significantly, the debates provided the space where secularism as a democratic and republican ideal was discussed and affirmed as the basis of citizenship, even as the relationship between citizenship and religion, the principles on which mobility could be made legible, questions of loyalty and allegiance, and the centrality of birth or descent as the source of citizenship, remained disputed. In what was a deviation from Ambedkar's opening statement explaining that the Parliament would have the power to make 'altogether a new law' on citizenship 'embodying new principles', Nehru's speech towards the end of the debate conveyed that the *objective* of the deliberations in the Constituent Assembly was different. The Constituent Assembly was a body that was articulating *policy*—the *norms and principles* that would define citizenship—and *not* the details of acquisition and termination of citizenship. While these details should appropriately be in the domain of law for the Parliament to decide, deliberations in the Constituent Assembly, Nehru declared, *must* lay down *the principles which would guide future law*. As the theory of *constitutional moments* (Ackerman 1991) tells us, constitution-making processes represent 'extraordinary' moments of intense participation and deliberation which are of a different order from the 'normal politics' of deliberations in legislative bodies. Constitutional moments do not produce merely the *text* of the constitution, but an inscription of the principles that would be adopted by 'We, the people'.

The Assam Exception

From 1979 to 1985, Assam saw an enduring movement against the presence of foreigners in the state. Assam has a long history of in-migration as a consequence of the colonial policy of settlement of peasants from East Bengal on forest land and tea plantations. The war with Pakistan in December 1971 and the atrocities in East Pakistan (now Bangladesh) committed by the military regime in Islamabad led to a huge inflow of refugees into Assam. While the 'foreigners question' in Assam has a complex history,[12] even at the risk of simplification, it may be argued that its contours were framed by anxieties around dilution of cultural identity, and demographic changes and consequent pressure over land and other scarce economic resources in the state. These anxieties festered for a long time and erupted in 1979 in the context of a controversy over electoral rolls in the by-election in Mangaldai Parliamentary constituency, which revealed an 'alarming rise' in the number of voters.[13] A sustained struggle was launched with a mass rally led by AASU on 6 November 1979, imploring the governments in the Centre and the state to *protect* Assam against 'the harmful effects of continuous immigration' which had changed the composition of the electorate and gathered enough strength

---

[12] For the details of the complex ways in which the foreigners question has unfolded in Assam see Baruah (1999; 2005; 2009), Dutta (2021), Gohain (2019), Hussain (1993), Misra (2000; 2014; 2017), and Pisharoty (2019).

[13] In a speech to state-level election officers before the General Election in 1979, the Chief Election Commissioner Shakdher referred to the census records of 1971 to report the 'alarming situation' arising out of unprecedented inflation in electoral rolls in Assam (Hussain 1993, 102). See Weiner (1983, 282–285) for a discussion on and estimation of the growth in the population of the state in Assam, and Baruah (1986) for the difficulty of estimating the number of foreigners/immigrants in Assam (Baruah 1986, 1189–1190).

to influence political decisions (Barpujari 2006, 3-4). Supported by several regional parties and major literary associations of Assam, the AASU called for a civil disobedience movement. The period between the launch of the movement and the signing of the Assam Accord in 1985, as a negotiated settlement between the leaders of the movement and the central government, was marked by political instability and deferral of the electoral process, interspersed with violence. Even as the movement waged, and the question 'who was entitled to vote' remained crucial, in what was considered an 'illegal election', the Congress formed government in the state in 1983. The Congress government of Hiteswar Saikia in Assam and the Congress government in the Centre sought to wrest control over the resolution of the citizenship question in Assam. This was manifested in the enactment of the Illegal Migrants (Determination) by Tribunals Act (IMDT Act) in 1983 by the Central government. Enacted to enable the identification of illegal migrants in the entire country, the IMDT Act was notified only in Assam. Unlike the Foreigners Act 1946, which applies to the entire country, the IMDT Act installed a parallel regime for the identification of illegal migrants in Assam and became another source of discontent in Assam, till it was repealed by the Supreme Court in 2005.[14]

The citizenship question in Assam today continues to be framed by the two 'events' that marked out the 'Assam exception' in the 1980s. An 'event', according to Shahid Amin, may be fixed in time or it may become a metaphor gathering significance outside this time frame. It may also become 'momentous' having ramifications for other events in future (Amin 1995, 3).[15] Events, Veena Das has pointed out, become *critical* when they 'institute a new modality of historical action which was not inscribed in the inventory of that situation' (Das 1995, 5). Through successive accumulation and aggregation of practices of signification, an event may acquire criticality in the same or in a different time/space (Roy 2014). The first event

[14] The Preliminary chapter of the IMDT Act 1983 stated that 'a good number of foreigners who migrated into India across the borders of the eastern and north-eastern regions of the country on and after the 25 day of March [1971] have, by taking advantage of the circumstances of such migration and their ethnic similarities and other connections with the people of India and without having in their possession any lawful authority to do so, illegally remained in India'.
[15] In his book, *Event, Metaphor and Memory: Chauri Chaura 1922-1992* (1995) Shahid Amin focuses on 'Chauri Chaura' as 'a momentous event' in the history of the anti-colonial movement in India. In the course of all India non-violent civil disobedience movement called by Gandhi against British rule in India, a mob of villagers burnt down a police station in Chauri Chaura, causing the death of twenty-three policemen. Gandhi immediately suspended the movement.

consisted in the enactment of the IMDT Act in October 1983, which became critical in exacerbating the field of contest around citizenship in Assam. The perception that the Act was discriminatory in marking out Assam as an exception festered, and the discontent over it figured in the Assam Accord and in later negotiations. Almost two decades later, the Supreme Court repealed the IMDT Act in what is commonly known as the Sarbananda Sonowal case (2005), reflecting the criticality that the Act had assumed in the anxiety around illegal migration and citizenship—an anxiety which the court averred spanned not just Assam but the entire country. The Supreme Court judgement scrapping the IMDT Act located the citizenship question in Assam in the dominant discourse of 'national security' and 'state sovereignty', characterizing 'illegal' migration as an act of aggression. It may be noted that the IMDT Act lay down a mode of identification of illegal migrants, which was considered more 'protective' of the interests of the immigrant by shifting the onus of proving 'illegality' onto the 'prescribed authority' instead of the migrant him/herself as was the case with the Foreigners Act. The IMDT Act was seen in Assam as an anomalous and unfair exception. In the judgement of 12 July 2005, which came five years after the petition was made by Sarbananda Sonowal—former President of AASU, and former Chief Minister of Assam—a three-Judge Supreme Court bench consisting of Chief Justice R. C. Lahoti, Justice G. P. Mathur, and Justice P. K. Balasubramanyan, declared the IMDT Act unconstitutional on grounds of legal procedure. But the general principles which were laid down by the court in removing the discriminatory law, articulated citizenship as a vital aspect of state sovereignty, with the policing of national boundaries critical to its entrenchment. Discussing the demographic shifts in Assam the judgment endorsed the evidence of an increase in the Muslim population in the state, presenting the figure of the illegal migrant as both an alien and an Islamic fundamentalist—a threat not only to Assam but to the country as a whole. The court justified the 'legal regime of suspicion' of the Foreigners Act, which placed the burden of proof on the person identified as illegal, on grounds of *restoring state sovereignty* (which was diminished by the IMDT Act since it deprived the 'Union of the right to expel foreigners who violated the Citizenship Act'); and of *restoring to the Union its constitutional duty of protecting the State from external aggression* under Article 355 of the Indian Constitution (which makes it the duty of the Central government to protect every state against 'external aggression and internal disturbance') (Judgement, *Sarbananda Sonowal vs. Union of India & Anr*, 12 July 2005, para. 38).

The second 'event' was the signing of the Assam Accord in 1985, which put in place exceptional provisions for the determination of citizenship in Assam. The accord purported to take into consideration the 'genuine apprehensions of the people of Assam' and pledged 'constitutional, legislative and administrative safeguards ... to protect, preserve and promote the cultural, social, linguistic identity and heritage of the Assamese people'. While binding the Central government to this promise, the accord effectively affirmed the Central government's decisive role in matters concerning citizenship. While the IMDT Act was an expression of how a law could become a political instrument for the resolution of the problem of 'illegal migration', the Assam Accord opened up the space for a 'negotiated settlement' of the issue. In the process the accord prepared the ground for two exceptions in the legal order of citizenship: the establishment through the law of *a hierarchical order* of *graded citizenship* in Assam and the *extension of the chronological boundary* of citizenship for Assam to 24 March 1971. The Citizenship Act was amended in December 1985 to implement the accord and Section 6A was inserted to address the special circumstances of Assam. The amended Act provided for two categories of 'immigrants' who could become citizens on the basis of the cut-off dates of their arrival into Assam from 'a specified territory' (meaning present Bangladesh). The first category consisted of those persons of Indian origin who had entered Assam before 1 January 1966 and had been 'ordinarily' residents in the state—who would be considered Indian citizens. The second category consisted of those who had entered Assam after 1 January 1966 but before 25 March 1971. These persons, 'detected' under the provisions of the Foreigners Act 1946 and Foreigners (Tribunals) Order 1964, would be considered citizens of India only after ten years from the date of their detection as a foreigner. This category would have deferred citizenship since they would enjoy all privileges of an Indian citizen including the possession of an Indian passport, but their names would be struck off the electoral rolls and restored only after the stipulated period of ten years. The graded model confirmed a hierarchical ordering of citizenship, in which those who were 'originally' resident in Assam were entitled to undisputed citizenship. The rest were 'residual' citizens, whose citizenship was rendered ambivalent by their linguistic identity or their religion. This ambivalence was sought to be resolved *legally* by conferring confirmed or deferred citizenship on some. The rest, that is, those who entered India after 24 March 1971, were *aliens*, and the *illegality* of their presence was to be confirmed by the IMDT Act. Since both the Foreigners Act and the IMDT Act applied simultaneously and prescribed different modes of determining citizenship, the residual citizens came to occupy a zone of perpetually indeterminate citizenship and suspect legality. The sanctity of the accord as a 'public contract', the dispute over the cut-off date prescribed by it which was different from the rest of the country, the 'additional load' that Assam had to subsequently bear, and the long-standing question of Assamese identity, which the accord also promised to protect, lingered on and became critical in the churning in Assam over the NRC and the CAA.

The Hinge Point

The third regime of citizenship was inaugurated by the amendment in the Citizenship Act in 2003. This amendment became definitive in affirming the tendency towards *jus sanguinis* that had been put in place by the 1986 amendment in the citizenship act which made changes in the provisions concerning citizenship by birth. The 1986 amendment provided that a person will be a citizen of India by birth if one of her/his parents was an Indian citizen at the time of his/her birth. This was a change from the 1955 Act under which anyone born in India, with a few exceptions, would be a citizen of India by birth. The 2003 amendment constrained birthright citizenship further to confine it to only those born in India, both of whose parents were Indian citizens or one was a citizen of India and the other was not an illegal migrant. With this amendment, the category 'illegal migrant' which was inserted in the citizenship act to address the specific context of Assam through the 1985 amendment, made its appearance in the provision of citizenship by birth. The amendment, moreover, by further constraining citizenship by birth, decisively ensured citizenship's association with the principle of blood, as descent from parentage of Indian origin became the defining principle for consideration of citizenship by birth. Alongside constraining citizenship by birth by making it dependent on descent, the 2003 amendment inserted the category of 'overseas citizen of India' (OCI). The OCI was an ambivalently articulated category, in so far as it recognized de-territoriality of citizenship by extending the privilege of holding an overseas citizen of India card to persons of Indian origin who had acquired citizenship of another country. Yet, the de-territorialization of citizenship through the OCI was deceptive, since it did not allow dual citizenship. Even as it created the possibility of 'affective belonging' for those who had lost Indian citizenship after they acquired the citizenship of another country, the OCI continued the foreclosure for those persons of Indian origin who had opted out of Indian citizenship in preference for the citizenship of Pakistan at the time of Partition. Not only did the OCI then sustain the original contexts of nation-state citizenship, it also manifested the dominant political and ideological contexts of Hindutva within which the OCI as a legal category was made effective. While the Indian Diaspora was dispersed across the world, the High-Powered Committee on the Indian Diaspora which recommended the OCI concluded, wherever in the world they were, their *punyabhumi* remained India.[16] The Committee carefully emphasized their common identity: 'They live in different countries, speak different languages and are engaged in different pursuits. What gives them their common identity is their Indian origin, their cultural heritage, their deep attachment to India' (Report of the High-Level Committee on Indian Diaspora [RHLCID] 2002, v). The 2003 amendment was brought by the BJP led NDA government and the prioritization of descent over birth was integral to both—the amendments in the provisions pertaining to citizenship by birth and the insertion of the category of the OCI.

The principle of parentage and blood ties was affirmed through another change that the 2003 amendment brought in the citizenship law, which made 'lineage' an integral part of Indian citizenship. The 2003 amendment empowered the Central government to prepare a National Register of Indian Citizens (NRIC) and issue national identity cards to persons identified as Indian citizens. The rules framed for the implementation of this provision lay down an exceptional procedure for Assam,

---

[16] The eagerness to include Non-Resident Indians (NRIs) and Persons of Indian Origin (PIOs) residing abroad has been a continuous feature of the Hindu Right and especially the Vishwa Hindu Parishad (Van der Veer 1996, 126, Deshpande 2003, 80).

whereby those seeking for a place in the NRIC in the case of Assam would be required to provide documentary evidence showing descent from those who were citizens of India of Assamese origin. The regime of documentary citizenship (Sadiq 2009) to prove citizenship through descent, along with the constraints on citizenship by birth, produced a regime of citizenship based on the logic of a 'bounded' community, based on ties of belonging to a dominant 'we' within a Hindutva imaginary of nationhood and citizenship.

Blood and Belonging

Citizenship in contemporary India represents a coalescence of tendencies that have emanated from successive citizenship regimes spawned by the earlier periods of change in the citizenship law. The amendment in 2003 may be considered a hinge point from which the NRC and the CAA 2019 emerged and became an integral part of the ideological landscape of citizenship in contemporary India. Having appeared as discrete tendencies out of the 2003 amendment in the Citizenship Act, the NRC and CAA 2019 have become conjoined to produce a spectre of national citizenship based on the logic of descent as the organizing principle. While the NRC, as the experience in Assam has shown us, is a legal regime of enumeration of Indian citizens based on evidence that establishes a legacy of inherited belonging, it is simultaneously, and often primarily, presented as a modality of identifying illegal migrants. The CAA 2019 is embedded in the idea of national-majoritarian citizenship with religion as its distinguishing principle. It makes a distinction among illegal migrants to identify those among them who would be considered eligible for Indian citizenship through naturalization. These two principles—of descent as the organizing principle of citizenship and religion-based citizenship—have coalesced in the ruling practices of the current political regime to become decisive in determining who belongs to the political community.

The inscription of the 'Assam exception' in the Citizenship Act, the IMDT Act 1983 and its repeal in 2005, and the Assam Accord have reverberated in the contemporary landscape of citizenship. Indeed, the framing of illegality within which immigration from Bangladesh came to be seen in a national security framework, was reiterated in the Supreme

Court judgement in the Assam Sanmilita Mahasangha case in December 2014, in which the court laid down the framework for updating the NRC in Assam. Indeed, in an extension of the court's position in the Sarbananda Sonowal Case (2005), it made the fortification of territorial boundaries as well as the protection of population a function of state sovereignty. The persistence of the Sarbananda Sonowal judgement in contemporary debates on citizenship is seen in the manner in which the JPC in recommending the CAB 2016 for the consideration of the Parliament, quoted the judgement to assert that 'misconceived' ideas of secularism must not come in the way of extending the protection of citizenship to non-Muslim religious minorities who faced persecution in Afghanistan, Bangladesh, and Pakistan.

Law, State, and the Politics of Belonging

The contestation around the CAA 2019 in institutional spaces of the state such as the legislature and the courts and sustained protests in the streets calling for a repeal of the law, raise a fundamental question pertaining to the meaning of law, and further questions concerning legal obligation, that is, *What* is it that makes a person obey a law? and, why *must* a person obey a law? Article 13 of the Constitution of India defines a law—the only place in the Constitution where an attempt has been made to state what a 'law' means—as 'laws in *force*', referring to its enactment by a 'competent authority'. Article 13 also specifies that all laws, even if they have been enacted by a competent authority, can be held void if they are inconsistent with the fundamental rights guaranteed in Part III of the Constitution of India. In defining law in terms of its *enforceability* and the *limits* that apply to it, Article 13 captures the debates that have surrounded the meaning of law with reference to its *usage* and the 'conceptual commitment' that any 'usage entails' (Dworkin 1967, 15). John Austin wrote of law as the *command* of the *sovereign* (Austin 1832). The sovereign for Austin is a determinate source of authority, not in the habit of obeying another person, and obeyed habitually by others because of the 'threat' of *consequences* that would follow non-compliance. This 'simple relationship' between 'subjects rendering habitual obedience and a sovereign who renders habitual obedience to no one'

INTRODUCTION 23

constitutes 'a vertical structure composed of sovereign and subjects' (Hart 2011 [1961], 50).

This relationship is, however, complex since there would exist within a society different orders of command, so that those who obey, do so not merely because of a threat of coercion but because they are *obligated* or bound by a law even in the absence of coercion. A fundamental characteristic of law that *binds* a person to obedience is that it has emanated from a source that has the *authority* to make laws. The nature of deference to this form of authority is different from that wielded by 'a gunman' who would force compliance by threatening physical harm. The question of authority is a normative one and does not simply refer to the 'physical power' of the author of the law (Dworkin 1967, 20). At one level it requires that the authority to make law must itself come from another higher-order law, which would constitute what Hart calls the secondary rules of validation (Hart 2011 [1961]). Such a test of validity is concerned not with the 'content' of laws but 'with their *pedigree* or the manner in which they were adopted or developed' (Dworkin 1967, 17). Ascertaining pedigree would serve to *distinguish* 'valid legal rules from spurious legal rules' and also from 'other sorts of social rules (generally lumped together as "moral rules") that the community follows but does not enforce through public power' (Dworkin 1967). The 'distinguishability test' is made up of rules of recognition that require that the validity of a rule may be traced through a complicated chain of validation to the source of its authority (Hart 2011 [1961]). Unlike the 'monopoly of power' constituting the authority of laws as seen by Austin, Hart traces the authority of laws 'in the background of constitutional standards' that have been accepted as the fundamental rule of recognition by the community which they govern. This background 'legitimates the decisions of government and gives them the cast and call of obligation' (Dworkin 1967, 22). In tracing law's authority to constitutional standards, laws may no longer be seen as orders backed by threats of coercion.

The 'field' of law is also imbued with a 'moral order' with justice serving as the link uniting the fields of law and morals (Hart 2011 [1961], 7). Hart speaks of justice as a virtue that is especially 'appropriate to law and the most legal of the virtues'. Yet, the unity of the moral and legal fields is fractured by a 'paradox' which arises when one speaks of 'justice according to law' and often of the 'justice or injustice of the laws'

(Hart 2011 [1961], 6–7). Both formulations, which are also articulated as procedural justice and foundational violence of law (e.g. Mbembe 2001), resonate with Bentham's formulation in which he claims that law 'shows itself in a mask'. Bentham's claim aims at 'demystifying' law by removing its 'mask' (Benaham, cited in Hart 1982, 2). While putting forward the principles of utility as a good reason for framing laws, Bentham argued that regardless of what form law takes, it is fundamentally structured by the *basic imperative* of 'command' (Hart 1982, 24). While laws 'conferring powers' may not appear to be issuing commands or prohibitions, 'the conventional formulation of such laws conceals their imperative character' so much so that 'frequently they appear to be describing something already existing, not prescribing something to be done' (Hart 1982, 23). Differing from what he considered the persistence of a positivist understanding of law in Hart, Dworkin inserted in his formulation of law and obligation, a standard of validation that is not dependent on *another set of rules*. Making a case for looking for standards that are not in the nature of rules, Dworkin writes of 'principles' as constituting a standard 'that is to be observed, not because it will advance or secure an economic, political, or social situation deemed desirable, but because it is a requirement of justice or fairness or some other dimension of morality' (Dworkin 1967, 23). In invoking 'principles' rather than 'rules' as a standard of validation, Dworkin goes beyond *constitutional conformity* to introduce *morality* as consideration for completing the chain of validation.

The contests around the CAA at one level have been about the validity of a law on a subject over which the Parliament has the authority to legislate. This authority is traced to the legislative powers inscribed in Article 11 of the Constitution and the distribution of legislative powers between the Centre and the states in the Constitution, in which citizenship is a subject assigned to the Central government. The argument based on legislative competence has been disputed by those who shift the rules of recognition to the realm of *principles* invoking justice as the standard on which a law must be tested. While the Constitution provides the framework of morality that would serve as the grounds on which the justness of law could be evaluated, there is a strong strand in this contest that would like to see the mere presence of a duly enacted law as authoritative, lending itself to legitimate enforceability.

The complex relationship between law, coercion, and morality may remain unexplained and the validation tests may be inadequate for our understanding of law, if the 'idiomatic expression', that is, the *'force of law'*, is not explored sufficiently to understand what constitutes 'enforceability' and the 'mystical foundation of authority of law' (Derrida 1992). Derrida tells us that the expression—force of law—reminds us that '... there is no such thing as law (*droit*) that does not imply in itself, in the analytic structure of its concept, the possibility of being "enforced", applied by force' (Derrida 1992, 6). Would the chain of validation and rules of recognition that Hart talks about and the satisfaction of conditions of morality make a law 'just'? Examining the relationship between law and violence, Derrida points towards the problem of distinguishing between the force of law which can be construed as just and the unjust violence of law. This problem pertains to the legitimacy of the 'originary violence' of the installation of the legitimating authority itself: 'How are we to distinguish between the force of law of a legitimate power and the supposedly originary violence that must have established this authority and could not itself have been authorized by any anterior legitimacy, so that, in this initial moment, it is neither legal nor illegal—or, others would quickly say, neither just nor unjust?' (Derrida 1992). It is this moment of 'originary violence' which 'rips apart the homogenous tissue of history' that constitutes the 'founding inauguration, justifying law' which consists of 'a coup de force, of a performative, and therefore interpretive violence that in itself is neither just nor unjust and that no justice and no previous law with its founding anterior moment could guarantee or contradict or invalidate' (Derrida 1992, 13). Any justification of institutive authority would then meet a 'mystical limit'—'the mystical foundation of authority of laws' (Đokić 1998, 451). It is interesting that while deliberating the principles that would be appropriate for the legal frameworks of citizenship in India, the Constituent Assembly worked with the determination of inaugurating a momentous phase for India, with principles of a republican, and secular order serving as the foundations of Indian citizenship. This founding moment was expected to substitute the order of command through which colonial power was constituted as the colonizer's right to exercise absolute dominion over the native (Mbembe 2011). Violence was imbricated in the imaginary of 'command' specific to state sovereignty in the colonial context. This included *foundational violence* which was imbricated in the assumption of a right to conquest, the subsequent *legitimation* of violence through narratives of justification expressed as in terms of a necessity, and finally, its *sustenance* in everyday practices, whereby the state claimed a shared life in society. Through these claims, the colonial state *domesticated* the colonized, who could challenge it 'only at the risk of being declared a savage and an outlaw' (Mbembe 2001, 6–7).

The protests over the CAA, which began in December 2019 and continued in Indian cities till March 2020, when the Covid-19 pandemic precipitated a national lockdown, recalled constitutional politics in the urban streets that became sites for the elaboration of citizen democracy. The ubiquitous recourse to the Constitution in street protests made it 'popular' and 'familiar'—belonging to the people. Unlike the engagement of the people with the Constitution in Rohit De's *A People's Constitution*, where the Constitution became a tangible experience for the people in 'situations of mundane everyday life' (De 2018, 3), those protesting against the CAA were re-installing the Constitution in a field of morality, to bring the legislative authority of the state to scrutiny. The rules of validation thus invoked referred not to the 'force' claimed by law because of its pedigree, but the notion of justice as a legal virtue. While unmasking law's violence, the protestors justified civil disobedience as an ethical means of questioning what they considered an unjust law.

A Map of the Book

This work explores the contemporary regime of citizenship by examining how it is structured around the amendment in the Citizenship Act in 2019 and the field of contestation generated by the amendment. Each chapter focuses on specific features of the regime of citizenship spawned by the present and past changes in the citizenship law. The following chapter (Chapter 1) puts forth the argument that the documentary regime instituted by the NRC in Assam, with the requirement to establish a clear link to Assamese 'legacy' generates a form of 'hyphenated citizenship' within Indian citizenship. The responsibility given to the Central government to establish and maintain a national register of citizens and issue national identity cards through the citizenship amendment act of 2003 and the rules framed under it, required it to carry out 'house-to-house enumeration' and collect particulars of individuals and families, including their citizenship status. Making an exception to this procedure, the NRC in Assam was prepared by *inviting applications* from all residents with particulars relating to each family and individual, including their citizenship status, which was based on NRC 1951, and the electoral rolls up to the midnight of 24 March 1971. By tracing the pedigree of Indian citizenship to an Assamese legacy, the citizenship act opened up the possibility of *hyphenated citizenship* for Assam, hitherto alien to the legal vocabulary of citizenship in India. The category 'hyphenated' helps capture the 'Assam exception' in the preparation of the NRC, especially the invocation of the citizenship identity of an Indian citizen of Assamese origin, which is an innovation in the legal vocabulary of citizenship in India. The use of the term hyphenated as a prefix to citizenship denotes a variant of citizenship that associates citizenship to an identity, which gets accommodated within a common national citizenship. The process of accommodation, as in the case of Assam, was inflected by competing and contentious articulations of belonging. Hyphenation served as a tool to alleviate the contest, but it also, as seen in the opposition to CAA in Assam, presented a challenge to the 'national order of citizenship' (Baruah 2009, 593). The chapter traces the process of accommodation and discord through an examination of the institutional, juridical, and documentary practices associated with the preparation of the NRC in Assam, the debates on the NRC in the political domain, and the arduous contests over legal delineation of categories in the Gauhati High Court and the Supreme Court of India. The experience with the preparation of the NRC through a Supreme Court-monitored process shows disparate strands where amidst the desire for closure of a festering issue in the state, deep uncertainties were generated as people in Assam presented themselves for registration as citizens to the NRC authorities.

Synchronous with the process of preparation of the NRC in Assam, a distinctive regime of citizenship was put in place through the CAA. As seen in the discussion on the three regimes of citizenship in India, the CAA represents a tendency in the ideological formulation of citizenship that redefines the idea of the political community. If the NRC as it has unfolded in Assam congealed the relationship between legal status and blood ties, the CAA has installed exclusionary nationhood under the veneer of liberal citizenship. The CAA 2019 purports to extend the protection of citizenship to those facing religious persecution and simultaneously puts in place a regime that discriminates on the ground of religion. Amidst the possibility of a nationwide NRC, the CAA made the question of 'documentary citizenship' (Sadiq 2009) more perplexing. Chapter 2 in this book focuses on the category of *bounded citizenship* to explain the contours of the legal regime of CAA. The concept of bounded is used in the sense of a 'boundary condition' (Walzer 1983), whereby citizenship installs 'strict walls of separation' (Sadiq 2009) to distinguish citizens from non-citizens and establishes the association of citizenship with 'the idealized notion of a bounded national territory with a clearly defined community of citizens' (Baruah 2009, 593). The chapter examines the discursive frameworks surrounding the CAA, the different figuration of the 'illegal migrant' when compared to the NRC, the idea of national citizenship based on the concept of a homeland, and the assertion of parliamentary sovereignty through law-making powers of the Parliament.

The chapter details, in particular, the two premises on which CAA has been justified: the invocation of legislative competence of the Parliament, drawn from Article 11 of the Constitution of India and a higher-order normative claim drawn from the Constituent Assembly, which ascribed this power to the Parliament. Through a detailed examination of the debates in the Constituent Assembly on the question 'who is an Indian citizen', and the debates in the Parliament in December 2019 on the CAA, the chapter discusses the ideological framing of citizenship in the constituent moment and its interpretation in 2019. In doing so, the chapter also examines ideas of popular sovereignty, the question of the source of law-making powers of the Parliament and its limits, along with the notion of power itself as it is elaborated itself in everyday politics driven by the political rationality of the ruling regime.

The JPC which studied the CAB and recommended it for the consideration of the Parliament invoked the power of the Parliament to make laws on any matter pertaining to citizenship. However, while invoking the legislative competence of the Parliament, in an exception to the foundational principles of citizenship, the CAA sought to introduce religion as a principle in making a distinction among persons—a principle that had been discussed and emphatically rejected by the Constituent Assembly of India. It is significant that both the NRC and CAA are concerned with the legal category of 'illegal migrant' but in different ways. The NRC is a modality of affirming citizenship through the detection and expulsion of illegal migrants. The CAA paves the way for exemption of specified groups of illegal migrants identified on the basis of religion from the category of illegal migrants to enable them to become citizens. The NRC and CAA come together in an ideological alignment in so far as both make citizenship dependent on lineage, spelling out ideas of belonging which are tied to descent and blood ties.

The idea of liminality—which could be understood both as a threshold condition as well as a condition of uncertainty—becomes important for understanding the experiences of those impacted by NRC and CAA. While the process of preparation of NRC generated documentation practices whereby people made themselves legible by placing themselves within identification regimes, it also opened up the spectre of statelessness for those who were not 'detectable' (Ghosh 2019) by the state. The CAA has exacerbated the uncertainty since it has come to be perceived as a citizenship regime responding to closures precipitated by the NRC. Coincident with the NRC process and initiation of the CAB through executive orders in 2015 and 2016 making changes in the Passport Act and the Foreigners' Act, a treaty between India and Bangladesh facilitated the exchange of territory and population along their borders in West Bengal, Assam, and Tripura. This exchange did not entail any amendment in the Citizenship Act of India but offered the possibility of citizenship to Bangladeshi enclave dwellers to become Indian citizens under Section 7 of the Citizenship Act of 1955. This meant that 'aliens', who otherwise ran the risk of being labelled as illegal migrants and infiltrators, could be absorbed as Indian citizens along with the territory. While the extension of citizenship in this context was largely seen as an effective resolution of a long-standing border problem, actual experiences of exchange— for those who continued to reside in India and became Indian citizens and those Indian citizens who were 'displaced' from what now became Bangladeshi territory—were replete with the ambivalence of belonging and fragmentation of their lifeworld as citizens. Chapter 3 examines the Land Border Agreement Treaty (LBAT) of 6 June 2015 between India and Bangladesh as an example of the resolution of 'illegality' through an agreement between the two governments to resolve long-standing disputes pertaining to the demarcation of the boundary. Till the summer of 2015, residents of enclaves were citizens of the country to which the enclave belonged; but governmental machinery had meagre or no access to the enclaves since its legal-juridical sovereignty over the enclaves was interrupted by the territorial sovereignty of another state. Enclaved citizens did not reside within the contiguous nation-state boundaries of either country, and for all practical purposes they were displaced persons with disputed citizenship, were denied political rights and constitutional protections, and led a precarious life of perpetual liminality bordering on illegality. The chapter is based on fieldwork conducted at five sites in Cooch Behar district in West Bengal—three transit camps for Indian 'returnees' in Dinhata, Mekhliganj, and Haldibari and two chhits with 'new citizens', Balipukhuri, and Dhabalsati Mirgipur. The fieldwork was conducted in December 2016, more than a year after the LBAT was signed and the exchange of land and population took place, and about six months after the state assembly elections in West Bengal in which both the returnees and the new citizens voted for the first time. The camps in Dinhata, Mekhliganj, and Haldibari were set up as transit accommodation for two years for Indian citizens 'returning' from Indian enclaves, and Balipukhuri and Dhabalsati Mirgipur were Bangladeshi enclaves that had become part of the Indian territory inhabited by the 'new' Indian citizens. The LBAT 2015 is largely considered a moment of closure in the history of contests over territory along the border with Bangladesh by ensuring correspondence/alignment between territorial boundaries and political sovereignty. Seen in the context of the preparation of the NRC in Assam around the same time, this chapter seeks insights from the field to argue that the exchange of enclaves generated split-citizenship among both the *returnees* and the *new citizens*, which was expressed through idioms of loss and betrayal.

The invocation of 'crisis' in citizenship generated by the spectre of *indiscriminate* immigration and the risks presented by 'strangers' among us (Miller 2016), has become the source for extraordinary legal regimes of citizenship. These regimes have recalled the sovereign's power to command and control the movement of people and prescribe the terms of belonging. Yet, the moments of crisis are also those of iteration of constitutional moments—of 're-discovering' the set of principles that came to be adopted by 'We, the people' (Ackerman 1991, 5)—that have the power to 'break the causal chain of process and launch something unprecedented' (Pitkin 1987, 168). These moments embody powerful acts of political courage that have the power to re-iterate not just a constitutional order but a democratic order as well. A range of innovative protests against the CAA and NRC sought to re-claim the constitutional moment to re-articulate citizenship as dissidence, recalling the constitutional ethics of fraternity and public conscience. Chapter 4 discusses the new idioms of constitutional citizenship that were iterated in rallies and sit-ins, through street art and theatre, and in institutional practices of public action litigation (PIL) asking for a democratic conversation about the Constitution and law and federal processes where states have resisted an imposition of the 'national order of things'. The chapter examines the ethic of citizenship in relationship with constitutional morality, and looks at the spate of protests against the CAA/NRC from December 2019 to March 2020, before the pandemic put in place a different order of public life. The title 'recalling citizenship' refers to *what* was being recalled in these movements, that is, the constitutional ethic of citizenship that informed the constituent moment, and the invocation of constitutional morality which B. R. Ambedkar considered indispensable for the durability of constitutional democracy. Describing this period as one of enhanced consciousness about citizenship, the chapter focuses on specific sites of protests that became iconic elaborations of dissident citizenship. It raises the question of why the constitution of India became emblematic of an idiom of politics that was insurgent and democratic at the same time. The movement can be seen as part of contemporary movements across the world which seek to restore democracy, for example, Hong Kong, or resurrect a constitutional politics that has become integral to the consciousness of being a citizen, for example, 'Black Lives Matter' movement in USA. In contexts of dominant politics where citizenship is itself under siege, dissident citizenship demands, in particular, the *restoration* of equality as the non-negotiable foundational premise of democracy. Yet, this process of restoration is a fraught one and has to contend with competing ideas, and indeed, claims to what it means to be a citizen.

With the help of interviews with public officials, accounts by displaced persons, and 'new citizens', government reports, case law, parliamentary debates, constituent assembly debates, and archival material, this work builds a narrative of contemporary citizenship that reflects the distinctiveness of the present, with residues of the past lingering on either as reminders of what is lost, or as unresolved questions that continue to fester.

The objective is to present a legal-anthropological account of citizenship in contemporary India, by examining the changes in law and judicial interventions as a manifestation of the contests that occur in the domain of the state. This work also attempts to trace anthropological accounts of the law through people's experiences, and the spaces in civil society that emerge out of dissident citizenship practices which aim at enhancing the deliberative content of the law.

1
Hyphenated Citizenship
The National Register of Citizens

In October 2019, Dulal Paul, a 65-year-old villager from Alisanga in Assam, died in Guwahati Medical College Hospital. Paul was declared a foreigner in 2017 and had since been living in a detention camp in Tezpur. Paul's family refused to take his body home unless the government declared that he was an Indian citizen. How could they accept the body of a Bangladeshi man as their own family? Dulal Paul's name did not figure in the final National Register of Citizens (NRC), which was published on 31 August 2019. All his family members, including his son, found a place in the NRC. His son claimed that despite possessing all documents from 1965 Paul was declared an illegal migrant and remained in detention until his death.[1]

The Citizenship Amendment Act of 2003 made it the responsibility of the Central government to prepare an NRC for the entire country and issue National Identity Cards to all citizens. The NRC is premised on the assumption that it is possible to distinguish citizens from aliens on the basis of documents as evidence of citizenship. While an NRC exercise for the entire country is yet to take place, the process of 'updating' the NRC in Assam, which was prepared in 1951 under a different legal regime, was initiated in 2015. The citizenship regime installed with the updating of NRC in Assam was marked by another innovation—that of *legacy*. This made the legal status of an Indian citizen in Assam dependent upon proving lineage with a person whose name figured in the 'legacy data' specific to Assam. From the time the court-monitored process of identification of citizens in Assam was set in motion with the Supreme

---

[1] 'NRC: Family of Dulal Paul, Who Died at Detention Centre, Accepts his Body after CM's Intervention', 23 October 2019, https://scroll.in/latest/941454/nrc-family-of-dulal-paul-who-died-at-detention-centre-accepts-his-body-after-cms-intervention (accessed on 5 December 2019).

Citizenship Regimes, Law, and Belonging. Anupama Roy, Oxford University Press. © Oxford University Press 2022.
DOI: 10.1093/oso/9780192859082.003.0002

Court judgement in *Assam Sanmilita Mahasangha and Others vs. Union of India and others* (December 2014) to the publication of the final 'list' of citizens in August 2019, the NRC left a trail of confusion or *kheli meli* in Assam.[2] This *kheli meli* persisted throughout the preparation of the register and beyond, as the uncertainty over the status of 1.9 million (nineteen lakh) people whose names were not part of the final NRC remained unresolved.

Taking the reader along the course of the NRC *Kheli Meli* in Assam, this chapter makes the argument that the NRC bears affinity to a model of citizenship in which the 'crisis' generated by immigrants and aliens is resolved by prescribing 'a thick and solidarity based model of citizenship' (Walzer 1983). Under the terms of this model, being an Assamese was ultimately about developing strong bonds of integration, which could also absorb migrants. But, the solidarity of citizenship was simultaneously driven by the logic of closure. Resembling 'a boundary condition', this solidarity was premised on a circumscribed world comprised of 'a group of people [who] commit themselves to dividing, exchanging, and sharing social goods, first of all *among themselves*' (Walzer 1983, 31, emphasis added). The NRC also produced a *hyphenated citizenship*, a category hitherto alien to the legal vocabulary of citizenship in India, by producing an 'Assam exception', and subsequently accommodating it in the 'order' of national citizenship. The chapter traces this process through four sections, by looking in the first section at the production of the Assam exception through the citizenship law, followed in the second section by a discussion of the interpretative practices of adjudicating citizenship in the courts, the bureaucratic practices of identification unleashed by the NRC in the third section, and finally, an exploration of the unsettled zone of citizenship produced by the accumulation of these practices, and the insertion of the CAB/CAA in the field of contest 2016 onwards.

---

[2] Parasmita Singh, 'NRC: This Graphic Novelist Sketches the Citizenship Test that May Render Millions in Assam Stateless', *Huff Post*, 8 January 2018.

The Assam Exception

The citizenship question in Assam has a contentious history which is reflected in successive amendments in the citizenship law. Equally, the citizenship law has become a source of continuing conflict over matters of citizenship in the state. The Citizenship Act of India enacted in 1955 was amended in 1985 to inscribe an exception in the law in recognition of the extraordinary conditions prevailing in Assam. The 1985 amendment came in the wake of the Assam Accord, and pertained to the identification and sifting out of foreigners and illegal migrants who had entered Assam and had been residing there. Migration into Assam from Bangladesh has a long history imbricated in colonialism and state formation after independence from colonial rule. It was, however, the year 1971, which has become a signpost in this history, when several lakhs Hindu and Muslim refugees fled into Assam to escape being ravaged by the war between what was then East and West Pakistan. The war ended with the formation of Bangladesh as a sovereign nation. On 8 February 1972, the Prime Ministers of India and Bangladesh issued a joint declaration whereby the Government of India assured 'all possible assistance to the Government of Bangladesh in the unprecedented task of resettling the refugees and displaced persons in Bangladesh' (Baruah 1999, 119).

The apprehension that a large number of 'foreigners' had entered Assam and continued to do so instilled a sense of unease in the state. The anxiety over changes in demography, language, and culture, and pressure over resources was expressed with increasing intensity. A powerful popular movement erupted in the early 1980s, led and steered by the All Assam Students Movement (AASU) demanding the ouster of foreigners. The movement lay claims to a distinctive Assamese identity and based on this—a differentiated citizenship (Young 1989)—to overcome what was considered to be a 'crisis' in citizenship. On 15 August 1985, an accord was reached between the leaders of the Assam movement represented by the AASU and the All Assam Gana Sangram Parishad (AAGSP), and the Indian government. Through the accord the Indian government made a commitment to address 'the profound sense of apprehensions' of the Assamese people 'regarding the continuing influx of foreign nationals into Assam and the fear about adverse effects upon the political, social, cultural and economic life of the State' (Clause 2, Assam Accord 1985).

Clause 5 of the Accord pertained to the 'Foreigners Question' and listed the measures that the Indian government would undertake to resolve it.

In 1985, an amendment in the Citizenship Act 1955 incorporated Clause 5 of the Assam Accord putting in place a template of graded citizenship in Assam. The amendment inserted Section 6A in the Citizenship Act with 'special provisions as to citizenship of persons covered by the Assam Accord' adding a sixth category of citizenship in India. Citizenship by birth, descent, registration, naturalization, and by incorporation of foreign territory into India were the existing five. This new category of citizenship applied exclusively to Assam and was expected to address the problems emerging from the presence of illegal migrants in the state. The 1985 amendment in the Citizenship Act identified two cut-off dates with corresponding regimes of legality and illegality. Section 6A prescribed 1 January 1966 as the initial cut-off date for the identification of citizens in Assam. Accordingly, all persons who had entered Assam from Bangladesh before 1 January 1966 and had been 'ordinarily resident' in the state would be considered citizens of India if they so wished. However, persons who had been residing in Assam and had been 'detected' under the Foreigners Act 1946 and Foreigners (Tribunals) Order 1964 as foreigners having entered India from Bangladesh 'on or after 1 January 1966 but before 25 March 1971', constituted a distinct category. A foreigner under this category would be considered a citizen of India, but only after a period of ten years from the date of detection as a foreigner. In the intervening period, she or he would enjoy all the privileges enjoyed by an Indian citizen, including holding an Indian passport, but would not have the right to vote. All other persons who entered the state on or after 25 March 1971, upon identification as 'illegal migrants' under the Illegal Migrants (Determination by Tribunals) Act (IMDT Act), 1983, would be deported.

These changes in the Citizenship Act were in accordance with Clause 5 of the Assam Accord in which 1 January 1966 was agreed upon as the 'base date and year' for the 'detection and deletion of foreigners'. All those who came before that date, including those whose names figured in the electoral rolls of the 1967 elections, were to be 'regularised' as citizens. The names of those who came after the base date and year up to 24 March 1971 would be deleted from the electoral rolls for a period of ten years after detection. These persons would be required to register themselves with the registration officers in their districts. Persons entering Assam after the 25 March 1971 deadline would be 'expelled'.

The Assam Accord installed a hierarchized/graded citizenship in Assam constituted by the 'universal we'—the Assamese people—whose claim to citizenship was undisputed. The universal 'we' was superimposed on residual citizens, whose citizenship was rendered ambivalent by their linguistic and religious identity. The government sought to resolve this ambivalence through the citizenship law, by conferring deferred citizenship onto some. The rest, that is, those who arrived in India on or after 25 March 1971, were illegal aliens, to be identified under the (now repealed) IMDT Act 1983, and deported from India. In actual practice, both the Foreigners Act and the IMDT Act applied simultaneously till 2005—the year the IMDT Act was repealed—and prescribed different modes of determining citizenship. As a consequence, the residual citizens continued to occupy a zone of indeterminate citizenship and suspect legality. Unlike the Foreigners Act in which the burden of proving whether or not a person was a foreigner fell on the person whose citizenship status was questioned, the IMDT Act was more 'protective' of the interests of the immigrant. It shifted the burden of proof to the 'prescribed authority' and demanded a *locus standi* from those who approached the prescribed authority with an 'application' alleging the presence of an illegal migrant in their vicinity. Under the Assam Accord, the government of India had promised to give 'due consideration' to the difficulties expressed by the AASU and AAGSP regarding the implementation of the IMDT Act and the low rates of identification of illegal migrants under it.

The IMDT Act 1983 was enacted to set up Tribunals for the determination of whether or not a person was an illegal migrant in the context of what the objectives of the Act described as the migration of 'large number of foreigners across the borders of the eastern and north-eastern regions of the country on and after the 25th day of March', who had 'taken advantage' of the 'the circumstances of such migration and their ethnic similarities and other connections with the people of India and without having in their possession any lawful authority so to do, illegally remained in India'. While the Act extended to the whole of India, it was notified only for the state of Assam, where it became effective on 15 October 1983. The Supreme Court scrapped the IMDT Act in 2005 removing what was perceived in Assam to be an anomalous and unfair exception in its application only to one state. In its judgment, delivered on 12 August 2005, almost five years after a petition seeking its repeal was moved by Sarbananda Sonowal—former President of AASU, former MLA of the AAGSP, presently a BJP member, and the Chief Minister of Assam from May 2016 to May 2021—a three-Judge Supreme Court bench, declared the IMDT Act unconstitutional. The declaration was premised specifically in questions of legal procedure, but the general principles articulated in the process had ramifications for the way in which citizenship has been defined and interpreted in India. While declaring the IMDT Act unconstitutional, the court described immigration from Bangladesh not simply as illegal entry, but *as an act of aggression*, which made the identification of illegal migrants an essential function of state sovereignty requiring the fortification of national territorial boundary and protection of its population from 'infiltrators' who posed a threat to national security.

An amendment to the Citizenship Act in 2003 brought about three significant changes: Section 7A was inserted in the Act introducing the category of Overseas Citizens of India (OCI) whereby a person who was a citizen of another country, but was a citizen of India at the time of, or after the commencement of the Constitution, or was a descendant of such a person, could be registered as an OCI. The 'Statement of Objects and Reasons' of the Bill introducing the amendment stated that the High Level Committee on the Indian Diaspora that had been set up by the Central government recommended the grant of 'dual citizenship' to persons of Indian origin in specified countries. The OCI was strictly speaking not a dual citizen—a citizen of two countries simultaneously—but enjoyed certain privileges, including a lifelong visa for visiting India. Section 3 was amended to constrain the conditions under which a person would be a citizen of India by birth. The process of constraining citizenship by birth had begun with the 1986 amendment, which had laid down that a person could be an Indian citizen by birth, only if *one* of his/her parents was an Indian citizen. The 2003 amendment further confined citizenship by birth to those born in India, *both* of whose parents were Indian citizens or one of the parent was an Indian citizen and the other was *not an illegal migrant* at the time of his/her birth.

A new section—Section 14A—was inserted in the Act through the amendment which provided that the Central government '*may* compulsorily register every citizen of India and issue a national identity card to him

[sic]'. The Central government was given the responsibility of maintaining a National Register of Indian Citizens (NRIC) and establishing a National Registration Authority for that purpose. Under Section 14A (3) of the Act, the Registrar General of India would act as the National Registration Authority and function as the Registrar General of Indian Citizen Registration. Section 14A (5) provided that the procedures to be followed for 'compulsory registration of citizen shall be such as may be prescribed'. The procedures for the 'preparation', 'establishment and maintenance' of the NRC were prescribed by the Central government through the Citizenship (Registration of Citizens and the issue of National Identity Cards) Rules of 2003. Section 4 of these rules made it the responsibility of the central government to carry out 'a *house-to house enumeration*' throughout the country to collect 'specified particulars', including *the citizenship status*, of each family and individual 'residing in a local area' for the preparation of the NRIC.[3] In November 2009, an amendment to the Citizenship Rules of 2003 was made through a Government Statutory Rule (GSR) issued by the Ministry of Home Affairs (Foreigners Division). This amendment made an exception in the procedure laid down in section 4 of the Citizenship Rules 2003 so that nothing in the section was any longer applicable to the state of Assam. Section 4A and its Schedule, inserted through this amendment, made 'special provisions' for the preparation of the NRC in Assam, different from those prescribed for the rest of the country.[4] A separate procedure was laid down for Assam, which replaced house to house enumeration with one where applications were 'invited' from all residents for the collection of 'specified particulars of each family and individual, residing in a local area in the state including the citizenship status based on National Register of Citizens 1951 and the electoral rolls up to the midnight of 24th March 1971' (Section 4A Citizenship Rules 2003 as amended in 2009).

---

[3] As per section 3(3) of the Citizenship Rules 2003, the National Register of Indian Citizens would contain the following particulars of every citizen: (i) Name; (ii) Father's name; (iii) Mother's name; (iv) Sex; (u) Date of birth; (vi) Place of birth; (vii) Residential address (present and permanent); (viii) Marital status—If every married, name of the spouse; (ix) Visible identification mark; (x) Date of registration of Citizen; (xi) Serial number of registration; and (xii) National Identity Number. [emphasis added]

[4] As amended by 1. G. S. R. 803(E), dated 9 November 2009 (with effect from 9/11/2009.) 2. Ministry of Home Affairs (Office of Registrar General, India), Order No. S.O. 596(E), dated 15 March 2010, published in the Gazette of India, Extra, Part II. No. 504 S.3(ii).

The 1951 NRC was prepared exclusively for Assam. On the directions of the MHA, the data which was collected for the census of 1951 was used to prepare the NRC for Assam. The 1951 NRC of Assam was prepared in the context of the Immigration (Expulsion from Assam) Ordinance of January 1950, which was replaced in February the same year with the Immigration (Expulsion from Assam) Act (Pisharoty 2019). The Immigration Act of 1950 gave the Central government the 'power to order expulsion of certain migrants' whose presence in Assam would be 'detrimental' to the 'interests of the general public of India' or of any section of the people of India or 'any Scheduled Tribe in Assam'. However, the Act did not apply to any person who had been 'displaced' from Pakistan 'on account of civil disturbances or the fear of such disturbances' and had been subsequently residing in Assam. The protection from expulsion to a class of foreigners allowed the influx of large numbers of persons fleeing persecution into Assam. Communal violence in areas bordering East Pakistan, including in the Indian states of Assam, West Bengal, and Tripura led to some immigrants fleeing to East Pakistan. The Liaquat–Nehru Pact of 8 April 1950 was signed by the governments of India and Pakistan which agreed to protect and restore the property of those who were displaced to facilitate their return. The NRC was prepared in these circumstances in the form of additional information based on individual, family, and household data (Dutta 2021, Pisharoty 2019). Sanjay Borbora (2019) refers to Sanjib Baruah (2018)[5] and Matthew Hull (2012) to point out that the preparation of NRC 1951 took place under conditions where the government lacked 'preparedness in conducting such a process' and amidst the absence of adequate communication between the government and the people, unlike the 'robustness' of the 2015 NRC, the response of the people to the NRC was difficult to ascertain in 1951.

In its judgement scrapping the IMDT Act in 2005, the Supreme Court had directed that all persons whose citizenship was suspect be brought under the purview of the Foreigners Act 1946. The then Chief Minister Tarun Gogoi proposed that the NRC prepared in 1951 in the state be updated to resolve all disputes over the presence of foreigners in the state, and put to rest the apprehensions of both the AASU and the Assam United Democratic Front (AUDF). A separate directorate was

---

[5] Sanjib Baruah, 'Stateless in Assam', *Indian Express*, 19 January 2018.

established by the Government of Assam to update the NRC, which, however, did not make any progress beyond the computation of available data, partly because the NRC 1951 for all the districts of Assam was not readily available with the state government.[6] In 2007, the Chief Minister reiterated the desirability of having an updated NRC but also drew attention to the intricacies of the process and the problems accruing from the fact that a large number of legitimate residents of Assam, such as the tea garden workers, may not have any documentary evidence to trace their residence in the state to 1971 or 1951. A pilot project launched in the assembly constituencies of Barpeta and Chhaygaon in 2010 showed mixed results.[7] A Cabinet sub-committee was subsequently set up by the state government to draw up the modalities for the finalization of the procedure for establishing the link of every person to the electoral rolls of 1971, which could then be connected to the NRC of 1951. In the course of his deposition in the Gauhati High Court in the case *Manowara Bewa @ Manora Bewa vs. Union of India and the State of Assam* (WP(Civil)2364 of 2016), the then NRC Coordinator Prateek Hajela informed the court that the modalities pertaining to updating the NRC and the list of admissible documents which would serve as evidence were finalized by the Cabinet Sub Committee. These were forwarded to the Central Government on 5 July 2013, and were subsequently approved.

The process remained desultory till the Supreme Court intervened and fixed a time frame for its completion. Based on the court's order, the Assam government fixed 31 October 2015 as the date for publishing the draft NRC and 31 January 2016 as the deadline for the final NRC. The entire process was closely monitored by the Supreme Court of India, which set up a schedule for the publication of the drafts.[8] The process stretched beyond the prescribed timeline. A 'part draft' of the NRC was

---

[6] Samudra Gupta Kashyap, 'Assam Yet to Update National Register of Citizens', *Indian Express*, 6 August 2007.

[7] The Chhaygaon NRC was successfully updated but the process at Barpeta was terminated because of protests by the All Assam Minority Students' Union (AAMSU). While the AAMSU believed that there has been no 'infiltration' from Bangladesh into Assam, other groups like the AASU wanted the process to be completed. Samudra Gupta Kashyap, 'In Assam, an Ongoing Effort to Detect Illegal Bangladeshi Migrants', *Indian Express*, 17 August 2015.

[8] As provided under the CAA 2003, the funds were provided by the Central government and the process was carried out by the state government under the guidance of the Registrar General of India. Prateek Hajela, a senior IAS officer was appointed as the NRC commissioner and co-ordinator. Samudra Gupta Kashyap, 'In Assam, an Ongoing Effort to Detect Illegal Bangladeshi Migrants', *Indian Express*, 17 August 2015.

released on 31 December 2017. The 'complete draft NRC' was released six months later on 30 July 2018. It left out 40 lakhs (4 million) of people from among those who had applied for inclusion. The 'final draft' released on 31 August 2019 left out 19 Lakhs (1.9 million) of people from the 39 Lakh (3.9 million) who had applied for insertion after being left out. Those left out were assured that they could present their claims before the Foreigners Tribunals, but the process is yet to start.

Adjudicating Citizenship

The Supreme Court's intervention in the process of updating the NRC in Assam came in the wake of a cluster of writ petitions. In 2009, Assam Public Works (APW), a Non-Governmental Organisation (NGO) actively involved in spreading, what it calls, 'social awareness' in Assam against terrorism and illegal migration into the state, filed a writ petition in the Supreme Court questioning the constitutional validity of Section 6A of the Citizenship Act of India. Section 6A, as discussed earlier, was inserted by the 1985 amendment in the Citizenship Act to lay down exceptional provisions for Assam. This petition was impleaded with two separate petitions by Assam Sanmilita Mahasangha (ASM) and the All Assam Ahom Association (AAAA), filed in 2012 and 2014, respectively. The ASM is a Guwahati-based organization that was formed in 2007 at the Talatal Ghar premises, the Rajdarbar of the Ahom kingdom in the present Sibsagar district. Matiur Rahman, the working president of ASM describes the organization as a 'confederation of 90 indigenous organisations of the state representing diverse ethnic communities living from time immemorial in the state', formed to protect the rights of the indigenous people living in Assam.[9] The AAAA, an organization whose origins go far back into the early Twentieth Century, has been described as having a history of participation in the anti-colonial movement and a

---

[9] Sangeeta Barooah Pisharoty, 'Interview: August 31st NRC Can't Be Final Without Constitutional Bench Verdict', *The Wire*, 3 September 2019.

sustained commitment towards 'the restoration of the rightful place of the Ahoms in independent India'.[10]

The three writ petitions by APW, ASM, and AAAA raised a common concern—the constitutionality of Section 6A of the Citizenship Act inserted by CAA 1985—which they argued, promoted indiscriminate influx into the state, and put the security of the state and its people at risk. The petitions focused on that part of section 6A which granted Indian citizenship to Bangladeshis who had entered Assam before 1 January 1966 and between 1 January 1966 and 24 March 1971. This, they argued, gave a large number of illegal migrants the benefit of Indian citizenship, either immediately—for those who had migrated before 1 January 1966 or deferred—for those who had migrated after this date but before 25 March 1971. The ASM had petitioned the Supreme Court in 2012 with a primary concern for the protection of the rights of indigenous people and sought direction from the Supreme Court for the implementation of the provisions of the UNDRIP (United Nations Declaration on the Rights of Indigenous People). It also challenged the exclusive citizenship cut-off date of 24 March 1971 for being against the Assam Accord in which, according to it, 1 January 1966 was identified as the 'base year' for the identification of non-citizens. There was no mention in the Accord that an enumeration of citizens should be done by updating the 1951 NRC. Indeed, the NRC was not mentioned as the mechanism to detect and delete the names of foreigners at all. In its writ petition [WP (Civil) No. 562 of 2012] the ASM appealed to the Supreme Court to 'order' the Central government and the government of Assam (henceforth, governments) not to update the NRC in Assam by taking the electoral rolls till the midnight of 24 March 1971 as cut-off, but treat 1951 as the base year to detect and deport illegal immigrants from Assam.

The Supreme Court admitted the Writ Petitions by ASM, APW, and AAAA on the grounds that they represented the interests of an *entire people*—the tribal *and* non-tribal population—of the state of Assam. These interests, the judges observed, related to the protection of the Assamese culture, but had larger ramifications for the sovereignty and

---

[10] Romesh Buragohain, The All Assam Ahom Association and Ahom Politics of Surendranath Buragohain, Proceedings of North East India History Association, Twenty Sixth Session (ed.), Manorama Sharma, North-Eastern Hill University, Shillong, 2004, 186.

integrity of the country as a whole. In its judgment delivered on 17 December 2014, Justice Ranjan Gogoi and Justice Rohinton Nariman left the question of the constitutional validity of section 6A (3) and (4) of the Citizenship Act, particularly its compatibility with the citizenship provisions in the Constitution, in prescribing for Assam a cut-off date which deviated from Article 6 of the Constitution, to be decided by a constitutional bench.[11] A substantial part of the text of the judgement focused on the historical contexts in which the need to protect the interests of Assam assumed importance. Tracing the different constitutional, political and legal signposts through which the citizenship question became significant in Assam, the judgement flagged the ceding of Assam by the Burmese to the British in 1826 under the treaty of Yandabo—the point at which the rule of the Ahoms came to an end and Assam became an administrative unit of Bengal—as a critical moment in this history. The judgement cited the 1931 report of the Census Superintendent C. S. Mullan, to emphasize the significance of this event:

> Probably the most important event in the province during the last 25 years—an event, moreover, which seems likely to *alter permanently the whole feature of Assam* and to *destroy the whole structure of Assamese culture and civilization* has been the *invasion of a vast horde of land-hungry immigrants mostly Muslims*, from the districts of East Bengal.... wheresoever the carcass, there the vultures will gathered together. (Judgement, *Assam Sanmilita Mahasangha & Others vs. Union of India & Others*, 17 December 2014, para. 2, emphasis added)

It must be kept in mind that the analogy of immigration into Assam as 'invasion' by 'land-hungry' Muslims has been a persistent trope in the discursive practices that have attributed illegality to the movement of people across the eastern borders. In this context, while the Foreigners Act 1946 has been the primary law invoked for the detection and expulsion of foreigners, it is the Immigrants (Expulsion from Assam) Act 1950, which has been foregrounded by those stressing the protection of the cultural

---

[11] Judgment delivered by Justice Ranjan Gogoi and R. F. Nariman on 17 December 2014 in the case *Assam Sanmilita Mahasangha and Others vs. Union of India and others* [Writ Petition (Civil) No. 562 of 2012].

identity of Assam. The Foreigners Act is applicable to the entire country and does not make a distinction on any grounds among 'foreigners' for detection and expulsion. The Immigrants (Expulsion from Assam) Act 1950, comes with the specific objective of protecting the indigenous inhabitants of Assam from what the statement of objects and reasons of the Act calls '... a serious situation [that] had arisen from the immigration of a very large number of East Bengal residents into Assam... disturbing the economy of the province, besides giving rise to a serious law and order problem'. The Act empowered the Central government to order the expulsion of 'any person or class of persons' who had been ordinarily the residents of places outside India but were residing in Assam before or after the Act came into effect, and their 'stay' in Assam was construed 'detrimental to the interests of the general public of India or of any section thereof or of any Scheduled Tribe in Assam'. While enabling the government to expel such persons, the Act made an important exemption. The provisions of the Act did not apply to a person 'displaced' from 'any area now forming part of Pakistan', who had 'left his place of residence' due to 'civil disturbance' and had 'been subsequently residing in Assam'. The Assam Accord, the amendment in the Citizenship Act in pursuance of the Accord, and the Supreme Court judgment in *Sarbananda Sonowal vs. Union of India* (2005) were all cited in the judgement as significant developments through which the trajectory of citizenship in Assam had taken shape.

The Supreme Court judgment in Assam Sanmilita Mahasangha case charted two *distinct* and mutually *contradictory* courses: One of these placed Section 6A of the Citizenship Act before a constitution bench, opening up the legal resolution of the citizenship question in Assam following the Assam Accord to judicial scrutiny; the other placed the extent to which the Central government had been able to implement the various components of the Assam Accord before the court for evaluation. The trajectory of the first scrutiny, that is, the examination of the validity of Section 6A has remained desultory.[12] The second, that is, the evaluation of the implementation of the Assam accord, ironically, led to a Supreme

---

[12] A five-judge Bench of the Supreme Court headed by Justice Madan B. Lokur was set up to examine the constitutionality of Section 6A. The bench held its hearing on 19 April 2017 but was dissolved when Justice P. C. Pant retired in August 2017. Faizan Mustafa, 'Who is an Indian Citizen? How is it Defined? Explained', *Indian Express*, 29 September 2019.

Court-monitored preparation of the NRC according to the exceptional procedure laid down in Section 4A of the Citizenship Rules 2003. It may be recalled that while the Assam Accord required the identification and expulsion of foreigners, it did not ask that this should be done by updating the 1951 NRC. Indeed, the preparation of the NRC based on the 2003 rules follows the cut-off dates specified in Section 6A of the Citizenship Act, which was entrusted to the scrutiny of the constitution bench in the same judgement.

The judges referred thirteen questions to the constitution bench, all of which called for an interpretation of the Constitution. These questions pertained to the consistency of Section 6A of the Citizenship Act with specific provisions of the Indian Constitution, especially those pertaining to citizenship, the fundamental rights of Indian citizens protecting them against discrimination by the state, and principles of rule of law that constrained those actions of the state which were arbitrary or were guided by political expediency rather than 'government according to law'. At the root of these was the fundamental question pertaining to the scope of Articles 10 and 11 of the Constitution of India which empowered the Parliament to make provisions for the 'acquisition and termination of citizenship', and all other matters pertaining to citizenship, including the continuation of citizenship under the constitutional provisions laid down in Articles 5 to 9. This question assumed significance, because in the exercise of its legislative powers over matters concerning citizenship as laid down in Article 11 of the Constitution, the Parliament inserted exceptional provisions for citizenship in Assam to specify a cut-off date—24 March 1971—which was different from the constitutional deadline for citizenship identified in Article 6 of the Constitution—19 July 1948. The legislative competence of the Parliament over matters of citizenship and the constitutional constraints over its law-making powers under Article 368 were, therefore, put under scrutiny. Section 6A was subjected to judicial scrutiny also for possible violations of other Articles of the Constitution: Articles 325 and 326 of the Constitution of India which provided universal adult suffrage and the right to be placed on the electoral rolls—for its dilution in the case of Assam; Article 29(1) of the Constitution which assured cultural rights to communities residing in any part of territory of India: for the purpose of this scrutiny the scope of Article 29(1) as well as the meanings of its content, such as, 'culture' and 'conserve', were to be ascertained; Article

355 of the Constitution pertaining to the duty of the Union to protect the states against 'external aggression' and 'internal disturbance': in this context the judges posed the questions—whether an influx of illegal migrants into a state of India constituted 'external aggression' and/or 'internal disturbance' and whether the expression 'state' occurring in Article 355 referred to a territorial region or included the people living in the state. If it was also the people, would the expression then also include their culture and identity; Article 14 of the Constitution for 'singling out' Assam from other border states, which would comprise a 'distinct class' for the application of exceptional measures: the question being asked in this case was—did the 'isolation' of Assam and the prescription of a separate cut-off date amount to discrimination; Article 21—the right to life and personal liberty of the people of Assam—and whether this right was affected by the 'massive influx of illegal migrants from Bangladesh' (Judgement, Assam Sanmilita Mahasangha 2014, para. 33).

While the above questions pertaining to the constitutional validity of Section 6A of the Citizenship Act began with the acknowledgement by the court of the presence of large numbers of illegal migrants in Assam, question eight in the list wondered if there was a possibility of 'any relief' to these 'large number of migrants from East Pakistan' who had enjoyed 'rights as Citizens of India for over 40 years'; Question nine raised the possibility of Section 6A being contradictory to other provisions of the citizenship Act *and* the Constitution of India by conferring dual citizenship to persons who had not lost the citizenship of East Pakistan (now Bangladesh) by making them 'deemed Citizens of India' in violation of Sections 5(1) and 5(2) of the Citizenship Act, in permitting them to become citizens of India 'without any reciprocity from Bangladesh and without taking the oath of allegiance to the Indian Constitution'; the possibility of the application of Immigrants (Expulsion from Assam) Act 1950, which was a special law brought for the specific purpose of curtailing immigration from East Pakistan into Assam, instead of the Foreigners Act and the Foreigners (Tribunals) Order 1964, which were applicable to the entire country.

Examining the rest of the petition, the judges decided that the legal modalities for conferring citizenship to resolve the 'foreigner's question' was only a part of the Assam Accord. The other and equally substantial components of the accord consisted in securing the international border against future 'infiltration' and the 'preservation of Assamese culture and identity'. In October 2006, the government of Assam had constituted a Committee of Ministers to examine the implementation of the Assam Accord and the complex task of defining the 'Assamese people'. The committee met with political parties, literary bodies, and student groups to deliberate on an appropriate definition. In July 2011, a Cabinet Sub-Committee was constituted by the Central government to examine the question. Leaving it to the government and the Assamese people to deliberate and decide on what constituted Assamese culture, the Supreme Court concentrated on issuing specific directions to the central and state governments under Article 142 of the Constitution of India. Article 142 of the Constitution empowers the Supreme Court to pass an order 'for doing *complete justice* in any cause or matter pending before it' (emphasis added). Such an order is enforceable throughout the territory of India in a way that may be laid down by a law of Parliament and in its absence by a Presidential Order. In the exercise of its powers under Article 142, the Supreme Court issued three directions to the Central government and the government of Assam: the fortification and surveillance of the eastern border including Assam, the reinforcement of the Foreigners Tribunals in Assam, and the augmentation of the process of identification and expulsion of 'declared illegal migrants'. The fortification of the India-Bangladesh border through double-coil fencing, building roads along the border, and continuous patrolling, especially in the riverine and other vulnerable areas, was in line with the Supreme Court judgment in Sarbananda Sonowal case in 2005 in which illegal entry into Indian territory was construed as an act of aggression. This placed a corresponding responsibility on the state to protect its territory, and the Supreme Court decided to monitor the progress made in this direction by the government, by preparing a roadmap for its completion.[13]

The court, however, concerned itself also with securing the territory 'internally' by expediting the process of sieving out foreigners. To this end, it asked the Gauhati High Court to hasten the process of selection of chairpersons and members of the Foreigners Tribunals to ensure that they became operational. The Chief Justice of the Gauhati High Court

---

[13] In May 2015, the court appointed a court commissioner to visit the border areas to study and report the progress made.

was to monitor the tribunals by constituting a special bench to oversee their progress. The Central government was asked to streamline the process of deportation of illegal migrants after discussions with the government of Bangladesh, and to place the outcome of these discussions before the court:

> While taking note of the existing mechanism/procedure for deportation keeping in view the requirements of international protocol, we direct the Union of India to enter into necessary discussions with the Government of Bangladesh to streamline the procedure of deportation. The result of the said exercise be laid before the Court on the next date fixed. The implementation of the aforesaid directions will be monitored by this Court on the expiry of three months from today. In the event it becomes so necessary, the Court will entrust such monitoring to be undertaken by an empowered committee which will be constituted by this Court, if and when required. (Judgement, *Assam Sanmilita Mahasangha*, 2014, para. 47)

Referring specifically to the petition by Assam Public Works (Writ Petition (C) No. 274/2009), the judges laid down a time schedule for updating the NRC by the end of January 2016. Significantly, the preliminary procedures for preparation of the NRC had already been initiated under an order of the Supreme Court delivered on 27 November 2015. In its administrative guidelines, the Supreme Court followed its decision in Sarbananda Sonowal (2005) in construing the 'influx of illegal migrants into the state of India as external aggression'. At the same time, however, it broadened the notion of security to include 'internal disturbance', which involved being alert to and eliminating risks to the Assamese people from outsiders. To this end, it directed the attention of the larger bench of the Supreme Court which would examine the constitutional questions precipitated by the petitions, to consider whether the expression 'state' occurring in Article 355, referred only to a territorial region or included also the people living in the state, their culture, and identity. For its part, by prescribing a deadline for updating the NRC, the court reinforced the responsibility of expulsion of foreigners from Assam on the Central and state government, by a modality that was not mentioned in the Accord.

The second set of petitions filed by the NGOs Swajan and Bimalangshu Roy Foundation in 2012 in the Supreme Court also questioned the constitutional validity of Section 6A. The set of petitions submitted by Swajan and Bimalangshu Roy Foundation focused, however, on that part of section 6A, which treated all Bangladeshi migrants who had entered Assam *after 24 March 1971* as *illegal* and required that they be *deported* by the state. The petitioners lamented the clubbing of all such migrants as illegal and asked that a distinction be made between *illegal migrants* and *displaced persons*, who they identified as Hindu, and other minority groups fleeing Bangladesh to escape religious persecution. Displaced persons, they pleaded, must not be bracketed with illegal migrants to be slotted for deportation. Pointing out the protection given to displaced persons in Section 2 of the Immigrants (Expulsion from Assam) Act 1950, the petitioners asked that displaced persons should constitute a distinct category for legal protection, and that Hindus seeking shelter in Assam should be given citizenship on the same grounds that they were given in Gujarat and Rajasthan between 2004 and 2007.[14] This petition was joined in 2014 by the Joint Action Committee for Bengali Refugees (JACBR). JACBR sought direction from the Supreme Court to the Central government and the government of Assam 'not to expel/push-back the displaced persons belonging to minority communities of Bangladesh, who had been forced to take shelter in various parts of Assam' and to ensure that they were 'not harassed and enjoyed basic human rights and reasonable living conditions, including access to courts, facility of primary education, of residence, permission to work and to travel, and also to protect their life and liberty'. The JACBR had been mobilizing groups around their demand of full and unconditional citizenship for displaced persons and considered the CAA 2003 deleterious for their rights. Sukriti Ranjan Biswas, a Namasudra community leader and president of the JACBR, pointed out that CAA 2003 turned all refugees into 'illegal migrants'. By constraining citizenship by birth it 'disenfranchised their children born on Indian soil', and Section 14(a), inserted by CAA 2003, 'nationalised the process of mandatory registration of citizens' (Chatterjee 2020).

[14] 'Bengali Hindu Refugees: Supreme Court Fixes April 7 for Final Hearing', *The Sentinel*, 31 May 2016.

On 5 December 2013, while the petition challenging 6A by ASM, APW, and AAAA was still being heard, the Ministry of Home Affairs (MHA) issued a notification on updating the NRC.[15] The AAAA, which was one of the three petitioners, filed another petition on 27 July 2014 in the Supreme Court of India challenging Rule 4A of the Citizenship Rules 2003 and the notification issued by the MHA under its provisions (WP(Civil)130 of 2014). This petition, filed about five months before the Supreme Court delivered its judgement in ASM and others, which directed the Central government to update the NRC, requested the Supreme Court to stay the process of updating the NRC in Assam. The AAAA challenged Rule 4A of the Citizenship Rules and the notification on the grounds that they went against Articles 14, 21, and 29 of the Constitution of India. The petitioners submitted that the updated NRC would allow the registration of large numbers of 'illegal migrant populations' from Bangladesh in the NRC as Indian citizens, making it impossible to remove them from Assam in the future. Citizenship would also retrospectively validate their occupation of land and acquisition of property rights in the state, which were otherwise illegal in their capacity as non-citizens. [Filed by Somiran Sharma, advocate for the petitioners on 28 July 2014, copy with the author.]

Following the Supreme Court decision in the case of Assam Sanmilita Mahasangha and others, concerns around a legal affirmation of the citizenship of illegal migrants through the NRC took the route of various petitions. The petition by AAAA discussed earlier was an attempt to halt the process of preparation of NRC in Assam by seeking a stay on the government notification initiating the process. Another petition was submitted to the Supreme Court *after* the process had begun, which raised the concern that *children of illegal migrants* who had entered Assam after 25 March 1971, might become citizens of India by birth (*Deepak*

---

[15] Following the sub-rule 3 of the Citizenship Rules 2003 which require that the Registrar General of Citizen Registration 'shall notify the period and duration of the enumeration in the official gazette', the notification issued by the MHA stated the following: And Whereas the Central Government has decided to update the NRC in Assam; Now pursuant to the provisions of sub rule (3) of rule 4A of the Citizenship (Registration of Indian Citizens and the Issue of National Identity Cards) Rules 2003, the Registrar General of Citizens Registration hereby notifies that the enumeration in respect to the State of Assam shall take place from the date of publication of this notification and shall be completed within a period of three years [F.N.9/5/2009-CRD(NPR) Vol. V issued by C. Chandramouli, Registrar General of Citizens Registration—5219/GI/2013].

Kumar Nath vs. Union of India, WP (Civil) no. 311/2015). The petition contested the constitutionality of section 3 of the Citizenship Act pertaining to citizenship by birth, as amended in 1986 and 2003. The petitioner intervened in the *Assam Sanmilita Mahasangha and Others vs. Union of India* case before the larger bench of the Supreme Court which was to decide on the constitutional questions around section 6A of the Citizenship Act. The petitioners premised their plea on what they presented as an absence of clarification and disregard of 'intervening facts' in the notification ordering the 'updation of the NRC'. Since this process was being undertaken thirty years after the signing of the Assam Accord and forty-four years after the prescribed cut-off date in Section 6A of the Citizenship Act 1955, the 'intervening facts' regarding the citizenship of the descendants of large numbers of 'illegal migrants' in the state had, according to the petitioners, become the *single most important issue* in the 'updation' of NRC: '. . . illegal migrants constituted in the state-around 20% of the state population and it is the children born to such illegal migrants and their citizenship status on which no clarification is forthcoming'. To support their argument, the petitioners cited the 17 December 2014 judgment of the Supreme Court in *Assam Sanmilita Mahasangha and Others vs. Union of India* which referred to the presence of 50 lakh illegal migrants in Assam in 2001:

> On 14th July 2004, in response to an unstarred question pertaining to deportation of illegal Bangladeshi migrants, the Minister of State, Home Affairs, submitted a statement to Parliament indicating therein that the estimated number of illegal immigrants into India as on 31st December was 1.20 crores out of which 50 lakhs were in Assam. (Judgement, *Assam Sanmilita Mahasangha and Others* 2014, para. 16)

Noting that the 2001 National Census had placed the population of Assam at 2.61 crores, 50 Lakhs illegal migrants would comprise 20 per cent of the population of the state, the petitioners drew a connection between the increase in state's population because of an influx of illegal migrants, the majority of whom were Muslims, and the increase in the Muslim population in the state:

It is an admitted fact that the number of migrants have since increased due to continued influx and the census figures for 2011 show that 34.23% of the population in 2011 were Muslims increasing from 30.9% in 2001. The illegal migrants being Muslims, rate of growth of the Muslim population is benchmark of the rate of extent of the infiltration which has been referred to by this honourable court in its earlier judgments in Sarbanand Sonowal and Assam Sanmilita... (Judgement, *Deepak Kumar Nath vs. Union of India* WP (Civil) no. 311/2015)

The petitioners pointed out the inconsistencies within the Citizenship Act and the 'curious situation' that had emerged in Assam as a consequence: Section 6A applicable to Assam granted citizenship to migrants coming into the state only up to 25 March 1971 but Section 3 which lay down the citizenship by birth provisions permitted the grant of citizenship 'unconditionally' to those born in India between 26 January 1950 to 1 July 1987, and to those born up to 3 December 2003, 'even if' only one of the parents was an Indian citizen. Arguing that Section 3 cannot be construed 'to confer a right to citizenship by birth' to children of illegal migrants, the applicants referred to the 'cloud of suspicion', and 'a growing tension in the air', generated mostly by political parties that children of illegal migrants would be entitled for registration in the NRC under Section 3 of the Citizenship Act. Appealing to the court to confirm that the expression 'every person born in India' in Section 3 refers only to children of Indian citizens and of foreigners who are not illegal migrants, the petitioners considered it the statutory duty of the state to 'detect and deport' them. To ensure that the NRC did not include the children of illegal migrants who would claim citizenship by birth under section 3 of the Citizenship Act, the petitioners asked that the consolidated list prepared by the Local Registrar of Citizen Registration after verification should contain the names of persons whose name appeared in any of the electoral rolls prior to the year 1971 or in National Register of Citizens 1951 and their descendants. They requested that a list of descendants of illegal migrants who had migrated after 25 March 1971 be prepared separately.

The arguments in the petition assume significance in affirming descent as a principle of citizenship identity. Yet, the questions being raised in the petition and the appeal to halt the preparation of NRC are important for understanding how the process was being understood in the specific context of Assam. Unlike a National Register of Indian Citizens (NRIC) for the entire country, which would be potentially an exercise in preparing a register where no such register is in existence, in Assam the preparation was being referred to as an exercise of 'updation'—of building upon a pre-existing NRC of 1951. Yet, it was also being argued that the process of updation was being framed erroneously as one of 'identifying citizens' instead of 'identifying and deporting illegal migrants' which had been the understanding in the Assam Accord. It was this displacement of the objective of 'updation' from what was mandated in the Assam Accord, which made the NRC procedure deviate from the promise of the Accord under Clause 5.8 which required that all foreigners who came to Assam on or after 25 March 1971, 'shall continue to be detected [and] deleted' and Clause 10 of the Accord which required 'all land under encroachment to be cleared'.

The Supreme Court resolved the question of citizenship of children born to illegal migrants on 13 August 2019, a couple of weeks before the final NRC was published. The inconsistency within the citizenship Act between citizenship by birth and Assam specific provisions was implicitly acknowledged by the judges as they prioritized the principle of descent rather than birth in addressing the question of citizenship of descendants of illegal migrants in updating the NRC. In an earlier order of 2 July 2018 the Supreme Court had issued directions that the names of *both*—persons who had been identified as Doubtful Voters (DVs) or whose cases were pending before foreigners' tribunals (PFTs) *and* their descendants—could not to be included in the updated NRC. A report was subsequently submitted by Prateek Hajela, then NRC Coordinator, to the court on 10 July 2019 with recommendations laying down a framework that took into consideration the citizenship of the parent from whom legacy was being traced and the constraints on citizenship by birth inserted through amendments in 1986 and 2003. Accordingly, the eligibility of the 'descendants' would be guided by the following principle, stated in Hajela's report:

> . . . . while deciding eligibility of descendants, provisions of Section 3(1) (b) & (c) of the Citizenship Act, 1955 may be important to be taken into account, *though citizenship purely by birth and not by descendance*

(Section 3(1)(a)) is not eligible for inclusion in NRC. It is humbly felt that the substance of Section 3(1)(b) & (c) is that while determining citizenship of any descendant born up to 3 December, 2004, citizenship eligibility of any one of the parents suffices, while for those descendants born on or after 3 December 2004, citizenship eligibility of both the parents needs to be taken into account.[16]

Accordingly, the course of action suggested in the report was as follows:

From a conjoint reading of Hon'ble Supreme Court's order dated 2 July 2018 and the provisions contained in Section 3(1)(b) & (c) of the Citizenship Act, 1955, the following appears to be the best course of action:

a. For any NRC Applications/Claimants, if parent/legacy person through whom eligibility is sought to be established is a DV or DF or PFT, then such persons will not be included in NRC irrespective of the status of the other parent.

b. For those persons born before 3 December 2004, if the parent through whom legacy is drawn is not DV or DF or PFT and is found eligible for inclusion in NRC, but the other parent from whom legacy is not drawn is a DV or DF or PFT, then, such descendants may be included in NRC.

c. For those persons who are born on or after 3 December 2004, they will not be included in NRC if any of the parents is DV or DF or PFT even if the parent from whom legacy is drawn is clear from all angles.[17]

It must be noted that in the course of monitoring the preparation of the NRC, a Supreme Court bench consisting of Justice Ranjan Gogoi and Rohinton Nariman handed out orders regularly to address and resolve contests over definitions of particular categories. The State Coordinator of NRC for Assam, Prateek Hajela was often reporting and appearing before the court. In this instance, the court had 'ordered' the NRC coordinator to issue a public notice to invite 'contests' to the proposals in

---

[16] Judgement, Assam Public Works vs. Union of India, 13 August 2019 (WP (Civil) No. 274 of 2009).
[17] Ibid.

his report by 'stakeholders', which would be taken up in the court. The judges decided to go with the course of action suggested by the NRC coordinator finding it 'infeasible' to order new modalities of preparation of the NRC:

> The entire NRC exercise having been performed on the aforesaid basis, the same cannot be now ordered to be reopened by initiation of a fresh exercise on certain other parameters that have been suggested on behalf of the intervenors/applicants on the strength of the provisions of Section 3(1)(a) of the Act.[18]

Hajela's proposals had been contested by Interlocutory Applications on the ground that they contradicted the provisions of Section 3(1)(a) of the Citizenship Act 1955 under which 'every person' born in India on or after 26 January 1950 but before 1 July 1987, would be a citizen of India. In its order, the judges noted that the 'purport and effect' of the provisions of Section 3(1)(a) and (b) was already before the Constitution Bench of the Supreme Court in Writ Petition (Civil) No. 311 of 2015, where the expression 'every person born in India' was being examined.

The adjudicatory regime of citizenship in Assam can be seen as having two trajectories. The 'illegal migrant' figures centrally in both these trajectories. One of these can be traced to the Sarbananda Sonowal judgement, which continues to provide the referential frameworks for citizenship in the state. Not only did the judgement structure the discursive field in which the illegal migrant figured as a legal category, it provided the imperative for an emphatic display of the sovereign power of the state in buttressing the territory against border transgressions. A second trajectory emerges as a recursive field structured around the Assam Accord so that the legal framing of the illegal migrant would be validated or found wanting with reference to the accord. The NRC traversed both trajectories as the Supreme Court in ASM judgment 'recalled' its judgement in Sarbananda Sonowal case to reinforce the logic of the security state. The NRC as an outcome of the ASM judgement has continually been tested against the Assam Accord. There has also been, however, an alternative trajectory where the exceptional citizenship provisions for

---

[18] Ibid.

Assam—reflecting the agreement reached through the Assam Accord—have been contested to erase the exceptions for Assam in the citizenship Act to go back to the 1951 NRC as the source of Assamese legacy.

Documentary Regime

It is the middle of March in 2016. Guwahati is dusty and just about getting warm. The dates for Assembly polls in Assam have been announced and the Model Code of Conduct regulating electoral competition is in place. Speculations around the fate of the ruling Congress party, whose Chief Minister Tarun Gogoi was seeking re-election for a fourth term, and the BJP's prospects of reversing its fortunes in the state in an alliance with the AGP, are rife. The election campaign is, however, still tepid. Driving down the Guwahati–Shillong Road to the NRC office, a gigantic poster of JNU Students Union President Kanhaiya Kumar behind bars, painted across almost the entire front of an abandoned flour mill asks, '*have achche din come?*' (Have the good days [as promised by the BJP], come?). The poster invokes the possibility of a political culture that was grounded in questions of constitutionalism and rule of law. Yet, quite like the façade of the abandoned building that it served, the poster occluded the simmering desire within the state for aspirational citizenship embedded in the continuum of Assamese identity. This continuum has made itself manifest along two overlapping axes of political and cultural identities—with the resolution being sought in one case through the 'updation' of the NRC and in the other through the establishment of successive committees that would determine what constitutes an authentic Assamese identity in pursuit of the provisions of Clause 6 of the Assam Accord. The foreigner's question, which became integral to the Assam movement in the 1980s, has persisted. Its resolution was, however, no longer being sought in the violent elimination of the non-Assamese outsider, but through a political consensus on identifying those who *belong* through legal and bureaucratic intervention. It is towards this end that Assam saw an unprecedented and exceptional exercise of identifying 'citizens' to prepare a *National* Register of Citizens for the state of Assam. My visit to Guwahati took place in March 2016, a few weeks before the State Assembly election in April, which saw the ouster of the 15 years long Congress rule in the state, and the installation of a BJP government with Sarbananda Sonowal as the Chief Minister.

'It is a register of *Indian* citizens', an eminent journalist from Assam, who has written extensively on the preparation of the NRC, corrects me, when I ask him about the preparation of the NRC for *Assamese* citizens. The register being prepared in Assam is indeed of *Indian* citizens. But the pedigree of Indian citizenship is traced to an Assamese *legacy*, which makes the NRC in Assam a register of Assamese-Indian citizens or Indian citizens who have an Assamese origin. The identification of Indian citizens simultaneously as Assamese recognizes a hyphenated citizenship, hitherto not found in the legal vocabulary of citizenship in India. Significantly, the harmonization of what was a conflicting relationship in the 1980s has been achieved by marking out the illegal alien ('Bengali speaking, Muslim, Bangladeshi infiltrator'), as the constituent other. The conceptual apparatus of citizenship summoned by the components of the hyphenated citizen—'Indian' and 'Assamese'—iron out the multiple layers and corresponding contestations within each.

The auto driver waxes eloquent on the prospects of the BJP in the coming election. As for the NRC, he felt fortunate for having been able to muster the documents required to trace his Assamese legacy through his grandfather to the 1951 NRC, and through his mother's refugee card issued in 1962; his son's birth certificate could be traced to him, and eventually to his Assamese legacy—his grandparents. Three generations and three identification registers, each testifying to and affirming his pedigree as an Indian citizen in Assam. 'What do you think—is the NRC any good?', I persist, expecting him to raise a rant against it. He surprises me, however: 'It will be very beneficial. NRC is a good thing. It will stop those coming from outside, and our future generations will live here through our link. Hindus can also come and stay, but will not get any government facilities'. Looking forward to the post-NRC future, he is torn between reminiscing about the trauma of the 1980s and the mass killing of Bengali Muslims, and the closure that he now finds in the affirmation of his status as a citizen, his Assamese legacy traced and confirmed through all prescribed signposts.

The NRC in Assam works on the principle of tracing citizenship to a legacy of Assamese descent going back to the 1951 NRC and to the next signpost of 1971—the 'additional load'—as Prateek Hajela called it, in an interaction with the author during this visit. The cab driver's relief at being able to produce the documents for identification and enumeration in the NRC, was indicative of the promise the process held of bringing closure to the burden of suspect citizenship Bengali speaking migrants have carried. On the other hand, it also revealed affinity to a model of citizenship in which the 'crisis' generated by migrants and aliens is resolved by prescribing terms of inclusion that are premised in a 'solidarity based model of citizenship'. Under these terms, being an Assamese was ultimately about developing strong bonds of integration, marked by the logic of closure.

Yet, the NRC was not *only* about integration and closure, or even the recognition of an Assamese identity by descent or through the affirmation of legal residence in Assam. It was equally about a humongous bureaucratic exercise of identification and enumeration, of putting in place efficient and effective identification regimes, and documentation practices, often associated with the exercise of state power, and state-formative practices. A body of scholarship has established that such practices produce the structural effect of the state, whereby the state appears to exist through palpable ruling practices. Fixing territorial boundaries and making its inhabitants legible are important ingredients of statecraft, which seek to make the citizen a stable and enumerable category, amenable to specific governmental practices. Identification practices are mechanisms through which the state builds enduring relationships with its citizens (Torpey 2000). Passport regimes, for example, have historically embodied the imperative to monopolize the control over people's movements. Documents such as driving licenses, passports, voter ID cards, ration cards, etc., are commonly used identification documents. Yet, they are not primarily identity documents, but documents devised to serve other purposes. Documents such as these, and now the Aadhaar card, for example, establish identity to enable access to specific rights and privileges, and also welfare benefits. The regimes of national Identity systems, enumerating entire populations of nation-states, make these systems more comprehensive, and consequential. In recent years, digitalized and biometric identification systems have made identification regimes more efficient and more intrusive than the older paper-based documentation regimes, for their potential for surveillance of citizens. The diverse components of surveillance, viz., tools and technologies of survey, measurement, census, etc., have long been used for marking what lies within the purview of the state's powers of extraction and control, enhancing, and entrenching its powers of revenue collection, garnering military service, law enforcement, and policing. Over the years these tools have become more sophisticated, specialized, and differentiated, and increasingly more nebulous, which does not require the constant proximity between the law enforcers and the people (Singh 2014, 42). It is indeed possible to see the NRC as part of the continuing legacy of governmental practices of the state, and its potential for surveillance and control.

Yet, the NRC regime is also a manifestation of citizenship practices that seek to resolve the crisis in citizenship generated by the difficulties states face in establishing and reinforcing the separation between citizens and aliens. In his book on how illegal immigrants acquire citizenship in developing countries, Kamal Sadiq posits that the idea that states can make a separation between citizens and immigrants/aliens is based on the 'distinguishability assumption' (Sadiq 2009, 7)—that states can allocate, distribute, and manage national citizenship by setting up a wall between citizens and aliens. This assumption is, he argues, conceptually blind to the role that documents play in bridging the gap between citizens and foreigners. A more adequate conception for citizenship would be 'documentary citizenship', which 'emphasises the role that documents play in acquiring citizenship, whether the documents are legal or not and whether the newly admitted citizen is a legal immigrant or not' (Sadiq 2009, 8). While making this argument, Sadiq challenges the 'commonsense idea' that citizenship can be acquired through an 'orderly immigration processes based on clear, legally specified criteria'. The idea of 'documentary citizenship' put forward by Sadiq challenges 'deeply held beliefs about what citizenship is and how it functions', and makes the claims that documentary citizenship is as much a 'normal path of legally specified immigration' and 'provides a more empirically accurate description of the actual citizenship practices in countries like India, Pakistan and Malaysia' (Sadiq 2009).

The documentary regime spawned by the NRC in Assam shows an inversion in the relationship between documents and citizenship. Instead of the assumption that one would possess certain documents only because one was a citizen, the NRC has made it possible to say that one is a citizen on the authority of the documents one possesses. A citizenship regime founded on documents as 'evidence of citizenship' (Sadiq 2009), relies on identification practices that activate the bureaucratic apparatus of the state, which invokes a model of rationality based on efficiency and procedural certainty, to elicit trust in the integrity of the model. Yet, the NRC in Assam unleashed a process that produced estrangement and vulnerability among large sections of the people who sought insertion in the register of citizens but were caught up in the legal and adjudicatory imbroglio over the definition of categories and the uncertainty of outcome. The political consensus around the NRC ultimately proved to be fragile. It was fractured by the fraught history of the NRC, its imbrication in past and contemporary electoral politics, and the overwhelming control of the Supreme Court on the process of identification, all of which became exacerbated with the introduction of the CAB by the BJP government in July 2016.

Identification and Bureaucratic Rationality

Elaborating the complex modalities of updating the NRC, Commissioner, and State Coordinator of NRC, Prateek Hajela foregrounds aspects of the NRC, which are distinct from the political imperatives of tracing an Assamese legacy.[19] With a degree in Engineering from an Indian Institute of Technology (IIT), Prateek Hajela professes a bureaucratic rationality, which is propelled by the logic of efficiency, and driven by the objective of developing a foolproof mechanism of identifying Indian citizens who can give evidence of being a 'legatee'. At the same time, since the efficiency of the identification system depended on the active and willing participation of the people of Assam, the technical model had to be made acceptable and comprehensible to the Assamese people as a whole. The question of acceptability may be seen as distinct from comprehensibility, although the two are consonant with each other. To be acceptable, a system needs to be made familiar, which would, however, be possible only after confidence was built. Indeed, in the sequence communicated by the NRC Commissioner, generating trust for the NRC was the first essential step before the actual process of enumeration could begin. Ajupi Baruah,

---

[19] Conversation with Mr Prateek Hajela, NRC Headquarters, Guwahati, 18 March 2016.

Project Manager with the NRC, described the process as akin to invoking a sentiment—of creating a frenzy—which could then be channelled into winning people's trust, alleviating their apprehensions, and ensuring their participation.[20] The NRC hoardings and visual promos played in cinema halls and television channels included *Bihu* songs and dances around the NRC theme. Using familiar cultural tropes, these promotional videos intended to build curiosity and subsequently anticipation, which would translate into popular acceptance for the NRC, enabling collective participation in a massive and complex exercise. Traditional dance forms like the *bihu* were effective in communicating the message of the NRC through the trope of a festive dance that is performed collectively. Indeed, the NRC anthem sung by the popular Assamese singer Zubeen Garg (actual name, Jibon Borthakur), wove together pleasing visuals of plurality and cultural diversity, promising the following:

> *We are the citizens of this country*
> *NRC represents our each and every soul.*
> *We hold each other's hands*
> *NRC gives courage in our hearts.*
> *Our identity, security, rights,*
> *Peace, progress, and unity together.*
> *Rashtriya nagarik panthi*
> *National Register of Citizens, NRC, NRC*

The emotive appeal of the NRC anthem lay in the promise of citizenship as a collective national political identity, juxtaposed on visuals affirming an inclusive Assamese identity characterized by cultural plurality. A leaflet issued by the State Coordinator NRC, Assam, invoked the spirit of *responsible* participation, by reminding citizens of their civic role in 'standing united and making the NRC a success story for *us and our future generations*'.[21]

Once curiosity had been generated and anticipation built, the second and more difficult step was to make people familiar with the complex

---

[20] Conversation with Ajupi Baruah, NRC Headquarters, Guwahati, 18 March 2016.
[21] 'Updation of NRC in Assam', NRC leaflet no. NRC Assam/Leaflet/L.D.PUBL-APPLCN/ 2015. Emphasis added.

procedures of application and verification. A range of strategies were adopted by the office of the NRC in Assam to make the system comprehensible to people. These included educational videos and television advertisements, newspaper advertisements, leaflets, pamphlets, and posters with illustrative examples of registration of a fictitious family, public meetings, community-level meetings, and gram sabhas, etc., to build, as the NRC Commissioner expressed it, people's 'capacity' to register themselves.[22]

It may be recalled here, that the ASM's petition before the Supreme Court questioned the constitutional validity of the 1985 amendment and consequently Section 6A of the Citizenship Act for being at variance with Article 6 of the Constitution of India, in setting a chronological deadline for Assam (24 March 1971) which was different from the constitutional deadline. The court entrusted the question of validity to the constitutional bench and confined itself to issuing instructions to the state government to expedite the process of updating the NRC for Assam and to the Gauhati High Court to accelerate the process of identification of foreigners and illegal migrants. The entire process of preparation of the NRC was to be monitored by the Supreme Court. The thumb rule for the identification of a citizen was to trace his or her pedigree to an ancestor who had resided in Assam on or before the deadline of 24 March 1971, by referring to what the NRC called the 'legacy data'. The data of the 1951 NRC and the electoral rolls published in Assam up to 24 March 1971 cumulatively comprised the legacy data. Finding an ancestor in the legacy data to whom a person could trace direct descent was the most common mode of identification for inclusion in the NRC. Before the process of tracing legacy could begin, the NRC office had to coordinate the compilation of large and dispersed data of the 1951 NRC and the electoral rolls which were available at district levels into one consolidated computerized database. The statutory publication of the legacy data was done alongside the launch of 2500 NRC Seva Kendras (NSKs) on 27 March 2015, marking the inauguration of the process of updating the NRC. Spread across the state, in districts, and clusters of villages, the NSKs housed the published legacy data, provided access to the digital database, and also served as

---

[22] See, *Government of Assam, National Register of Citizens*, http://nrcassam.nic.in/faq01.html accessed on 14 May 2016.

application receiving centres. The legacy data was also available online to facilitate the search. Having searched an ancestor, the computerized database assigned a unique code—the Unique Legacy Data Code—to each record. The Unique Legacy Data Code was an 11 digit number, which was issued to an applicant, giving a numerical code to link up with an ancestor in the legacy data. The applicant quoted the legacy data code at the time of submission, and while the legacy code became the basis for the verification of the applicant's claims, it also linked him or her to others who would have the same code because of 'common ancestry'. Apart from obtaining the legacy trace through the legacy data code, the applicants furnished a number of *prescribed* 'linkage documents' to establish eligibility for inclusion in the updated NRC. Linkage documents established connections with the ancestor appearing in the legacy data and included documents, which carried the names of both the ancestor and applicant.[23]

Apart from those who could trace their legacy to the 1951 NRC, there were other categories of persons eligible for inclusion, namely, those who came to Assam on or after 1 January 1966 but before 25 March 1971, and had registered themselves with the Foreigners Registration Regional Office (FRRO) and had not been identified as illegal migrants or foreigners. The 'original inhabitants' of Assam and their descendants, whose citizenship could be ascertained by the registering authority, were another category. Subsequent Supreme Court orders permitted Indian citizens and their children and descendants who moved to Assam after 24 March 1971 to apply for inclusion, if they could furnish evidence that they were resident in any part of the country outside Assam on 24 March 1971. The project officer with the NRC clarified that in the absence of any proof of residence, and no legacy data code, original inhabitants like the Karbis could be registered without documents, through the affirmation of their status by what was called a 'speaking order'. Through such

---

[23] According to the NRC website, the following documents were admissible: birth certificate, land documents, pan card, board university exam certificate, bank, LIC policy, Post Office documents, GP Secretary certificate, electoral roll, etc. In case an ancestors name was not found in the legacy data, application for inclusion could be made for inclusion in the NRC by providing any of the other admissible documents issued before 24 March 1971 (midnight), namely (i) land and tenancy records; (ii) citizenship certificate; (iii) permanent residential certificate; (iv) refugee registration certificate; (v) passport; (vi) LIC policy; (vii) Government-issued license/certificate; (viii) government service/employment certificate; (ix) Bank/post office accounts; (x) birth certificate; (xi) Board/university educational certificate; (xii) court records/processes. See http://nrcassam.nic.in (accessed 14 March 2016).

an order, the Local Registrar of Citizen Registration (LRCR) could certify that even though they possessed no documents, on the basis of their language, food, clothes etc., it could be assumed that they were 'original inhabitants' of the state.

After the publication of the legacy data and the launch of the NSKs, the process of actual application began. The forms were distributed to the public at their houses but could also be downloaded from the website. Photocopies of the forms could be used as well. It was the head of the family who was expected to apply for the entire family, including the daughters. All members of the family residing in Assam or outside it, in any other part of the country or abroad, had to be included in the application. In the case of institutional homes, like orphanages, old age homes, asylums, etc., the head of the institution could apply for the inmates.[24] Photocopies of all documents, showing the names of the persons in the family who figure in the legacy data, and additional linkage documents showing relationship with the ancestor in the legacy document were submitted at NSKs designated for particular localities, whose officials would be responsible for conducting the physical verification of the details by visiting the addresses mentioned in the form.

At the time of my visit, the process of updating the NRC was at the stage of verification of 68.33 Lakh application forms which had been received, along with the 5 Crore supporting documents.[25] Verification was being done as per the provisions of the Citizenship (Registration of Citizens and Issue of Identity Cards) Rules 2003, which consisted of two parts—office verification and field verification. Office verification entailed the scanned and uploaded copies of all the documents being sent to the issuing authority to confirm whether the document was in fact issued by it and whether the details in the document corresponded with the records that existed with the issuing authority. If official verification was intended to weed out forged documents, field verification consisted of house-to-house visits by the verification team intended to check identity proof, verify submitted documents for validity and establishment of the relationship, and collect details of the 'family tree' (list of family

---

[24] NRC, Leaflet on application form receipt, filing, and application, 2015 (not numbered).
[25] NRC, Leaflet on verification of NRC application forms and family tree detail submission for an error-free NRC, Leaflet no. NRC Assam/leaflet/verification-1/2015.

members) to match the detail with those submitted by various applicants across Assam. Matching the family tree submitted by applicants with the one generated by the computer software on the basis of forms received was designed to detect false claims.[26] The *family tree* was an innovation where the authenticity of claims to residence and citizenship were expected to be affirmed through the kinship network. A family tree form was filled up by the visiting team from the information given by the applicant in the form and to the visiting team. This 'manual family tree' was checked against the computer software generated family tree carrying the details of all the persons who had claimed to be children or grandchildren of the same legacy person.[27]

Kheli Meli: Estrangement, Documents, and Legacy

'NRC Ulaigol', a *Bihu* video in the music album 'Taxi Driver Bihu' presents a satire on the NRC. Lyrics saying that NRC will make the 'bidexi' (foreigners) 'swadexi' (nationals), with a visual elaboration of the foreigner and the citizen, the video strings together clips showing who benefited from the NRC and who lost.[28] The lyrics translated from the Assamese are:

> NRC emerged, what happened, what happened
> O foreigners became nationals;
> The kings and emperors smiled
> We only had to lose some money... Some touts became rich...
> The village headman's brother became rich...
> The photographers have increased their business...
> When NRC emerged, they came, they came;
> The sisters who eloped, they came... The brothers who live afar, they came...
> It is very good, very good, that NRC emerged
> O friend, the relation between two families remained...

[26] Ibid.
[27] Ibid.
[28] The link to this Bihu song video is https://www.youtube.com/watch?v=w_5wAFtyacc (accessed on 17 May 2016).

The video captures the social perception of the manner in which the documentary regime set in motion by the NRC involved middlemen and the exchange of money in which the people had to spend money to procure documents. Simultaneously, with the family becoming integral to proving 'legacy', all those who had become strangers or were estranged 'returned' to the fold. As discussed before, the NRC in Assam was prepared by *inviting applications* from all residents with documents that established their Indian citizenship traced to an Assamese legacy. The list of 'admissible documents' were segregated in two. List A consisted of those documents issued before the midnight of 24 March 1971 which provided proof of residence in Assam for 'self' or 'ancestor' up to midnight of 24 March 1971. List B consisted of 'link documents' which would establish lineage with an 'ancestor' in List A. List A included the 1951 NRC and the electoral rolls up to the midnight of 24 March 1971 as well as specific 'public documents' issued by the government. These 'public documents' were land or tenancy records, citizenship certificate, permanent resident certificate, refugee registration certificate, passport, any license, or certificate issued by the government, government service employment certificate, bank/post office accounts, birth certificate, board/university educational certificate, and court records/processes. A person possessing *any one* of these documents with his or her name on it could establish through them his/her claim to be part of the NRC. Two other documents—Circle Officer/Gaon Panchayat (GP) Secretary Certificate in respect of married women migrating after marriage, which could be of any year *before or after* 24 March (midnight) 1971 and Ration Card issued up to the midnight of 24 March 1971 could be presented as supporting documents. These could be accepted as evidence only if accompanied by any one of the documents in List A. In case the name in any of the documents of List A was not of the applicant himself/herself but that of an ancestor, the applicant had to submit a document mentioned in List B to establish a relationship with an ancestor whose name figured in List A. These documents had to be 'legally acceptable' and 'clearly prove such a relationship'. Birth certificate, land document, board/university certificate, bank/LIC/post office records, circle officer/GP Secretary certificate in case of married women, electoral roll, ration card, and any other *legally acceptable* document, were listed under this category.[29] The discussion in this section shows how the conditions of legal acceptability would become a matter of dispute in a large number of cases. The ability of a document to *clearly prove a relationship* could similarly remain in the domain of ambiguity, opening spaces for interlocution, and interpretation by the executive and judiciary.[30]

To sum up, the data of the 1951 NRC, the electoral rolls published in Assam up to 24 March 1971, cumulatively comprised the legacy data. Finding an ancestor in the legacy data to trace direct descent was made necessary for inclusion in the NRC for those who were not themselves its part. The rules devised for the preparation of the NRC gave the 1951 NRC legitimacy by inscribing it in a *national* identification regime and installing it as the core around which incremental electoral rolls could cluster. Applications to be placed in the NRC were made on the basis of specified documents that alone could prove citizenship. The power of evidence assumed by documents drew from their capacity to establish linkage with the legacy data. An eleven digit Unique Legacy Data Code provided the applicant with a numerical link with the ancestor. The legacy code embodied a personal claim for verification for the applicant but also acted as a *legacy trace* linking the applicant with others who had been allotted the same code because of common ancestry. The legacy trace could be authenticated only through 'linkage documents' carrying the names of the applicant and the ancestor who was present in the legacy data.

In an inversion of the relationship between documents and citizenship, the evidentiary paradigm invoked in the preparation of the NRC in Assam listed documents which would, under specified conditions, become 'proof of citizenship' (Sadiq 2009). Under these conditions, the meaning of documents such as the voter ID card, which are identity documents that can be obtained only by citizens changed, as they became part of the identification regime spawned by the NRC in Assam. These documents acquired evidentiary worth only by becoming part of a serialized link in relationship with other documents. Significantly, all

---

[29] Website of the Office of the State Coordinator of NRC, Government of Assam. http://nrcassam.nic.in/admin-documents.html (accessed on 10 March 2019).

[30] See Sahana Ghosh (2019) whose anthropological study of the 'detectability' of the 'illegal migrant' by the Foreigners Tribunals refers to modalities of policing in the process of detection and Akhil Dutta (2018) on the judicial interventions and the NRC process in Assam.

these documents, which were discrete in their origin and purpose, were connected together to serve another purpose—to establish the lineage of the applicant—which would henceforth constitute the proof of citizenship. Indeed, categories such as 'legacy', 'legacy documents', 'legacy data', 'legacy trace', and 'unique legacy data code', were innovations that made documents meaningful or irrelevant for the purposes of NRC.

In this process, documents got re-inscribed in a register alien to its original inscription and purpose. When it was being prepared in 1948, the electoral roll came to be seen as an extraordinary and unprecedented 'act of faith'. It inserted 'the people' into the administrative structures of the state by linking the abstract text of the Constitution to their everyday lives as a popular narrative, and prepared the ground for 'the conceptions and principles of democratic citizenship' (Shani 2018, 7). Writing about the first general election in India in a short story titled 'The Election Game', R. K. Narayan recounts the election fever that had seized the people participating in what he called a 'large scale rehearsal for political life'. No one, young or old, was left untouched 'as though a sense of sovereignty [was] aroused even in the most insignificant of us' (Narayan 1952). The coincidence of citizenship with voting rights and universal adult franchise, involved a governmental activity of identification different from any other similar exercise since its objective was not the enhancement of the governmental power of the state, but the affirmation of popular sovereignty and transition to a democratic republic.

As a legacy document, the electoral roll was recalled on a different register which changed its *authority* from a text embodying popular sovereignty to a document providing legacy trace, to serve the imperatives of the identification regime of the state. The worth of the legacy document depended on the extent to which it strengthened the regime of legibility and evidentiary framework of which it was now a part. This was evident in a 2019 Gauhati High Court judgement that rejected a petition by Babul Islam against a Foreigners Tribunal order pronouncing him a foreigner. Babul Islam had placed before the court his Electoral Photo Identity Card (EPIC) as proof of citizenship. While the EPIC is a voter identity card and not a citizenship card, the fact that only citizens can vote makes for a stable relationship between the two. The Gauhati High Court refused to recognize the EPIC as evidence of citizenship on the grounds that it did not possess the attribute of 'due' proof which could make the EPIC 'admissible' evidence. The EPIC would be an evidence of citizenship only if it could be inserted in the chain of validation linking it up with the pre-1971 voter list.[31]

Close on the heels of the judgement in Babul Islam's case, the same bench of the Gauhati High Court rejected a petition by Jabeda Khatun, a 50-year-old woman from Guwahari village refusing to consider the 15 documents she had submitted as evidence proving citizenship.[32] Jabeda Khatun had petitioned the Gauhati High Court challenging the Foreigners Tribunal opinion of 31 May 2019, declaring her a foreigner 'of the post-1971 stream'. Under the procedure laid down in the Foreigners Act 1946, Jabeda Khatun was issued a notice to appear before the Foreigners Tribunal in Baksa, Tamulpur, Assam to prove her Indian citizenship. Maintaining that she was a citizen of India by birth, Jabeda Khatun filed a written statement before the Tribunal along with documents to support her claim. In her statement, she claimed to have been born to Jabed Ali and Jahura Khatun in Bangalpara. Due to river embankment erosion, her father had shifted from Bangalpara to Dongoragaon and lived there till his death. She was married to Mohammed Rejak Ali of the same village and her name appeared in the voter lists of 2008. Her name had figured in the voter list in 1997 too, but she was marked in the list as a 'D' voter. Among the documents submitted by her were land revenue payment receipt, bank passbook, voter lists, and Permanent Account Number (PAN) Card. The NRC 1951 and voter lists of 1966 and 1970 where the names of her grandparents and parents figured were submitted by her as proof of her parentage. In addition, Jabeda Khatun had also submitted certificates by the *gaon bura* (village headman) which stated that she was the daughter of Jabed Ali, a permanent resident of village Dongoragaon, and that she had married Rajek Ali. Jabeda Khatun's citizenship claims were turned down because of the absence of *appropriate* legacy documents. None of the documents she presented before the court could establish her links with her parents in the legacy documents. The

---

[31] Writ petition (WP(C)7426/2019 by Babul Islam against an order of the Foreigners Tribunal, where he was declared as a foreigner of post-1971 stream. See also, 'Gauhati High Court Says Electoral Photo Identity Card Not a Proof of Indian Citizenship', *India Today*, 17 February 2020.

[32] Writ petition no. WP(C) 7451/2019 before the Gauhati High Court. Also, 'Land Revenue Receipts, PAN Card, Bank Documents No Proof of Citizenship: Gauhati High Court', *The Hindu*, 18 February 2020.

evidentiary weight of *gaon bura's* certificate as a linkage document was limited by its subsidiary status among the admissible documents, where it was listed as a 'supporting document'. Court decisions in earlier cases had interpreted this status to mean that the certificate could only serve as proof of a woman's *migration* to her 'matrimonial village' after marriage, not of her citizenship. Affirming the decision of the Foreigners Tribunal, the Gauhati High Court decided that Jabeda Khatun was a 'foreigner' since she had 'failed' to prove her 'linkage' to legacy persons through appropriate legacy documents.[33]

The status of the Panchayat certificate as a *document* was made ambiguous through its listing as a 'supporting' document with no independent standing. While the list of admissible documents clearly says that the Panchayat certificate could be submitted by women who had migrated upon marriage, the purpose of such a certificate and its role in proving citizenship remained contested. The courts deliberated upon the principles that should guide the evaluation of panchayat certificates as evidence for the purpose of the NRC. It was in the Gauhati High Court judgement in February 2017 in the case of *Manowara Bewa alias Manora Bewa vs. Union of India and Others*, which was turned down by the Supreme Court of India in December 2017, that issues under contention were laid out for judicial scrutiny. On 17 March 2016, Manowara Bewa was declared a foreigner by a Foreigners Tribunal in Dhubri in Assam on the ground that she had 'failed to discharge her burden under Section 9 of the Foreigners Act 1946 to prove that she was not a foreigner'. Under the provisions of the Foreigners Act 1946, if a 'reference' has been made against a person that he or she is a foreigner, the burden of proving citizenship is on the person himself/herself, who has to be 'examined as her own witness' and must submit evidence to prove otherwise. Manowara Bewa had submitted five documents to the Foreigners Tribunal to prove her citizenship. Among these documents was a certificate issued by the gram panchayat of Sahebganj, a school certificate issued by the Headmaster of Khagrabari School, and land documents. Along with these, she submitted the NRC 1951 and the voter list of 1966. Her father's name appeared in both. The Tribunal, however, noted discrepancies in the spelling of her father's

---

[33] Jabeda Begum @ Jabeda Khatun vs. The Union of India and Others, WP(C)7451/2019, decided by the Gauhati High Court on 12 February 2020.

name in the linkage and legacy documents and concluded that they were different persons. Based on this, the Tribunal decided that the evidence submitted by Manowara Bewa was not 'trustworthy' and that she had 'failed miserably to discharge her burden of proof', 'with cogent and reliable evidence that she is born through genuine Indian parents'.

The Gauhati High Court found 'no error or infirmity' in the Foreigners Tribunal's view. It concluded that 'a cumulative analysis of the evidence adduced by the petitioner' presented 'a bundle of confusing and contradictory statements making the contention of the petitioner of being an Indian citizen totally unreliable'. The High Court found Manowara Bewa an unreliable witness because of what it called 'material discrepancy' in her written statement and evidence submitted. The court found the absence of information regarding the date, year, and place of birth, lack of coherence on significant biographical signposts pertaining to the place where she was born and went to school and where she migrated after marriage, and the fact that she obtained the school certificate and GP certificate *only after* the enquiry proceedings against her had started, suspicious. All the documents submitted by her, the court argued, could, therefore 'amount to admission of content but not its truth'. In both the cases—of Manowara Bewa and Jabeda Khatun—the court had refused to accept the testimony of relatives as evidence of *relationship* with the legacy person. It rejected the certificate issued by the village panchayat on the ground that the petitioner failed to establish the authority of the documents through a corroborating oral testimony of the issuing authority in the court.

What is, however, significant about the Gauhati High Court's decision in Manowara Bewa case is the long discussion in the judgement from paragraph 33 to 75, after the dismissal of the petition had been announced in paragraph 31, and directions to the Deputy Commissioner of Police, and Superintendent of Police (Border) had been issued in paragraph 32. Under the head 'Larger Issue', this discussion focused entirely on the Gram Panchayat (GP) Secretary's certificate. In the course of its proceedings, the Gauhati High Court decided to take a 'closer look' at the modalities through which the certificate was obtained, whether issuing such a certificate was within the purview of the powers of the village panchayats as laid down in the Assam Panchayat Act 1994, and whether the Panchayat and Rural Development Department were taken into confidence when a Cabinet-sub-committee took the decision to include the Gram Panchayat certificate as a supporting document. In doing so, the High Court went beyond the merits of Manowara Bewa's case to what it called the 'larger issue' of resolving the ambiguity surrounding the evidentiary value of the GP certificate. It concluded that the GP certificate issued to women who had migrated to other villages after marriage or certificates issued by jurisdictional circle officers in urban areas, mentioned in the 'illustrative list of documents admissible' as a supporting document was invalid in law and would have *'no effect in the process of verification of claims for inclusion in the NRC'*.

While invalidating the GP certificate, the High Court found it contradictory that a document issued *after* 24 March 1971 could be considered admissible as evidence for inclusion in the NRC. Questioning the evidentiary relevance of a 'contemporary document', the only document in the 'illustrative list' which was permitted to have a date of issue after the prescribed cut-off date, the judges argued against the *necessity of new documents to facilitate the registration of migrating married women*:

> ... was it *really necessary* on the part of the State Government to create new certificates ostensibly for migrating married women *to enable them* to show linkage with their parents prior to the cut-off date of 24.03.1971. *Is it really the duty of the State to facilitate such an exercise when it is for the applicant to justify his claim for inclusion in the updated NRC by producing necessary documentary evidence? Are the remaining existing documents not enough?* Is it the duty of the State to facilitate creation of additional new documents, that too in millions, for inclusion of the certificate holder in updated NRC which would be prima facie proof of citizenship...? (Judgement, Manowara Bewa, 2017, para. 45, emphasis added)

Like most other judgements which referred to it to buttress their argument, in this case too, the judges held that *facilitation* of documentary evidence went 'against the grain' of the Supreme Court's judgment in *Sarbananda Sonowal vs. Union of India* (2005), which placed the burden of proof upon the person whose citizenship was disputed. There were sound reasons to do so, the judges argued, since information about date and place of birth, names of parents and grandparents—and *their* place of birth—which were relevant for proving citizenship, lay in the domain of 'the *personal knowledge* of the person concerned and not of the authorities of the State'. Reinforcing the regime of suspicion, the judges considered it imperative to *extract* this evidence rather than *facilitate* it, since 'Assam was facing "external aggression" and "internal disturbance" on account of large-scale influx of Bangladeshi nationals into the State ... making the life of the people of Assam wholly insecure' (Judgement, Manowara Bewa 2017, para. 47).

The judge rejected the certificate issued by the village panchayat on the grounds that the petitioner had failed to establish the validity of the documents through a corroborating oral testimony of the issuing authority in the court. Following the pattern in Jabeda Begum Case, the court refused to accept the testimony of relatives as evidence of relationship with the legacy person. It is significant that even when the information regarding relationships and blood ties was construed as 'personal knowledge', its affirmation in the court could only be done through 'public' documents. According to Section 74 of the Indian Evidence Act 'public documents' are documents 'forming acts or records of the act—(i) of the sovereign authority, (ii) of official bodies and tribunals, and (iii) of public officers, legislative, judicial and executive ... as well as public records kept in any state of private documents'. Certificates by gaon bura pertaining to relationships by marriage could not be considered public until they were 'heard' by the court for attestation of their veracity. The High Court ruled that the certificate of residence issued by the village panchayat could not be considered a 'public document' for a range of reasons. That the certificate was not issued from a 'record' that the Panchayat maintained under the provisions of the 1994 Panchayati Raj Act and Rules was among the most significant. The certificate could, therefore, only be a 'private' document expressing personal knowledge whose 'truthfulness' had to be attested by the issuing officer in the court, who would take 'full responsibility as to the contents of the certificate with all its attendant consequences'. In case the officer of the Gram Panchayat was not believed by the High Court, and the certificate holder was indeed a foreigner, the officer would be considered guilty of 'harbouring an illegal migrant', and guilty of 'gross misconduct' exposing him to 'departmental action' besides attracting penal consequences (Judgement, Manowara Bewa 2017).

The Supreme Court turned down the Gauhati High Court Judgement in Manowara Bewa case in its order in a petition by Rupajan Begum, on the grounds that the invalidation of 'an agreed document' affected a large number of claimants.[34] The Court observed that 'the exercise' undertaken by the Gauhati High Court in going into the 'larger issues' did not arise out of the 'proceedings before it' and the resolution of those issues 'was not indispensable for answering the writ petitions' under its consideration. The GP certificate had been agreed to 'by all stakeholders', had the approval of the Central and state governments, and as part of the list of illustrative documents had been brought before the Supreme Court in the course of proceedings: 'this Court was aware of the nature and effect of each of the documents mentioned in the list' (Judgement, Rupajan Begum 2017, para. 13–14, 12). The Court observed that while the Gram Panchayat certificate merely acknowledged the shift of residence of a married woman and did not by itself establish any claim of citizenship, it could be used as a 'supporting document' for the 'limited purpose of providing a linkage' between the claimant and the legacy person after 'due enquiry and verification'.

Apart from 'married migrated women' who were identified as a separate class for whom provisions of a separate supporting document was made, another category—that of 'original inhabitant' of the state of Assam—became contentious. As discussed earlier, various petitions questioned the applicability of section 3 of the Citizenship Act of India, which lay down the provisions of citizenship by birth in updating the NRC in Assam. The Supreme Court agreed the NRC recognized the claims of citizens not on the fact of their 'birth' as Indian citizens but for being 'descendants' of Indian citizens. The exceptional requirements of the preparation of the NRC in Assam validated the principle of descent to create a separate category of Assamese-Indian citizens. Yet, the concern that this principle could generate within Assam an exceptional, indeed, a superior class of citizens, was raised with respect to the special procedures laid down in the Schedule to the Citizenship Rules 2003, for 'originally inhabitant' citizens.

---

[34] Judgement dated 5 December 2017 in *Rupajan Begum vs. Union of India and Others*, Civil Appeal no. 20858 of 2017 [Arising out of Special Leave Petition (Civil) No. 13256 of 2017].

Clause 3 of the Schedule (Special Provisions as to the Preparation of the National Register of Citizens in Assam) to the Citizenship Rules 2003 under the head Scrutiny of Applications, elaborates the process of scrutiny of applications which would be made by 'comparing the information stated in the application form with the official records'. Persons whose information was found in order would be 'eligible for inclusion of their names in the consolidated list'. Clause 3(3), provided that 'originally inhabitants of the State of Assam and their children and descendants, who are Citizens of India, shall be included in the consolidated list if the citizenship of such persons is ascertained beyond reasonable doubt and to the satisfaction of the registering authority'. In *Kamalakhya Dey Purkayastha and Others v. Union of India and others* (WP (Civil) No. 1020 of 2017), with which a clutch of five more writ petitions were attached, the Supreme Court bench consisting of Justice Ranjan Gogoi and Justice Rohinton Nariman, was asked to issue directions 'as to the manner in which the expression originally inhabitants of the State of Assam' was to be 'understood' and 'the procedure' by which they would be 'identified'. Apprehensions, were, however, raised that the special process of identification of those who claim to be 'originally inhabitants' of the state may lead to the creation of a 'superior class of citizens' which may have ramifications for future claims to entitlement to opportunities of education and employment. The Judges clarified that Clause 3(3) provided only for a different *process* of identification, which would be 'less strict and vigorous'. A special process did not 'determine any entitlement for inclusion in the NRC' which could only be on the 'basis of proof of citizenship'. The NRC, they clarified, was not an exercise for the identification of original inhabitants of the state.[35] Yet the NRC process had ramifications for creating different kinds of citizens depending on their access to the modalities of inclusion, which produced unsettled zones of citizenship within the state.

Unsettled Zones of Citizenship

The NRC marks a continuity with a notion of citizenship that can be traced to the Assam Accord, the contestations around the amendment

---

[35] All the members of the tea tribes are covered under 'Original inhabitants of Assam'.

HYPHENATED CITIZENSHIP 77

of the citizenship act in 1985, and subsequently the Supreme Court judgment in the Sarbananda Sonowal Case 2005. The petitions by the ASM, APW, AAAA, Swajan, and Bimalangshu Roy Foundation questioning the constitutional validity of section 6A of the Citizenship Act, have added fresh dimensions to the debate, which became significant in the electoral competition in the state in the 2016 state assembly election. After the BJP formed the government in the Centre in 2014, leading a coalition of the NDA, its leaders spoke in rallies in Assam assuring citizenship to Hindus who had fled to India to escape religious persecution in Bangladesh. Indeed, the government promised to enact a law for the rehabilitation of Hindu refugees from Pakistan and Bangladesh, setting up a task force to expedite pending citizenship requests from refugees, and issuing long-term visas of 10–15 years, wherever citizenship requests were taking longer to process. At the same time, echoing the campaign speeches of Prime Minister Narendra Modi in the 2014 Lok Sabha election, Amit Shah convinced people in Assam that the BJP would get rid of 'infiltrators'. Indeed, the BJP declared immigration policy a major plank of its campaign in the Assam Assembly elections in 2016. On 9 April 2016, speaking in a rally at Sonari, Amit Shah promised to give the Assamese people a Bangladeshi-migrants-free Assam if BJP was voted to power.[36]

The political consensus on the NRC as a mode of resolution of the citizenship question in Assam was, however, fractured by contending strands—one which saw it as a continuing commitment to the Assam Accord and its potential to alleviate the crisis in citizenship, and the other which was suspicious of the Accord's capacity to resolve the problem. The petitions in the Supreme Court by organizations contenting that the modality of preparing the NRC in Assam under the 2003 Rules was at variance with the Assam Accord, and others contesting the constitutional validity of Section 6A represented these strands in the adjudication of the citizenship question. In the political domain, while Tarun Gogoi vouched for the efficiency of the tools developed by the NRC office to update the NRC, others expressed the fear that it may only legitimize the Bangladeshi immigrants. In the course of the campaign in state assembly elections, Himanta Biswa Sarma, who had migrated to the BJP from the Congress

---

[36] Samudragupta Kashyap, 'BJP will Rid Assam of Bangladeshis: Shah', *Indian Express*, 10 April 2016.

in 2015 and became its chief political strategist and the Chief Minister of the state in May 2021, declared his disagreement with the continuation of 1971 as the deadline for the NRC. Sarma reiterated the dominant BJP position that the party was committed to granting citizenship status to Hindus, who came to Assam after the 24 March 1971 deadline.[37] In addition, claiming that the Assam Accord's provisions pertaining to citizenship were disputed and had been challenged in the Supreme Court, Sarma chose to foreground that part of the Accord, which promised that the original inhabitants of Assam and their culture be protected. In line with this, Sarma preferred to see the citizenship signpost pushed back to 1951, and those who came to Assam between 1951 and 1971 be given refugee status and not full citizenship.[38]

It is important to note that not only had the BJP managed to weaken the faltering leadership and social base of the Congress Party in Assam with Sarma emerging as an alternative node of power within the Congress and later outside, but it also retrieved the 'foreigners question' in Assam and relocated it in a vocabulary of loss and reclamation. An AASU member in a political meeting in Sarbananda Sonowal's constituency Majuli communicated this as follows: 'The Tarun Gogoi government has to go. People will have to come out this time if they want the *Axomiya jati* (the ethnic Assamese) to survive. Or else we will become foreigners in our own land. It wasn't for nothing that Bhupen Hazarika sang long ago, "*Aami axomiya nohou dukhia buli santona lobhile nohobo*" ["It is not enough of a succour to believe that we Assamese will never be poor in our own land]."'[39] Indeed, the BJP's electoral campaign and victory in the state assembly election in May 2016, which ended the fifteen-year rule of the Congress Party in the state, was compared by the BJP's supporters to the battle of Saraighat in 1671. In this battle, the Ahom army led by the celebrated general Lachit Borphukan gave a crushing defeat to the Mughal emperor Aurangzeb's army, led by the Rajput ruler Ramsingh. The reclamation of a historical moment of pride for the Ahom people in their emphatic win

---

[37] Nilotpal Bhattacharjee, 'BJP, AGP in Migrant Divide', *The Telegprah*, 6 March 2016.
[38] 'Himanta Biswa Sarma: In this Assam Poll, Bangladeshi Immigrants Want Their Own CM too', *Indian Express*, 15 February 2016.
[39] Sangeeta Barooah Piharoty, 'BJP Pins Its Hopes on Anti-Immigrant Sentiment in Assam Polls', *The Wire*, 4 April 2016, https://thewire.in/politics/bjps-anti-immigration-strategy-in-upcoming-assam-polls (accessed on 16 May 2016).

against an invading army to draw correspondence with the landslide victory of the BJP invoked the familiar vocabulary of insider/outsider in the construction of a past and wove it in the narrative of the BJP's electoral victory.[40]

The narrative of change, drawing upon the idiom of past victories over invading armies, was, however, contingent and dependent upon the durability of the dominant narrative of crisis in citizenship in Assam and the appeal of the NRC as the mode of resolving it. The narrative of NRC in Assam soon became deeply conflictual with suspicion over its efficacy and the form in which it was envisaged mounting from different quarters. The judiciary provided one site where this conflict played out. The vulnerability and marginalization precipitated by the bureaucratic exercise among different sections of the Assamese people produced a fraught site where 'participation' in the preparation of the NRC and 'trust' in the process held out different meanings to people. The process was replete with innumerable stories of difficulties getting the right document (Borbora 2019), disputes over documents and their acceptability (Ghosh 2019), and the suspicion that the procedure was designed to exclude Muslims. Fears of disenfranchisement and elimination from the NRC and the angst against years of discrimination experienced by Bengali speaking Muslims was given vent in art genres, among them—'Miya poetry'. As Poetry of protest and anger, Miya poetry revived a form that had an earlier origin but became assertive in the context of the NRC. A movement to claim the 'Miya' identity used for long to deride Bengali speaking Muslims as illegal migrants, the poems 'threw back' the derision by an emphatic claim to 'identity'. The opening stanzas of a poem by Hafiz Ahmed considered to have pioneered the Miya poetry genre, therefore say, 'Write Down I Am A Miya':

> Write
> Write Down
> I am a Miya
> My serial number in the NRC is ... ..
> I have two children
> Another is coming

---

[40] See, for example, Sethi and Subhrashtha (2017).

Next summer.
Will you hate him
As you hate me?[41]

The road to the publication of the final NRC went through the publication of successive drafts, leading to anxiety among large numbers of people over the uncertainty of the final outcome. Before the publication of the complete draft in August 2019, an 'additional draft *exclusion* list' was released, which included the names of those whose names had figured in the earlier drafts, but were now being dropped after 're-verification'. The preparation of the draft exclusion list was approved by the Supreme Court under Clause 5 of the Schedule of the Citizenship (Registration of Citizens and Issue of National Identity Cards) Rules 2003. Some individuals whose names were dropped were 'detected' as 'foreigners' while they were appearing as witnesses in NRC-related hearings for other applicants. Others were dropped after they or their descendants were found to be DF, DVs, or DFTs—'categories which are exclusive to Assam'.[42] The exclusions prompted civil society members to write a letter to Chief Justice Ranjan Gogoi about the 'panicky situation' created by 'suspicious and mischievous' re-verification notices served by the NRC authorities.[43]

Those excluded were pushed yet again into uncertainty. For others, it was a message that mere inclusion in an earlier list did not mean closure. This uncertainty had, however, already been precipitated a year back, in August 2018, when the Assam government 'revealed' district-wise figures of exclusions in the state assembly. Through this 'revelation', the government raised doubts on the modalities of preparation and the integrity of the procedure based on the premise that the figures for some districts could not be relied upon since the percentage of exclusions for those districts was not, according to it, in correspondence with its demographic profile. Making a case for re-verification, the figures of Muslim-majority districts bordering Bangladesh—including Dhubri and South

---

[41] Aletta Andre and Abhimanyu Kumar, 'Protest Poetry: Assam's Bengali Muslims Take a Stand', *Al Jazeera*, 23 December 2016.

[42] 'Assam NRC Explained: Add, Delete and What Next?' *The Indian Express*, 31 August 2019.

[43] 'NRC Re-Verification Notices: Civil Society Members Write to CJI on "Panicky Situation"', *The Wire*, 8 August 2019, https://thewire.in/rights/nrc-re-verification-notices-panic-civil-soci ety-letter-cji-ranjan-gogoi (accessed on 10 August 2019).

Salmara—with a low percentage of exclusion, and in districts such as Hajoi—in Central Assam where 'indigenous people live ... where sons of the soil have been living for ages', where the exclusion rate was highest at 32.99 per cent, were cited as examples, to corroborate the point.[44]

On the eve of the publication of the 'complete' draft NRC, apprehensive of any 'crisis' that the list would generate, vigorous preventive measures were put in place along with what the officials termed 'public confidence building measures'.[45] While the Director General of Police in Guwahati was confident that Assam would remain peaceful, and that these measures were routine, 'prohibitory orders' were issued in 'vulnerable areas' under Section 144 of the CrPC to curb the assembly of more than five persons in any place and prevent any disturbance of public order. In the words of the police, 'foot patrolling, route marches and area domination patrols' were conducted in some districts as 'confidence building' measures. Fifty-five companies of paramilitary force that had only recently been withdrawn from Assam for deployment in Jammu and Kashmir were re-deployed in the state. District authorities were, in addition, instructed to enhance 'citizen contact' to assure them that mere absence of their names would not automatically make them foreigners.[46] That the 'post-NRC scenario' would be challenging was a dominant concern. To address the claims of those left out of the final list, the Central government contemplated setting up e-Foreigners Tribunals and also increase the number of Foreigners Tribunals from 100 to 1000 and appoint lawyers and retired bureaucrats and judges as members. It appeared that at this point, the government wanted to convince people that 'the NRC-rejects' would not be placed immediately in detention centres and they had the option of going to the Foreigners Tribunals and the judiciary thereafter. Assam's Additional Chief Secretary in charge of Home and Political Departments informed that all those whose names did not figure in the list could challenge their exclusion before a Foreigners Tribunal within a period of four months of publication of the list. Yet, the precariousness of

---

[44] Abhishek Saha and Tora Agarwala, 'Deadline Approaching: What it is to be a Name on NRC List—or Off it', *Indian Express*, 25 August 2019.
[45] Rahul Karmakar, 'Those Excluded from Final NRC Will Get a Window of 10 Months', *The Hindu*, 29 August 2019.
[46] 'Assam: Security Increased Across the State before Publication of Updated NRC', *The Wire*, 30 August 2019.

those left out of the NRC persisted with six central prisons serving as detention centres and separate detention centres coming up in other parts of the state. The assurance to the Bangladesh government by the External Affairs Minister that the NRC was an 'internal matter' of India made the context of identification more complex.[47]

Conclusion

By the beginning of 2020, the political and popular consensus around the NRC ruptured as it came to represent a field of contradictions for reasons which were different from the conflict over categories and procedures. While the final NRC had been published on 31 August 2019, the rejection orders had not been served to those excluded, deferring the claims process. The Assam government was dissatisfied with the outcome of the NRC, which did not appear to corroborate the claims of large-scale illegal presence of Bengali Muslims from Bangladesh and contested the integrity of the procedure. Prateek Hajela was returned to his 'Home Cadre' Madhya Pradesh, and replaced by Hitesh Dev Sarma, whose views on citizenship were perceived to be in affinity with the ruling dispensation. The passage of the Citizenship Amendment Act (CAA) 2019 exempting Hindus, Sikhs, Jains, Buddhists, Christians, and Parsis from the category of 'illegal migrants', making it possible for them to apply for citizenship, further unsettled the field of citizenship. In addition, the announcement by the Home Minister, which was later withdrawn, that a nationwide NRC would be prepared alongside the implementation of the CAA 2019, pushed the citizenship question in Assam onto the brink. A spate of agitations spread across the state. The question of 'illegal migrants' and citizenship regimes remained at the centre of these protests. It is these contestations precipitated with the announcement of the CAB 2016 that will be discussed in the Chapter 2.

---

[47] Baruah, Sanjib, 'A More Precarious Citizenship', *Indian Express*, 30 August 2019 https://indianexpress.com/article/opinion/columns/a-more-precarious-citizenship-assam-nrc-list-jammu-kashmir-5949158/ 8/11 (accessed on 8 September 2019).

2
Bounded Citizenship
The Citizenship Amendment Act 2019

On 20 December 2019, a minister in the Government of India handed out citizenship certificates to seven refugees of the Sodha community from Pakistan residing in Kutch district in Gujarat. Speaking on the occasion, the minister said that the Citizenship Amendment Act (CAA) would provide 'a new opportunity in life to the minorities who faced religious persecution in Pakistan, Bangladesh and Afghanistan'.[1] Reporting the event, most newspapers commented on the contrast between widespread protests against the CAA 2019 (henceforth CAA) and the jubilation among the refugees in Gujarat upon its passage. The news agency ANI's Twitter handle remarked that the refugees gathered at the ceremony 'welcomed' the CAA for 'restoring trust and faith in humanity' and celebrated 'by distributing sweets, bursting crackers and putting colours on each other ... their faces were full of happiness and satisfaction'.[2] *The Indian Express* report mentioned the 'violence [that] rocked parts of Vadodara and Ahmedabad over the new citizenship law', alongside the minister's speech claiming that the CAA would ensure a life of dignity to refugees of minority communities from Pakistan, Bangladesh, and Afghanistan, without 'taking away' anything from Indian citizens—an assurance that was being given consistently by the government.

Nathusinh Sodha, a resident of Bhuj, was a refugee from Tharparkar-Mithi district in Pakistan, who came to India in 2007 and acquired Indian citizenship. Sodha founded the Overseas Hindu Rehabilitation Committee, an NGO to help Hindus from Pakistan. At the event, he

---

[1] 'Shri Mansukh Mandaviya Hands Over Citizenship Certificates Issued by the Government of India to 7 Pakistani Refugees in Kutch, Gujarat Today', *Press Information Bureau*, Government of India, Ministry of Shipping, 20 December 2019.

[2] 'Union Minister Hands Over Indian Citizenship Certificates to 7 Pakistani Hindu Refugees', 20 December 2019, *India.com News Desk*, accessed on 10 May 2020.

Citizenship Regimes, Law, and Belonging. Anupama Roy, Oxford University Press. © Oxford University Press 2022.
DOI: 10.1093/oso/9780192859082.003.0003

recalled his trauma as a refugee in India, and thanked Prime Minister Modi for making the situation 'easier for refugees': 'We wanted to thank Modi and [therefore] organised this event today'.[3] Interestingly, the *Wikipedia* entry on CAA *erroneously* entered 20 December 2019 as the day when '[T]he implementation of the CAB began' stating that the seven refugees who received citizenship certificates were the first to become citizens under the CAA. The Rules laying down the procedure for giving citizenship under the CAA 2019 have not been framed so far. Under Section 18 of the Citizenship Act, the Central government has the power to make such rules, which must be placed before the Parliament. All seven persons of the Sodha community were given citizenship certificates not under the CAA but under the Standard Operating Procedure (SOP) followed for 'Pakistan Nationals of minority Hindu community'. The SOP was put in place through the Citizenship (Amendment) Rules 2004, which came into effect on 1 March 2004 to empower District Collectors in Rajasthan and Gujarat to 'grant citizenship' to Hindu migrants from Pakistan. The notification dated 28 February 2004 giving powers to District Collectors was an exception for the two states to facilitate the acquisition of citizenship by those 'who were forced to come to India due to persecution on religious grounds'. In May 2021, thirteen District Collectors in Gujarat, Chhattisgarh, Rajasthan, Haryana, and Punjab were empowered by the Central government to grant citizenship certificates to minority communities from Pakistan, Bangladesh, and Afghanistan.[4] The 2004 SOP supplemented the special Long-Term Visa (LTV) provisions that had been augmented through instructions issued from time to time by the Ministry of Home Affairs (MHA) to allow minority communities from Pakistan to stay in India.[5] In January 1986, revisiting India's policy towards 'illegal entrance and settlement in India of minority communities from Pakistan',

---

[3] 'Rajkot: Mandaviya Hands Over Citizenship Certificates to Seven Pak Refugees', *The Indian Express*, 21 December 2019.

[4] Vijaita Singh, '13 More District Collectors Empowered to Grant Citizenship to Applicants From 3 Countries,' *The Hindu*, 29 May 2021. https://www.thehindu.com/news/national/13-more-district-collectors-empowered-to-grant-citizenship-to-applicants-from-3-countries/article34674508.ece (accessed on 4 July 2021).

[5] As per the preliminary counter-affidavit submitted by the government of India, in response to the IUML's affidavit in the Supreme Court questioning the constitutionality of the CAA 2019. According to the counter-affidavit, it was on the request of Ashok Gehlot, then a Congress MLA and presently the Chief Minister of Rajasthan that these exceptional procedures for Rajasthan and Gujarat had been inserted in the citizenship rules. See https://www.livelaw.in/pdf_upload/pdf_upload-371370.pdf (accessed 3 July 2020).

the then Home Secretary had advised the Cabinet Committee on Political Affairs (CCPA) to make an exception for illegal migrants from the minority community and consider their request for long-term stay in India 'liberally'. In 2011, 'Christians' and 'Buddhists' were added to the preferential regime already in place for 'Hindu' and 'Sikh' communities. These 'executive instructions' were drawn from the powers that the Central government has under the Foreigners Act 1946 and the Passport (Entry into India) Act 1920.[6]

The Joint Parliamentary Committee (JPC), which recommended that the CAB be placed for discussion in the Parliament, went for field visits to Rajasthan, Gujarat, Assam, and Meghalaya to take inputs from 'stakeholders'. The refugees in Rajasthan and Gujarat, who had migrated to India from different parts of Pakistan, narrated their hardships to the JPC and requested changes in the citizenship law to facilitate the acquisition of citizenship. They also asked for the alleviation of the social and economic conditions of those who had already become citizens. The depositions from Assam and Meghalaya, on the other hand, were averse to the amendment and were apprehensive that the CAB would unsettle the peace that obtained in the region, especially in Assam after the 1985 Accord. The tension between the different 'stakes' that groups had in the passage or rejection of the CAB was evident in the debates in the Parliament and in the protests that occurred in the months before and after its passage into an Act. In this chapter, the CAB/CAA is seen as the culmination of a tendency that emerged out of the 2003 amendment in the citizenship Act with the NRC and the CAA as its two strands. While the NRC, which was provided for in the 2003 amendment, represented a citizenship regime driven by bureaucratic practices of identifying 'citizens' through documents that proved parentage, the CAA manifested consolidation of an ideological formation of citizenship that redefined the idea of the political community. By extending the status of citizenship to persons facing religious persecution and simultaneously discriminating against other persons on the ground of religion, the CAA unleashes exclusionary nationhood under the veneer of liberal citizenship. By invoking the idea of *bounded citizenship* to explain the contours of the legal regime of CAA, this chapter argues that citizenship under CAA installs strict 'walls of

[6] Ibid.

separation' (Sadiq 2009) and associates citizenship with 'the idealized notion of a bounded national territory with a clearly defined community of citizens' (Baruah 2009, 593). The idea of national citizenship in this formulation gains intensity by marking the national territory as a natural homeland of Hindus. The first section of the chapter details both the specific changes in the citizenship law brought by the CAA and the long-term tendencies which the contemporary changes represent. The subsequent sections take the question 'who is an Indian citizen' to three different sites of deliberation on citizenship—the Constituent Assembly, the Parliament, and the Joint Parliamentary Committee (JPC). The ideological framing of citizenship in the constituent moment and the debates on the CAA in 2016/2019, reveal the dissonance between the foundational principles of Indian citizenship—the secular-constitutionalism of the Constituent Assembly in 1949—and the national-communitarianism that prevailed in the Indian Parliament in 2019.

CAA 2003: The Hinge Point

The Citizenship Amendments Acts of 1985/86 and 2003 made emphatic changes in the citizenship law in India. The 1985 amendment which inserted special provisions for Assam was politically significant, having come as part of the process of resolution of 'the foreigners' question' in Assam. The 2003 amendment made changes in citizenship by birth and also introduced the category of the Overseas Citizens of India (OCI). Both these changes marked the transition in the citizenship law from the principle of *jus soli* to *jus sanguinis*. Neither of these amendments generated the kind of criticism, political polarization, and popular outrage, which was seen in the wake of the introduction of the CAB in 2016. Public protests against the amendments acquired fresh momentum breaking out of its concentration in the North-East to span the breadth of the country after the CAA 2019 was passed by the Parliament. In a triumphal note after its passage in the Lok Sabha, Home Minister Amit Shah declared that a nationwide NRC would follow soon. In a context where the NRC had come to be seen as targeting Muslims, the synchronization of NRC, and the CAA reinforced the perception that the CAA would shield non-Muslims, while the NRC would facilitate the exclusion of Muslims without affording them the protection of the CAA. The entrenchment of citizenship within the dominant Hindutva ideology, through a culmination of a process that had begun in 2003 under the NDA regime, precipitated the 'fear' that the NRC would target all Muslims regardless of their status as citizens.

The CAB 2016 was introduced in Lok Sabha on 19 July 2016, a couple of months after the conclusion of the State Assembly election in Assam. In these elections, held two years after the BJP led NDA came to power in the Centre, BJP leaders, including then party president, Amit Shah, spoke in rallies assuring a Bangladeshi-free Assam. Echoing the campaign speeches of Prime Minister Narendra Modi in the 2014 Lok Sabha election, Shah had been convincing people in Assam that the BJP would get rid of Bangladeshi 'infiltrators'. Simultaneously, the party also promised to protect Hindus who had fled to India to escape religious persecution in Bangladesh, enact a law for the rehabilitation of Hindu refugees from Pakistan and Bangladesh, set up a task force to expedite pending citizenship requests from refugees and issue long-term visas of 10–15 years, wherever citizenship requests were taking longer to process.

On 11 August 2016, a motion was passed in the Lok Sabha to entrust the CAB 2016 to a JPC, which was agreed to by the Rajya Sabha the following day. The JPC submitted its report on 7 January 2019, recommending that the CAB be discussed in Parliament. Nine members of the thirty-member committee submitted notes of dissent, indicating that there was no consensus on the final recommendation. The Bill was placed for discussion in the Lok Sabha on 8 January in the budget session, the last session of the 16th Lok Sabha. It faced opposition in the Lok Sabha but was passed with the force of the numerical majority of the ruling NDA. The Bill was placed for discussion in the Rajya Sabha on 9 January, a day when the proceedings in the house were dominated by the Economically Weaker Sections (EWS) quota bill, which ended in the adjournment of the house. With the dissolution of the Lok Sabha by the President in preparation for the next general election, the CAB lapsed. The BJP made CAB part of the party's campaign for the 2019 Lok Sabha election. In rallies in Assam and West Bengal in particular, but also in other states, BJP leaders made it clear that when the party returned to power, it would ensure the passage of the CAB into an Act. The manifesto of the Congress Party released on 2 April 2019 announced its opposition to the CAB.

The CAB 2016/2019 faced opposition in the North East, with large numbers of people across the states, taking to the streets in protest. The protestors raised concerns ranging from cultural estrangement to economic deprivation, forcing the chief ministers of the eight states, who were in all cases either from the ruling BJP or allied to it in a coalition partnership, on the defensive. These protests were in consonance with the position taken by civil society groups that had deposed before the JPC to express their objections to the Bill when JPC members visited Guwahati, Silchar, and Shillong from 7 to 11 May 2018 as part of their field study. In Assam, for example, civil society groups expressed outrage at what they called a violation of the Assam Accord of 1985, which they argued was in the nature of 'a public law contract' between the Indian government and the people of Assam. Any decision to change this 'negotiated agreement' which placed obligations on both the parties, they asserted, must have the 'informed consent' of the people of Assam.[7] The BJP leaders were at pains to convince them that any change in the citizenship act would take place only after a consensus was reached with the people. In the Rajya Sabha, speaking in defence of the CAB on 9 January 2019, then Minister for Home Affairs, Rajnath Singh assured the people of Assam that the government would take measures to protect the 'cultural identity' of the state. These measures would be in pursuit of Clause 6 of the Assam Accord which envisaged constitutional, legislative, and administrative measures to safeguard, protect, preserve, and promote the cultural, social, linguistic identity, and heritage of the Assamese people.[8] The Home Minister also enumerated a list of measures that the government would take to ensure recognition of special status of scheduled tribes in the region.

Following the BJP's return to power in May 2019, the CAB 2019, was introduced in the Lok Sabha by Amit Shah, Minister for Home Affairs in the new Cabinet, on 9 December 2019 with changes from CAB 2016

---

[7] The submission of Forum Against Citizenship Act Amendment Bill to the Chairperson of the JPC, dated 7 May 2018. (Copy with the author.)

[8] A Clause 6 Committee set up in July 2019 under the chairpersonship of Biplab Kumar Sarma, a retired Gauhati High Court judge, submitted its report to the Assam Chief Minister in February 2020. Justice Sarma reported that the committee had 'received over 1200 memorandums, took the views of all communities across Assam and noted our observations for Constitutional safeguards of the indigenous people and for defining the Assamese people.' The three representatives of the AASU who were part of the committee but were not present at the time of submission stated that the Centre seemed to have lost interest in the committee. 'Assam Accord Clause 6: Committee Submits Report to Chief Minister', *The Hindu*, 25 February 2020.

giving exemptions to parts of the northeastern states (see Table 2.1). The CAB was passed with 311 MPs voting in favour and 80 opposing it. It was debated and passed in the Rajya Sabha on 11 December with 125 MPs voting in its favour and 105 against it. JDU, AIADMK, BJD, TDP, and YSR Congress, were among the political parties that voted for it. The President of India gave his assent to the Bill on 12 December, and it came into force with gazette notification on 10 January 2020.

The Citizenship Amendment Act of 2003 constituted the hinge point, from which the NRC and the CAA emerged as two distinct modalities of regulating and determining citizenship. Both these modalities were concerned with addressing the problem of 'illegal migrants'. In preparing the NRC, the government was seized with devising ways to identify legitimate citizens and expel illegal migrants. The CAA came with the objective of 'exempting' a class of persons who would otherwise be considered 'illegal migrants' and denied access to citizenship under the new provisions inserted by the 2003 amendment. In 2003, the amendment to the citizenship act brought about two significant changes—the recognition in law of the category of overseas citizens of India, and the constraining of citizenship by birth by confining it to those persons whose parents were Indian citizens or one of the parents was an Indian citizen and the other was not an illegal migrant. In addition, by making changes in the provisions pertaining to citizenship by registration, the amendment disallowed persons from seeking citizenship through registration if they were illegal migrants. We may recall from the discussion earlier in this chapter that the provision of LTV that was in place for persons belonging to minority communities in Pakistan who had entered India with short-term visit visas was augmented in 2004 through amendments in the citizenship rules to give citizenship to persons belonging to specified religious communities from Pakistan who had sought refuge in Rajasthan and Gujarat. The 2019 amendment made this exception more definitive by extending it to the entire country and incorporating it within the statutory frameworks of the Citizenship Act itself.

The CAA exempts six 'minority communities', Hindus, Sikhs, Buddhists, Jains, Parsis, and Christians, from three countries—Bangladesh, Pakistan, and Afghanistan—from the category of 'illegal migrants' which was inserted in Section 3 (Citizenship by Birth) and Section 5 (Citizenship by Registration) of the Citizenship Amendment Act 2003.

Table 2.1 Amendments to the Citizenship Act of India

Citizenship Amendment Act	Objects and Reasons of the Act	Insertion	Ramifications
Citizenship Amendment Act 1985/1986	**Changes Pursuant to the Assam Accord** signed as a memorandum of settlement between the Government of India and the leaders of the Assam Movement. The amendment sought to implement Clause 5 of the Assam Accord pertaining to the detection and deletion of foreigners. **To make the acquisition of Indian citizenship stringent** in the context of large number of persons of Indian origin entering India from the neighbouring and some African countries	Section 6A was inserted into the Citizenship Act, 1955, via Act no. 65 of 1985 with effect from 07.12.1985, which set 1 January 1966 as the base-date for the identification of foreigners. Those who entered Assam from Bangladesh after that date and before 25 March 1971 would be considered Indian citizens, following identification under the Foreigners Act. Those who entered after that, as detected under the IMDT Act, would be deported as 'illegal migrants' Section 3 of the Citizenship Act 1955 was amended via Act no. 51 of 1986 to lay down that a person could be an Indian citizen by birth if one of his/her parents was an Indian citizen at the time of his/her birth	The amendment inscribed an exception for Assam in the citizenship law. It made way for a graded citizenship in Assam. The amendment had implications for the exceptional NRC regime for Assam in 2005 and also became the basis for petitions in the Supreme Court to declare Section 6A unconstitutional. Citizenship by birth constrained manifesting the tendency in the citizenship law towards *jus sanguinis*. Any person born in India after the amendment came into effect on 1 July 1987 would be a citizen by birth only if one of his/her parents was an Indian citizen.

| Citizenship Amendment Act 2003 | The Citizenship Act of 1955 was one of the 109 laws that were reviewed by the Commission on Review of Administrative Laws constituted by the Central government in 1998. The High Level Committee on Indian Diaspora constituted by the Central government also recommended the amendment of the 1955 Act. The CAA 2003 had the following objectives: (i) make the acquisition of Indian citizenship by registration and naturalization more stringent; (ii) prevent illegal migrants from becoming eligible for Indian citizenship; (iii) simplify the procedure to facilitate the re-acquisition of Indian citizenship by persons of full age who are children of Indian citizens, and former citizens of independent India; (iv) provide for the grant of overseas citizenship of India to Persons of Indian Origin belonging to specified countries, (v) provide for the compulsory registration and issue of a national identity card to all citizens of India; (vi) enhance the penalty for violation of its provisions, as well as the rules framed under it; and (vii) omit all provisions recognizing, or relating to Commonwealth citizenship from the Act | **Amended Section 3 of CAA 1955 Citizenship by birth** to lay down that every person born in India on or after the commencement of the CAA, 2003, would be a citizen by birth only if *both* parents are citizens of India; or *one of the parents is a citizen of India and the other is not an illegal migrant at the time of his/her birth.* **Inserted Section 7A** which provided for the 'registration of Overseas Citizens of India (OCI)' (subject to conditions and restrictions) **Section 7B** conferred the OCIs with certain rights which allowed them, among other things, the freedom of entry into India. The rights to equality of opportunity in employment and registration as voters, and to seek election to representative bodies at the central and state levels was not conferred. Section 7C provided the process of renunciation of OCI status, and Section 7D specified the grounds under which the registration of a person as OCI could be cancelled by the Central government if the registration was obtained by fraud, false representation or concealment of facts; disaffection towards the Constitution of India; the registration could be cancelled also as if 'it was necessary so to do in the interest of the sovereignty and integrity of | The CAA 2003, further constrained citizenship by birth consolidating the tendency towards *jus sanguinis*. Read with CAA 1986, citizenship by birth was now of three kinds—those born after the commencement of the Constitution and before the CAA 1986 came into effect (1 July 1987) would be citizens of India by birth; those born after 1 July 1987 but before the commencement of CAA 2003, would be citizens of India by birth only if one of the parents was an Indian citizen at the time of his/her birth; those born after the commencement of CAA 2003 would be citizens of India by birth only if they satisfied the conditions prescribed in CAA 2003. Confirmed the tendency towards *jus sanguinis* or the principle of parentage. The OCI was not dual citizenship and while it seemed to reflect a growing trend worldwide towards mobile/flexible citizenship in the context of global flows of population, the OCI manifested a tendency towards consolidating affective ties of belonging to a home country, which was different from the country of residence and work. |

(continued)

Table 2.1 Continued

Citizenship Amendment Act	Objects and Reasons of the Act	Insertion	Ramifications
		India, the security of India, friendly relations of India with any foreign country, or in the interests of the general public.'	The entrenchment of the power of the state to identify and enumerate citizens. The importance of documents as evidence of citizenship was established. The innovation of legacy as evidence of citizenship further strengthened the association of citizenship with parentage. In a manifestation of entrenchment of the national security state, the category of illegal migrant figures prominently in the justification for the exercise of preparing an NPR and NRC.
		Inserted Section 14A which lay down that 'the Central government may compulsorily register every person of India and issue national identity card to him'. The Citizenship (Registration of Citizens and Issue of National Identity Cards) Rules 2003 provided the procedure for the preparation of the National Register of Indian Citizens through house to house enumeration (Section 4). An amendment to the rules in 2009, prescribed an exception to the procedure in the case of Assam.	

Citizenship Amendment Bill 2016	According to the Statement of Objects and Reasons of CAB 2016, under the existing provisions of the Citizenship Act, persons belonging to minority communities, such as Hindus, Sikhs, Buddhists, Jains, Parsis, and Christians from Afghanistan, Bangladesh, and Pakistan, who entered India without valid travel documents or the validity of their documents had expired are considered illegal migrants and are ineligible to apply for Indian citizenship. The Act intended to make this category eligible for Indian citizenship.

Persons belonging to this category of minority communities as well as others of Indian origin who have been applying for citizenship under section 5 of the Act, are not able to give proof of their Indian origin and are therefore compelled to apply for citizenship by naturalization which requires twelve years of residency, depriving them of opportunities that Indian citizens have. The Bill proposed to make applicants belonging to minority communities from specific countries eligible for citizenship by naturalization in seven years. | The Act Amended Section 2 (b) of the CA 1955 to make an exception in the interpretation of the category 'illegal migrant' [Section 2 CAB 2016], to exclude the categories mentioned in the objects and reasons.

It amended the Third Schedule of the Citizenship Act pertaining to the requirements for naturalization to reduce the aggregate period of stay for persons belonging to minority communities identified in Section 1 CAB 2016 from 11 years to 6 years. [Section 4 CAB 2016]

Inserted Clause (*da*) to Section 7D of the Citizenship Act to lay down that the registration of an Overseas Citizen of India Cardholder would be cancelled, if he or she violated any of the provisions of the Act or provisions of any other law for the time being in force'. | The amendment sought to make changes brought in the Passport Act 1920 and the Foreigners Act 1946 part of the citizenship law.

It inserted for the first time the consideration of religion in decisions pertaining to citizenship.

Extension of control over the status of the OCI in relation to India, by making them subject to laws over which the Indian government had jurisdiction. This could have ramifications for the OCI status of those vocal in their opposition to political parties and regimes in power. |

(continued)

Table 2.1 Continued

Citizenship Amendment Act	Objects and Reasons of the Act	Insertion	Ramifications
	The Bill proposed an amendment which would enable the Central government to cancel the registration of an OCI, who had violated any *Indian* law a condition which had been absent in the 2003 provisions.		
Citizenship Amendment Act 2019	Same as CAB 2016, that is, 'removal of adverse penal consequences' for those belonging to specified minority communities from Afghanistan, Bangladesh and India under the Passport Act 1920 and Foreigners Act 1946, to grant them 'immunity' from any proceedings against them under the two Acts, and reduce the required period of stay for acquiring citizenship by naturalization to 5 years.	**Amended the Third Schedule of the Citizenship of India Act pertaining to the requirement of minimum period of stay for naturalization**–reduced from 6 years in Section 4 CAB 2016 to 5 years [Section 6 CAB 2019)	Same as CAB 2016. In addition, the accommodation of an exception for some states in North-East India, intended to assuage heightened opposition to the CAA in the region, introduced another system of gradation within the universe of Indian citizenship. While this garnered support for CAB 2019 in the Parliament, opposition to the law in the region, especially in Assam continued.

continued

In addition, the Bill made modification in the CAB 2016, 'to protect the constitutional guarantee given to indigenous populations of North Eastern States covered under the Sixth Schedule of the Constitution and the statutory protection given to areas covered under the 'Inner Line' system of the Bengal Eastern Frontier Regulation' 1873'.

To remove an anomaly in the earlier provisions pertaining to the cancelation of registration of the OCI Cardholder, the Bill sought to provide the OCI with an opportunity to be heard.

Inserted a new Section 6B (i, ii) [Section 3 CAB 2019] Empowering Central government to issue a certificate of registration or naturalization to persons specified under the CAB who would be deemed to be citizens of India from the date of entry in India. All proceedings against such persons upon the grant of certificate of citizenship would be cancelled.

Inserted a new Section 6B (iv) [Section 3 CAB 2019]
Excluding tribal area of Assam, Meghalaya, Mizoram, or Tripura as included in the Sixth Schedule to the Constitution and the area covered under 'The Inner Line' notified under the Bengal Eastern Frontier Regulation, 1873, from the purview of the new section 6B.

Amendment of Section 7D of the Citizenship Act 1955 [Section 4 CAB 2019]
The provision that the OCI would be given a reasonable opportunity of being heard, before an order of cancelation of OCI registration is passed was added.

A notification issued by the Ministry of Home Affairs on 4 March 2021 issued under section 7B of the Citizenship Act which allows the Central government to notify the rights of the OCI, placed constraints on those rights that had been given to them by the 2003 Amendment Act. The notification restricts the grant of multiple entry lifelong visas to OCI cardholders, by requiring some of them—those undertaking research, missionary, tabligh, or journalistic activities—to obtain 'special permission' from the 'competent authority' or the Foreigners Regional Registration Officer or the Indian Mission. These changes enhance the government's 'surveillance' over the OCI's activities in India.

While the OCI was never conceived as 'dual citizenship' status, the change in the definition of the OCI Cardholder in the notification to one where the OCI cardholder is 'a *foreign national* holding passport of a foreign country and *not a citizen of India*' is a distinct move towards consolidating the state's control over those whose activities it would consider 'undesirable'.

Under the existing provisions of the Citizenship Act, an 'illegal migrant' is someone who has entered India without valid travel documents or has overstayed, with the result that the validity of his or her documents has expired. The 'statement of objects and reasons' of the Bill introduced by Home Minister Amit Shah in Lok Sabha in December 2019 declared that special provisions for these communities were necessitated because they faced persecution on religious grounds in the three countries. The constitutions of all these countries provided for a state religion, with the result that the minority communities feared persecution in their 'day to day life' and restriction of their right to practice, profess, and propagate their religion. These persecuted persons, when they entered India without valid documents or overstayed, faced 'adverse penal consequences' under the Passport Act and the Foreigners Act. As 'illegal migrants' they were unable to apply for citizenship by registration. The Bill was, therefore, being brought with the purpose of 'granting' them 'immunity' from any penal action and enabling them to apply for Indian citizenship by registration in cases where they had the documents to show that they were persons of Indian origin or by naturalization by reducing the minimum period of stay in India to five years.

By exempting the specified communities from the category of illegal migrants, the CAA has sought to bring the citizenship law in line with the executive orders and rules issued by the government in 2015 and 2016. These orders had laid down exemptions for such 'migrants' from the 'adverse penal consequences' of the Passport (Entry into India) Act 1920 and Foreigners Act 1946 to ensure that the communities identified in the CAB 2016/2019 were not treated as illegal migrants under these Acts. The gazette notification dated 7 September 2015, which executed these exemptions, introduced the cut-off date of 31 December 2014. To become eligible for the exemption, the migrants should have entered India before this date. A PIL filed by the Assam Sanmilita Mahasangha (ASM) which is pending before the Supreme Court has contested the deviation in the cut-off date set for Assam by the Citizenship Amendment Act 1985, that is, 24 March 1971, from the date specified in Article 6 of the Constitution of India. The CAA is applicable to entire India and takes the cut-off date forward by several years. In addition to exempting specified minority communities from the category of illegal migrants, the CAA enables them to acquire Indian citizenship by naturalization, by reducing the minimum period of residence from twelve to five years. For this purpose, the CAA amended the Third Schedule to the Citizenship Act to make applicants belonging to minority communities from the specified countries eligible for citizenship by naturalization if they had stayed in India for an aggregate period of five years.

Constitutional Assembly Debates and the Citizenship Question

While justifying the need for the CAA, the JPC cited B. R. Ambedkar's statement in the Constituent Assembly in which he expressed difficulty in laying down *permanent* provisions for citizenship in the Constitution, and stressed the need to empower the Parliament to legislate on all future matters concerning citizenship. The debates in the CA from 10 to 12 August 1949, when the final provisions of citizenship were deliberated upon and approved, show the complexity that the citizenship question had assumed in the context of Partition and large-scale movement of people across the newly created borders amidst unprecedented violence along religious lines. It is evident from a reading of the CAD that the question 'Who is an Indian citizen?' elicited deep 'ideational disagreement' (Lerner 2016) and ideological dissonance among members of the CA and anxieties around the ramifications the constitutional inscription of citizenship would have on the definition of *Indian* citizenship. These disagreements arrayed along the familiar fault-line of whether 'birth' (the territoriality principle; *jus soli*) *or* 'descent' (the parentage principle; *jus sanguinis*) should be the foundational principle of citizenship. These were questions pertaining to both the *source* of citizenship and its expression as an *identity* attached to ideas of home and belonging.

A close reading of the debates shows that these lines were unevenly drawn and the arguments on different sides were framed in such a way that no position was absolute. Indeed, strong arguments in favour of one principle showed an irresolute overlapping with the other. Those who adhered to the constitutive principle of *descent* as the source of citizenship, for example, sought to make citizenship conditional for 'returnees' from Pakistan and were apprehensive of the 'dual ties' it would generate when extended to the diaspora community. Similarly, the apologists for the principle of *birth* as the basis of citizenship sought to constrain it by making it conditional on domicile and in some quarters by combining it with 'inheritance' or lineage from Indian parentage. The need to specify the *uniqueness* of Indian citizenship among countries that subscribed to one or the other form of citizenship was asserted amidst concerns that the inscription of 'birth' as a definitive condition of citizenship would make it 'cheap'. Anxieties were expressed that indiscriminate absorption of people migrating across borders would make Indian citizenship precariously flexible and embarrassingly indecisive. Those concerned with 'cheapness' of citizenship desired that birth should be aligned with descent. Flexibility of citizenship with respect to migrants was sought to be curbed by aligning citizenship with religious belonging, an alignment which remains fraught to this day.

Scholars have pointed at 'innovations' (Lerner 2016) by the CA as strategies of decision making and the 'original contributions' that it made in the modes of deliberation to reach those decisions (Austin [1966] 2010). 'Innovations' were prompted by the 'deep disagreements' that existed within the CA over the 'vision of the State', compelling its members to 'refrain from making unequivocal choices' and take recourse to 'constitutional incrementalism' based on 'creative use of constitutional language' (Lerner 2016, 61). *Deferral* of controversial decisions was among the strategies of 'constitutional incrementalism', which was deployed—as in the dispute over national language—to allow for 'the gradual emergence of a broader consensus' (Lerner 2016). For Granville Austin, the modalities through which decisions were reached in the CA constituted its 'original contribution'. Austin described these modalities as follows: *decision making by consensus* which gave emphasis to the *process* through which a decision was reached rather than the decision itself and *the principle of accommodation* whereby the CA displayed the ability to harmonize differences over categories, without changing the content of the categories themselves (Austin [1966] 2010, 311–318). In his later work, Austin focused his attention on the 'conflicts' in the 'seamless web' of the constitutional edifice which emerged in the working of the Constitution.[9] Apart from examining the 'inner conflicts' in the Constitution (Mehta

---

[9] These conflicts unsettled the harmony among the 'democracy', 'social revolution', and 'national unity and integrity' strands of the constitutional web (Austin 2002).

2002), scholars have reconsidered the idea that the Constitution was the result of a consensus pushed by nationalism (Elangovan 2018) and see it as a 'series of conflicts', of which several remained unresolved (De 2016). Constitutions often present the identity of a constitutional subject through narratives of 'sameness and selfhood' (Rosenfeld 2009, cited in Tushnet 2010, 673) or through a constitutional worldview that offers different possibilities of pinning an identity. Constitutions may also acquire salient features which give them a 'discernable identity' (Jacobsohn 2010, 3). Most constitution may, however, carry 'conflicting' and 'radically inconsistent' ideas (Tribe 1987, 173, cited in Jacobsohn 2010) with a potential for 'constitutional disharmony', which Jacobsohn considers 'critical' for the development of constitutional identity (Jacobsohn 2010, 4). More recently, Madhav Khosla has described the 'founding orientation' towards 'written constitutionalism' in the Indian context as a modality of creating 'common meanings' and 'explicating norms' that 'other societies could take for granted'. The text of the Constitution was devised, argues Khosla, not simply to empower or restrain political actors but as a 'pedagogical tool'—as an 'instrument of political education' to build a 'new civic culture' (Khosla 2020, 23).

Deferral and Interlocutory Spaces

The Constitution giving processes in the CA embodied the moment when a constitutional identity was being consciously crafted. The debates on citizenship in the CA show how integral the delineation of citizenship was for expressing both—the identity of the Constitution and that of the constitutional subject. In the course of the final reading of the draft Constitution, on 10 August 1949, B. R. Ambedkar proposed the citizenship articles immediately after the provisions pertaining to financial relations between the Union and the States and the establishment of a Finance Commission had been considered and passed. The two Articles, 5 and 6, dealing with citizenship, were presented for deliberation as a 'consolidated amendment', along with what Rajendra Prasad—President of the CA—termed a 'veritable jungle' of 130 to 140 amendments. These amendments—some of which were moved in the CA and voted upon—manifested the *dissonance* within the CA on the foundational principles of citizenship, even among those from the Congress Party, who would later become members of Nehru's first Cabinet. The introduction of the provisions immediately prompted a procedural question. Naziruddin Ahmed, elected from West Bengal on a reserved Muslim seat, queried how the consolidation of the amendments had been done by the drafting committee, and whether substantial departures from the original draft had taken place, which he argued, would amount to an amendment of the Constitution itself (CAD, 10 August 1949, 345). Representing West Bengal, Ahmed was a persistent and 'vocal critic of the draft Constitution', 'fuelled by an inward suspicion of the Drafting Committee itself' (Rathore 2020).[10] His angst at what he considered a daily departure from the draft constitution was reflective of *both*—the role that the various sub-committees and the drafting committee played in determining the final form of the Constitution *and* the concern this prompted within the CA over the loss of control over the draft and their reduction to simply a deliberative and approving body.

It may be recalled that the drafting committee, chaired by B. R. Ambedkar, was appointed by the CA on 29 August 1947. The committee prepared the initial draft of the Constitution in six months, which was discussed in the CA for almost a year, in the course of which amendments were discussed, voted, incorporated, or rejected. Several articles were entrusted back to the drafting committee or held in abeyance for a longer period to facilitate a consensus. Often the members of the drafting committee were not in agreement with each other and expressed their differences when these articles were brought back to the CA for deliberation and voting (Singh 1990, Austin 1966 [2010]). The citizenship provisions fell in this category of articles which required attenuation of disagreement. They were entrusted to the drafting committee, which received over 130 proposals for amendment. It subsequently presented a modified draft as its own amendment, for which it sought approval from the CA. The amended draft Articles 5 and 6 concerning citizenship, which would become Articles 5 to 11 in the Constitution of India, were proposed by B. R. Ambedkar.

---

[10] Ahmad believed that the drafting committee, led by Dr Ambedkar, had engaged in a drafting process that lacked transparency, making changes to the draft Constitution without the knowledge or consent of the Constituent Assembly (Rathore 2020).

The discussions which ensued show that the CA constituted itself into a discursive body in which contestations over the provisions unfolded in a deliberative mode.[11] The decision on citizenship was, however, not reached through a deliberative consensus. The positions taken in the CA on citizenship were strongly agonistic, expressed along plural, and intersecting axes of dissonance rather than parallel binaries. 'Plural' agonism paved the way for accommodation of the consensus that had been reached in the drafting committee. The grounds for accommodation had, however, been prepared through a prior agreement on procedures. It was in deference to this prior consensus that the CA agreed to the draft prepared by the drafting committee and proposed by Ambedkar.[12] The debate in the CA over a period of three days become important, however, for giving insights into the fraught nature of the citizenship question generated by uncertainties about the present and anxieties around the ramifications any resolution of the present problems would have for the future. The debate on citizenship in the CA tells us that among its many strands—some of which reverberated in the debates on the CAB 2019 in the Parliament—what prevailed was a prior consensus among the members of the CA, regardless of their own positions on specific issues, on their commitment collectively to the objectives of the Constitution. Thus, while what was discussed in the CA was the legal framework of becoming a citizen, it was elsewhere, during the debates on the various fundamental rights that the relationship between the state and citizens was elaborated. Yet, the debate on citizenship saw substantive questions concerning the nature of the political community being raised, with implications for both citizenship identity and belonging. Significantly, the debates provided the space where secularism as a democratic and republican ideal was discussed and affirmed as the basis of citizenship, even as the relationship between citizenship and religion, the principles on which mobility could be made legible, questions of loyalty and allegiance, and the centrality of birth or descent as the source of citizenship, remained disputed.

---

[11] Following Jon Elster's study of Constituent Assemblies, Udit Bhatia makes a distinction between discursive, political, and institutional features of the debates in Constituent Assemblies (Bhatia 2018).

[12] See Knops (2007) on the relationship between agonism as deliberation and Chantal Mouffe's theory of democracy.

In his opening speech inaugurating the debate on citizenship, B. R. Ambedkar stated that he was not proposing a *permanent* law of citizenship for the country:

> Now, Sir, this article refers to citizenship not in any general sense but to citizenship on the date of the commencement of this Constitution. It is not the object of this particular article to lay down a permanent law of citizenship for this country. The business of laying down a permanent law of citizenship has been left to Parliament, and as Members will see from the wording of article 6 as I have moved the entire matter regarding citizenship has been left to Parliament to determine by any law that it may deem fit (Ambedkar, CAD, 10 August 1949, p. 347–348).

Article 6 in Ambedkar's proposal which was incorporated in the Constitution of India as Article 11, lay down that nothing in the provisions pertaining to citizenship would 'derogate from the power of Parliament to make any provision with respect to the acquisition and termination of citizenship and all other matters relating to citizenship'. While presenting the proposal in the CA, Ambedkar explained the scope of the Article, which would later be cited by the JPC to draw support for CAA:

> The effect of article 6 is this, that Parliament may not only take away citizenship from those who are declared to be citizens on the date of the commencement of this Constitution by the provisions of article 5 and those that follow, but Parliament may make altogether a new law embodying new principles. *That is the first proposition that has to be borne in mind by those who will participate in the debate on these articles. They must not understand that the provisions that we are making for citizenship on the date of the commencement of this Constitution are going to be permanent or unalterable. All that we are doing is to decide ad hoc for the time being.* (Ambedkar, CAD, 10 August 1949, 347, emphasis added)

Both Ambedkar and Prasad admitted that the committee had found it extremely difficult to frame an appropriate draft. Their concerns were, however, alleviated by the understanding that the citizenship provisions were being proposed only 'for the time being'. In the manifestation of constitutional incrementalism (Lerner 2016), the CA kept the future course of citizenship open for the Parliament to determine through the legislative route. It was, however, in the space created by *deferral* that agonistic expression of difference *and* deference to a prior procedural consensus became possible. Yet, deferral was not complete nor was it unequivocal. In what was a deviation from Ambedkar's opening statement explaining that the Parliament would have the power to make 'altogether a new law' on citizenship 'embodying new principles', Nehru's speech towards the end of the debate conveyed that the objective of the deliberations in the CA was different. The CA was a body that was articulating *policy*—the *norms and principles*—that would define citizenship, and *not* the details of acquisition and termination of citizenship. While these details should appropriately be in the domain of law making and for the Parliament to decide, the deliberations in the CA, Nehru declared, *must* lay down *the principles which would guide future law*. Nehru's declaration was inconsistent with the premise on which Ambedkar initiated the discussion—of the impermanence of the constitutional provisions on citizenship—and the power of the Parliament, if it wished, to change their content, and even redefine the principles, on which consensus was being sought from the CA.

Ambedkar's proposal may, however, be seen as keeping open the possibility of 'interlocutory spaces' in the constitution giving process—spaces that served as a conduit between the past and the future, generating overlapping visions of a future society. The Constitution, as Upendra Baxi (2008, 93) puts it, was the culmination of 'prior [and continuing] histories of power and struggle', which shaped the specific project of writing a constitution and also the production of the legal ensemble which generated specific modes of governance and juridical norms. Yet, as the theory of *constitutional moments* which draws upon history to understand and explain constitutional *practice* (Ackerman 1991) tells us, constitutional moments are 'extraordinary' moments of intense constitutional participation and deliberation, which produce not simply the text of the constitution, but consist in the inscription of the set of principles that would be adopted by 'We, the people' (Ackerman 1991, 5).

Birth, Descent, and Secularism

While setting down the procedures to be followed in the debate, Rajendra Prasad asked the CA members to 'confine' themselves to 'the limited question of laying down the qualifications for citizenship on the day the Constitution comes into force' (Prasad, CAD, 11 August 1949, 351). The Drafting Committee identified the following 'classes of people' who would become citizens of India from the commencement of the Constitution, under specified 'terms and conditions':

(1) Persons domiciled in India *and* born in India who constituted the bulk of the population of India (Article 5(a) in the proposal);
(2) 'Indians abroad' or persons ordinarily residing outside India but whose grandparents or parents were born in India as defined in the Government of India Act, 1935. This class of persons, on an application to the Consular Officer or to the Diplomatic Representative of the Government of India in a prescribed form, could be registered as citizens before the commencement of the Constitution (Article 5(b) in the proposal);
(2) 'Persons domiciled but not born in India', who had resided in India for at least five years before the commencement of the Constitution (Article 5(c) in the proposal);[13]
(3) 'Migrants' into India from Pakistan, who were residents of 'the territory now Pakistan' and had 'migrated to the territory of India', would be considered Indian citizens if they or either of their parents or any of their grandparents was born in India as defined in the Government of India Act, 1935. The drafting committee lay down different modalities for those coming to India from Pakistan before and after 19 July 1948—the date on which a permit system regulating movement between the two countries became effective. Those who migrated *before* 19 July 1948 and had been 'ordinarily' resident in India since migration would be considered Indian citizens *automatically*; those who migrated *after* 19 July 1948 would

---

[13] Under this provision subject of the Portuguese Settlements in India or the French Settlements in India like Chandernagore, Pondicherry, or the Iranians who had come from Persia and although not born here, had resided for a long time with the intention of becoming the citizens of India, could become Indian citizens.

be able to enter India on the basis of a permit issued to them for 'resettling or permanent return'. A person to whom such a permit had been issued would be entitled to 'register' as a citizen of India by 'an officer appointed in this behalf by the Government of the Dominion of India on an application made by him therefore to such officer before the date of commencement of this Constitution in the form prescribed for the purpose by that Government'. A person applying for registration should have resided in the territory of India for at least six months before the date of application (Article 5A of the proposal).

(4) 'Returnees' to India from Pakistan: Exceptions were made for persons who were residents of India but migrated to the territory which subsequently became Pakistan after 1 March 1947, when the communal violence and movement across borders began. These person could become citizens of India if, 'having so migrated to the territory now included in Pakistan, they returned to the territory of India under a permit for resettlement or permanent return issued by or under the authority of any law and every such person shall for the purposes of clause (b) of article 5-A of this Constitution be deemed to have migrated to the territory of India after the nineteenth day of July 1948' (Article 5AA). It was the provision of citizenship for this class—of 'returnees' from Pakistan—which became the site of most contentious debates in the CA.

The first amendment to the provisions proposed by Ambedkar was moved by P. S. Deshmukh, a farmer's rights activist and satyagrahi against untouchability, who would later serve in Nehru's first cabinet.[14] Objecting to Ambedkar's proposal which he believed would make Indian citizenship 'the cheapest on earth', Deshmukh proposed the principle of parentage and descent for delineating Indian citizenship. The amendments proposed by Deshmukh to make Indian citizenship both *special*

---

[14] P. S. Deshmukh was a farmers' rights activist who established the Central Provinces and Berar Farmers' Association in the course of the independence movement, and participated in satyagraha against the practice of untouchability in Amba Temple in Amaravati. He was elected to the CA from Central Provinces and Berar and served in Nehru's Cabinet after independence as the Union Minister of Agriculture and later as the Union Minister of Cooperation. He was a member of the Lok Sabha from 1952 to 1962. https://www.constitutionofindia.net/constituent_assembly_members/ps_deshmukh.

and *stringent* was as follows: insertion of 'born of Indian parents' as an additional condition for citizenship for those born in the territory of India, the enhancement of the period for which a person has been 'ordinarily resident' in the territory of India immediately before the commencement of the Constitution to become eligible for citizenship from 5 years to 12, and the removal of the provision that allowed anyone who had migrated to Pakistan from India after the first day of March 1947 to become a citizen of India. In what would be among the first emphatic statements in the CA of a religious identification of citizenship, Deshmukh suggested that Article 5 proposed by Ambedkar should be modified to include: 'every person who is a Hindu or a Sikh by religion and is not a citizen of any other State, wherever he resides shall be entitled to be a citizen of India (Deshmukh, CAD, 11 August 1949, 352).

Deshmukh's proposals represented a strand within the CA which would have preferred to make citizenship a matter of inheritance, delineating a 'community of descent' (Brubaker 1992). This was aligned with the idea of a 'homeland' as the primary and inextricable unit of belonging and source of identity, to which one remained tethered and could eventually return. The question—who *belongs*—was central to this formulation, paving the way for making citizenship an instrument of closure, exclusion, and demarcation. Deshmukh's position presents the centrality of citizenship as an institution through which the modern state 'constitutes and continually reconstitutes itself as an association of citizens' (Brubaker 1992). As an instrument of 'closure' citizenship served to establish the sovereignty of the state in demarcating membership—internally and externally—which was not 'freely disposable' (Bockenforde 1995, in Kuenkler and Stein 2016, 319). Yet citizenship was also about 'the standardisation and intensification of state authority internally', so that the state could disempower other competing loci of power to territorialize its authority. Simultaneously, while establishing its authority, the state installed itself as the only 'politically relevant affiliation' for people, affirming citizenship as an organizational principle of the state, and the state as a union of persons (Bockenforde 1995).

Deshmukh made a case for religion as a consideration to spell out the terms of belonging and the criterion for membership. It was in this context that he also argued strongly against 'throwing open' *our* citizenship 'so indiscriminately', and saw no ground for doing so, unless it was, as he put it, '*the specious, oft-repeated and nauseating principle of secularity of the State*'. Such a principle could, however, only be sustained at the cost of 'wiping out *our own people*':

> Does it mean that we must wipe out our own people; that we must wipe them out in order to prove our secularity; that we must wipe out Hindus and Sikhs under the name of secularity, that we must undermine everything that is sacred and dear to the Indians to prove that we are secular? I do not think that that is the meaning of secularity and if that is the meaning which people want to attach to that word "a secular state". I am sure the popularity of those who take that view will not last long in India. (Deshmukh, CAD, Vol. IX, 11 August 1949, 354)

In a manifestation of mimetic longing Deshmukh pinned citizenship to an idea of a Hindu/Sikh homeland, espousing an idea of citizenship which would resonate seventy years later in the justification for the CAA:

> [E]very person who is a Hindu or a Sikh and is not a citizen of any other State shall be entitled to be a citizen of India. We have seen the formation and establishment of Pakistan. Why was it established? It was established because the Muslims claimed that they must have a home of their own and a country of their own. Here we are an entire nation with a history of thousands of years and we are going to discard it, in spite of the fact that neither the Hindu nor the Sikh has any other place in the wide world to go to. ... But we are a secular State and do not want to recognise the fact that every Hindu or Sikh in any part of the world should have a home of his own. If the Muslims want an exclusive place for themselves called Pakistan, why should not Hindus and Sikhs have India as their home? We are not debarring others from getting citizenship here. We merely say that we have no other country to look to for acquiring citizenship rights and therefore we the Hindus and the Sikhs, so long as we follow the respective religions, should have the right of citizenship in India and should be entitled to retain such citizenship so long as we acquire no other. I do not think this claim is in any way non-secular or sectarian or communal. If anybody says so, he is, to say the least, mistaken. (Deshmukh, CAD, 11 August 1949, 355–356)

Later in the course of the debate, K. T. Shah too lent his weight to Deshmukh, cautioning that being secular must not make them afraid of stating the facts:

> *Hindus and Sikhs have no other home but India,* and I do not see how we can include everyone in this category unless we say it bluntly in this form. We should not be ashamed in saying that every person who is a Hindu or a Sikh by religion and is not a citizen of another State shall be entitled to citizenship of India. That will cover every class whom we want to cover and will be comprehensive. The phrase 'Secular' should not frighten us in saying what is a fact and reality must be faced. (Shah, CAD, 11 August 1949, 376)

Interestingly, however, Deshmukh was averse to giving the Parliament unbridled powers to regulate citizenship by law. Objecting to Ambedkar's proposal of giving unfettered authority to the Parliament, Deshmukh wanted the CA to lay down precise provisions for citizenship which would be difficult to change later. Making a distinction between the Constitution as a higher-order law, and a law enacted by Parliament, he averred: 'And then, this [i.e., the citizenship provision] is not a definition in an Act of Parliament that is easily changeable. So, if by the Constitution you are going to give this right of citizenship in the way proposed in this article, you cannot change it later on and this will go against the interests of the Indian nation' (Deshmukh, CAD, 11 August 1949, 355–356).

Naziruddin Ahmed raised a procedural issue yet again, pointing out that the power of the Parliament in Article 6, would amount to an amendment of the Constitution itself through the Parliament's law-making function. To avoid a law made by Parliament having the 'effect of amending the Constitution itself', the provision should mention that any change would not be seen as a constitutional amendment (Ahmed, 11 August 1949, 359–360). Jaspat Roy Kapoor representing Uttar Pradesh[15] communicated his disagreement with the Parliament's law-making powers under Article 6: 'A definite article conferring the right of citizenship

---

[15] Jaspat Roy Kapoor had a degree in law. A member of the provisional parliament from 1950 to 1952, Kapoor served as a member of the Rajya Sabha for two consecutive terms from May 1952 to May 1962. Rajya Sabha Members Biographical Sketches, 1952–2003.

under the Constitution cannot, I think, be tampered with by any subsequent law made by Parliament' (Roy Kapoor, CAD, 11 August 1949, 362).

Migrants and Returnees

After the commencement of the Constitution, the Parliament enacted a law on citizenship in 1955. There existed a period of legal vacuum between 26 November 1949, when the citizenship provisions came into force, and 1955 when the Citizenship Act became effective. Similar hiatus in law existed before the constitutional provisions came into force. In these periods of hiatus, citizenship of those moving across the borders between India and Pakistan remained liminal and indeterminate. Within the CA, a debate ensued over two 'classes' of people who were to become citizens at the commencement of the Constitution: (a) 'Migrants' into India from Pakistan, among whom a distinction was made between those who came to India before 19 July 1948, when the permit system came into force, and those who came after that, and (b) 'Returnees' to India from Pakistan for whom exceptions were made to enable them to become Indian citizens after following specific procedures. The first category, which was more likely to be Hindus and Sikhs migrating to India, as a matter of choice and/or to flee violence against them in Pakistan, were according to Jaspat Roy Kapoor, at par with those who were residing in the Indian territory. They were 'citizens of India as of right' and not by 'way of grace', he argued. They 'took all the trouble' and experienced the 'misery and agony' of migrating from Pakistan to 'this *dear and sacred land* of theirs':

> All the while that they were on their way to this land, they were thinking of this beloved country of theirs, pining and praying to reach our borders, and immediately on reaching those borders, with a great sense of relief they cried out 'Jai Hind', a cry which touched every one of us. *They had such tremendous loyalty and affection for this country*. (Roy Kapoor, CAD, 11 August 1949, 364, emphasis added)

While arguing for the removal of what he considered an 'inconsiderate' and unbecoming distinction between those 'migrating' into citizenship and those 'found living' in India, he went on to urge the CA to specify the precise reasons for their migration in the provision itself, that is, '*civil disturbances or fear of such disturbances*'. While putting this condition, Kapur sought to bring the provision in line with laws pertaining to evacuee property in force in the country—the Evacuee Property Ordinance—in which an evacuee was defined as a person 'who has left a territory because of civil disturbances or because of fear of such disturbances' and also to communicate that it was not the intention of the CA to 'confer the right of citizenship on anybody who wanted to migrate to this country'. The right could be conferred only on those persons who 'found it difficult to stay in the place of their original domicile'. (Roy Kapoor, CAD, 11 August 1949, 364–365) While the suggestion was not incorporated in the final provision, in January 1950 the interim Parliament promulgated an Ordinance, followed by an Act a month later—the Immigration (Expulsion from Assam) Act 1950—to contain the influx of refugees from the eastern borders into Assam and the eruption of communal tensions in the border districts of Cachar, Goalpara, and Kamrup. Under the Act the government could direct a person to 'remove' himself from Assam and India, if the 'presence' of that person was 'found to be detrimental to the interests of the general public'. The Act, however, made an exception 'aimed at protecting mainly the Bengali Hindus fleeing in from East Pakistan' (Pisharoty 2019, 50), by providing that a person who had entered India on account of civil disturbance or fear of such disturbance and had been residing in Assam, could not be removed (Pisharoty 2019).

Objecting strongly to allowing 'returnees' (that is those who migrated to Pakistan after 19 July 1948 and returned to India with permits from the Indian Embassy) to become citizens, Kapoor brought considerations of 'loyalty' and 'allegiance', into the debate. Calling this provision 'obnoxious', he argued:

> It is a serious matter of principle. Once a person has migrated to Pakistan and transferred his loyalty from India to Pakistan, *his migration is complete. He has definitely made up his mind at that time to kick this country and let it go to its own fate, and he went away to the newly created Pakistan*, where he would put in his best efforts to make it a free, progressive and prosperous state. We have no grudge against them … (Roy Kapoor, CAD, 11 August 1949, 366)

Responding to Brajeshwar Prasad's interjection whether all those persons who fled to Pakistan 'did so with the intention of permanently settling down there' and because they owed 'allegiance to that State?' or they too, like those escaping to India 'fled in panic?', Kapoor insisted:

> ... To our misfortune, only a handful of nationalist Muslims were opposed to the idea of Pakistan. The vast majority of the Muslims and most certainly those of them who went away to Pakistan immediately after Partition had certainly the intention of permanently residing in Pakistan... They gave up their loyalty to this country and they gave their allegiance to the new country of Pakistan. *Their migration was therefore complete and absolute and, therefore, the right of citizenship which they had before their migration is eliminated altogether...* Now if they want to come back to India to settle down here permanently, we may welcome them as we would welcome any other foreigner ... You can come back again and settle permanently here if you like; but please do not think it is for the reason that you kicked this country once... (Roy Kapoor, CAD, 11 August 1949, 366–367, emphasis added)

The 'returnees' could be allowed to come back on a permit but could become citizens like any foreigner, after showing their eligibility under a law made by the Parliament. Alerting the Assembly to the possibility of the returnees reclaiming the property they had left behind, worth hundreds of crores, and now under the management and regulatory control of the Custodian of Evacuee Property, Roy Kapoor wondered if the costs of removing the anomaly between a person being simultaneously a citizen and an evacuee was not too high (Roy Kapoor, CAD, 11 August 1949). The argument that the constitutional provisions must make a distinction between 'returnees' and 'citizens' was reinforced by K. T. Shah, who sought an uneasy alliance between the republican ideal of citizenship as a 'proud privilege'—recalling its usage in the Roman Republic, where every Roman citizen could 'regard himself as equal to any King'—with the principle of citizenship as 'inheritance'. The 'pride' in being an Indian citizen flowed from the transition it symbolized from subjecthood, which Shah hoped, like Roman citizenship, would become emphatic: 'I hope the time is coming when the same proud boast may justly be made by Indians, *when the citizenship of India will not be merely regarded as a burden of our "nativity"—for we were used to be called "natives" in the dead and buried past*—but it would be regarded as something to which the rest of the world will look up with respect' (Shah, CAD, 11 August 1949, 366–370). Yet, the privilege of citizenship was to accrue unequally—on the ground of 'birth' but combined with 'inheritance'—*from the paternal side*. Shah professed to be a believer in 'the equality of men and women', but recommended a paternal lineage for citizenship—'because of the many complexities and difficulties involved in this tracing of inheritance from the maternal side, not the least of which is the problem of proof' (Shah, CAD, 11 August 1949, 370). The principle of inheritance would not, however, work for the 'returnees'—who had, Shah believed, 'indicated by every act in their power that they would have nothing to do with this country, that they belong to a different nation, that they are different in race, language, culture and religion, or whatever the reason that inspired then in, we would be justified in presuming that they have renounced their birthright' (Shah, CAD, 11 August 1949, 370). Even if the CA would consider giving them citizenship, it could not be on the basis of 'inheritance' but the requirement of 'sufficient evidence documentary or otherwise, not only to their right by descent but also to show their intention to permanently reside in this country, and be its loyal citizens' (Shah, CAD, 370–371).

Making a distinction between refugees and returnees, Thakur Das Bhargava too made a case against giving citizenship to 'those who were desirous to become the citizens of Pakistan on the 15 August 1947 or who left this country to become citizens of Pakistan with open eyes and with the song on their lips: *"Hanske liya Pakistan Ladke lenge Hindustan"'* (Bhargava, CAD, 11 August 1949, 380). In a striking similarity with the debates on 'illegal migrants' in Assam, even though the category is not used anywhere in the CAD, Bhargava draws attention to the problem of giving citizenship to persons on the mere fulfilment of residential requirements. Shah preferred the insertion of 'civil disturbance' as a reason for seeking refuge in India, particularly to make a distinction between Muslims who had come to Assam to make it a Muslim majority state for election purposes and those who came on account of disturbances in Pakistan or fear of disturbances: '... If any nationalist Mussalman who is afraid of the Muslims of East Pakistan or West Pakistan comes to India he certainly should be welcomed. It is our duty to see that he is protected. We will treat him as our brother and a *bona fide* national of India' (Bhargava, CAD, 11 August 1949, 380–386).

Like the previous speakers, Bhargava too was sceptical about giving citizenship to the returnees. Holding the position that 'a person who has once migrated from this country has migrated for all time' and abandoned his domicile, he argued: 'There is no question of partial abandonment'. Blaming the government for having allowed 'thousands of people' from Pakistan into India on permits of resettlement, Bhargava declared:

> Perhaps you are not conscious as to what difficult questions of property and propriety are agitating the minds of the refugees in this connection. ... Though *bona fide* refugees have not yet been rehabilitated, the houses in Delhi etc., were reserved for those who had yet to arrive from Pakistan and many of such returned people have got their houses back. ...apart from rights to property which may run to crores, I for one do not understand how, according to law and equity, we can hold to a proposition that if any person gets a permit for resettlement in India, *proprio vigro* he becomes a citizen of India. It means that the High Commissioner at Karachi has got the power of making any person he likes a citizen of India. It virtually comes to that. .... When the Act relating to these permits was placed in the House, we did not know that they would acquire this force. ... My submission is that any further issue of these permits would not be just and would not be conducive to the solidarity of this country. (Bhargava, CAD, 11 August 1949, 380–386)

Bhupinder Singh Maan too made a distinction between 'refugees' and 'returnees' and blamed 'a weak sort of secularism' that had 'crept in', to make the provisions of Article 5AA an exception to accommodate the returnees, showing 'an unfair partiality . . . to those who least deserve it'. Speaking as someone who was a refugee himself, Maan argued that this partiality had worked to the detriment of the refugees because of the claims the returnees could make to evacuee property:

> ... The Indian Government is already short of property as it is and it is unable to solve the rehabilitation problem. The difference of property left by Indian nationals in Pakistan and the one left behind by Muslims, in India—this difference of property cannot be bridged. ... The securing

of a chance permit from the Deputy High Commissioner's office or any other authority should not carry with it such a prize thing as citizenship of India, or that the holders be considered to be sons of Bharat Mata. ...I certainly grudge this right and concession being given to those people who had flagrantly violated and dishonoured the integrity of India. (Maan, CAD, 12 August 1949, 393–394)

Mahboob Ali Baig Sahib appealed to the CA to consider the matter calmly before making a distinction between a person who went to Pakistan and those who were compelled to migrate to India, 'under the same and similar circumstances': '... what happened was that after the transfer of power there was a holocaust, there were disturbances, there were tragedies which compelled persons to migrate' (Baig Sahib, 12 August 1949, 397). Baig asked the CA to remember Gandhi's exhortation to those [Muslims] who had gone to Pakistan to 'return to their homeland'. Surprised that those returning were being considered 'traitors', he reminded the CA that the invitation to return in Gandhi's framework was *open to all* (Baig, CAD, 12 August 1949, 397–398). Maulana Mohammed Hifzur Rehman placed faith in the local government and officials who would be required to conduct an enquiry to satisfy themselves of their eligibility under the prevalent laws. For Maulana Rehman it was not a problem of what should be the threshold of admissibility, but 'the difficulties which they have to face as *Indian citizens*' (Rehman, 12 August 1949, 408–409).

Citizenship provisions were seen as integral to the identity of a Republican constitution. Alluding to citizenship as an expression of constitutional identity, Alladi Krishnaswamy Aiyyar directed the discussion towards the *relevance* of citizenship provisions and their *necessity* for setting in motion the processes of establishing a representative and constitutional democracy. Aiyyar asserted the importance of procedures for democratic institutions: 'Otherwise, there will be difficulties connected with the holding of particular offices, and even in the starting of representative institutions in the country under the republican constitution' (Ayyar, CAD, 12 August 1949, 402). The idea of a 'permanent home' for Aiyyar was associated with domicile, different from what was posited in the speeches of earlier speakers as 'homeland'. At the commencement of the Constitution, the problem—*who wanted to make India their permanent home*—assumed primacy. It was in this context that birth and domicile became important considerations, to accommodate not only those living in tracts like Goa where people had settled down to make India their permanent home, and 'contributed to the richness of the life of the country' as well as 'all cases of mass migration' from Pakistan into India who too had made India their home. Apart from the obligation to extend the protection of citizenship to those who return, Aiyyar reminded the members that the CA 'was pledged to upholding the principles of a secular state':

> We may make a distinction between people who have voluntarily and deliberately chosen another country as their home and those who want to retain their connection with this country. But we cannot on any racial or religious or other grounds make a distinction between one kind of persons and another, or one sect of persons and another sect of persons, having regard to our commitments and the formulation of our policy on various occasions. (Aiyyar, CAD, 12 August, 404)

The commitment of the CA to Gandhian principles of non-discrimination was repeated by Brajeshwar Prasad, who described the proviso in 5AA as 'a tribute to the memory of the great Mahatma who worked for the establishment of good relations between Hindus and Muslims' (Prasad, CAD, 12 August, 404). In an argument against the identification of India with a Hindu homeland, Prasad described the proviso as an invitation to all the Muslims 'who had left this country, to come back and settle in this country'. Making a case for 'common citizenship' for India and Pakistan as a first step towards a common citizenship of the Asian people as the basis of peace and progress in the region, Prasad warned against 'the mischief of partition' being 'allowed to spread beyond the legal fact of partition'. Disagreeing with the assertion that partition was responsible for mass migration, Prasad, argued that India never agreed to Jinnah's principle of exchange of population. It was a logical implication of 'our' rejection of the partition based on an exchange of population [on the ground of religion] that 'the fact of partition would have no bearing on the question of loyalty of Muslims of this country. Partition or no partition, the Muhammadan will remain loyal to this country. That was the meaning of the rejection of the demand of Mr Jinnah. And how can we say that the fact of partition was responsible for mass migration? It must be realised that it was the riots and the disturbances in certain parts of the country which were responsible for mass migration' (Prasad, CAD, 12 August, 404–405).

Hriday Nath Kunzru described Articles 5A and 5AA as 'extraordinary provisions', 'arising out of the present extra-ordinary circumstances, created by the partition of India', with no 'counterpart' to them in the Constitution of any other country. To Kunzru, the criticism of 5A on the ground of being 'undesirably wide' throwing open 'the door of citizenship to people who have no moral right to be regarded as Indian citizens', was not justified. Asking the Assembly to consider the position of those 'who had to leave Pakistan for some reason or other after the partition of India or about that time', Kunzru spoke of the representatives of refugees who wanted to be regarded as Indian citizens 'unconditionally'. In an interesting intervention, which would resonate with the debates later on the CAA 2019, he referred to Thakur Das Bhargava's plea to include 'civil disturbances or the fear of such disturbances', as the reason to allow absorption into citizenship. To Kunzru, 'it would be very strange if such a condition is laid down', which would be difficult for a person to prove and for an officer to ascertain. In particular, people who migrated from East Bengal to West Bengal, who would find it difficult to prove that they have left their homes in Eastern Pakistan because of civil disturbances or fear of such disturbances, 'when millions of non-Muslims were still living in Eastern Pakistan' (Kunzru, CAD, 12 August 1949, 410–411).

Claiming to speak for 'Assamese Hindus' and on behalf of the 'tribal people' and 'Bengali Scheduled Castes of Assam', Rohini Kumar Chowdhury *only* wished to state what he called 'some plain facts without any fear'. Drawing clear boundaries between who should and who should not be considered for citizenship of India from the experience of Assam, Chowdhury clarified:

> I want to make it perfectly clear that I want citizenship rights for those people of East Bengal who had gone over to West Bengal or Assam out of fear of disturbance in the future or from a sense of insecurity and—also for those people who have come over from Sylhet, who at the time of coming had no fear of disturbance or anything of that kind, but who, on account of fear of disturbances now have decided to live here. (Chowdhury, CAD, 12 August 1949, 413)

Arguing that a sense of insecurity was pervasive among persons from East Bengal who had crossed over to West Bengal or Assam, a 'fear' which was 'latent in the mind of everybody', Chowdhury did not consider it desirable to demand a proof of this fear. Chowdhury represented a strand in the CA debates which expressed the anxieties of the border regions. Thus, while asking that those who entered Assam in the course of Partition or those who had come earlier and made Assam their home be considered citizens, Chowdhury wanted the exclusion of persons who came to the state 'surreptitiously' before Partition, 'mixed themselves with their own brethren' and now desired citizenship not because of any sense of insecurity but 'with a desire to exploit' Assam. These persons had 'set up the struggle for Pakistan', 'compelling the politicians of India to agree for partition'—and were now 'living peacefully' on property purchased cheaply which rightfully belonged to 'the minority' who came to Assam 'out of fear' (Chowdhury, CAD, 12 August 1949, 413–414). Chowdhury claimed to have the backing of all communities, including Muslims who 'belong to Assam', who had 'made Assam their home'. Even at the risk of being labelled a person who was 'against the entry of Bengalee Hindus into Assam', Chowdhury considered this important in order not to 'expose' the 'frontier' and through it the 'province', which would potentially become a source of danger to the country:

> Already I have been to Cachar, and I have seen in that district, from which crossing the Barak river you come into India, there is trouble; and if this amendment of Dr Ambedkar is accepted, this district of Cachar will be entirely one district of Pakistan, and who will be responsible for giving one district which should have been kept in our province and which was retained after a good deal of fight but which will be sent to Pakistan? It will be this amendment moved by Dr Ambedkar. (Chowdhury, CAD, 12 August 1949, 416–417)

The identification of citizenship as a legal status and a source of identity animated the members of the CA. The dilemma around what needed to be explicitly stated in the constitutional text and what could be left for future democratic majorities to legislate was expressed in terms of a fundamental contestation over parliamentary sovereignty and the status of the Constitution as a higher-order law embodying popular sovereignty.

In his speech in the CA, Nehru mounted his defence of Ambedkar's proposal by expressing the impossibility of drafting anything, with 'whatever meticulous care', which could address the 'difficult and complicated' situation precipitated by the Partition. Emphasizing yet again the importance of *principles*, Nehru considered a decision that involved 'the greatest amount of justice' and served as the most practical solution to the problems of the 'vast majority of cases', as a principled decision. Yet, the practicality of a decision would be subservient to the principles which gave the Constitution an identity. Troubled by the manner in which opposition to Ambedkar's proposal was built around the rejection of secularism—as an 'appeasement to Pakistan'—Nehru sought to register his 'strong protest' arguing that these positions eschewed considerations of equity and justice. To those denigrating secularism, Nehru responded:

> Another word is thrown up a good deal, this secular State business. May I beg with all humility those gentlemen who use this word often to consult some dictionary before they use it? It is brought in at every conceivable step and at every conceivable stage. I just do not understand it. It has a great deal of importance, no doubt. But, it is brought in all contexts, as if by saying that we are a secular State we have done something amazingly generous, given something out of our pocket to the rest of the world, something which we ought not to have done, so on and so forth. We have only done something which every country does except a very few misguided and backward countries in the world. Let us not refer to that word in the sense that we have done something very mighty. (Nehru, CAD, 12 August 1949, 398)

Nehru defended the 'permit system' on grounds of justice: 'to argue against the proposal was "to argue definitely for injustice, definitely for discrimination, for not doing something which after full enquiry has been found to be rightly done"' (Nehru, CAD, 12 August 1949, 401). Questions pertaining to the underlying basis of citizenship—descent/parentage or birth/territory—in other words subscription to a model of citizenship which envisaged a community of descent, prioritizing blood as a bond that linked up the political community with an inherited community of ancestors *or* a model based on the principle of territoriality offering a political relationship with the state for successive generations born on its land—were expressed as alternatives. The principle of *jus soli*, which prevailed through the amendment brought by the drafting committee, was seen by Nehru to be addressing the contexts of Partition in a *just* manner, and also as laying down non-discrimination and secularism as enduring principles of citizenship. Those in the CA who opposed Ambedkar's proposal advocated parentage as a principle, not only to prevent returnees from acquiring Indian citizenship but also to present citizenship as an identity emerging from distinctive nationhood. These strands in the CAD resurfaced in the debates around the CAA 2019. The JPC set up to examine the CAB 2016 presented the debates in the Constituent Assembly to reiterate the position that the contemporary predicament over citizenship had their roots in the flawed resolution of the citizenship question during Partition. It was in this context that the debates in the CAD on the Parliament's legislative powers over citizenship and the idea of 'national' citizenship associated with a 'Hindu homeland' assumed significance.

The JPC and the Spectre of National Citizenship

The CAB 2016 was introduced in the Lok Sabha on 19 July 2016 and entrusted immediately to the consideration of a JPC. The committee system had been installed in 1993 to enable Parliamentary oversight over the government through ad hoc and permanent committees consisting of Members of Parliament (MP). As an ad hoc committee set up to scrutinize specific issues which in the consideration of the Parliament required more detailed scrutiny, a JPC draws its members from both the Lok Sabha and the Rajya Sabha. It deploys a range of modalities including consultation with experts, reaching out to and receiving memoranda from those likely to be impacted by the government's decision and also talking to those in the ministries and the bureaucracy responsible for matters under the perusal of the JPC. The proposal to refer the CAB 2016 to a JPC was made in the Lok Sabha by Bhartruhari Mahtab of the Biju Janata Dal (BJD) and was supported by Jyotiraditya Scindia (then in the Indian National Congress, presently with BJP), Mohammed Salim of the Communist Party of India (CPI) and Sudip Bandyopadhyay of the All India Trinamool Congress (AITMC or TMC) on the ground that citizenship was a matter which required careful and focused attention. Interestingly, at this point in the life of the CAB, no member expressed any apprehension beyond indicating its sensitive nature, especially in relation to Assam.

Headed by Rajendra Agrawal from the BJP, the JPC was expected to submit its report by the last week of the Winter Session of 2016. In its 425-page report, submitted on 7 January 2019, the JPC stated its mandate and *modus operandi*, and included the minutes of its meetings and the dissenting notes of nine members, apart from its recommendations on the final Bill. The Committee undertook three 'study visits'—to Jodhpur from 18 to 20 December 2016, to Ahmedabad and Rajkot from 18 to 20 April 2017 and to Guwahati, Silchar, and Shillong from 7 to 11 May 2018, held discussions and received depositions from 'stakeholders' at the local level. In addition, it received 'evidence' in the form of written replies, clarifications, and documents from different state governments (Assam, Bihar, Gujarat, Jharkhand, Maharashtra, and West Bengal) and various ministries including the Ministry of Home Affairs, Ministry of Law, and Justice (Department of Legal Affairs and Legislative Department), and Ministry of External Affairs. 'Representatives' of these ministries were present in all sittings of the JPC and gave 'oral evidence' to the JPC. Oral evidence was also obtained from the Intelligence Bureau and the Research and Analysis Wing (RAW). Non-official 'witnesses' were also heard in the course of sittings. The categories invoked in the report refer to the nature of consultation attributed to different entities. Reading the report, one can identify two premises on which change in the citizenship law was justified: legislative competence and bounded citizenship.

Legislative Competence

The JPC invoked 'legislative competence' of the Parliament on all matters concerning citizenship, drawn from Article 11 of the Constitution of India, as the fundamental premise to justify the CAB. The assertion of legislative competence and authority was buttressed by the JPC by referring to a higher-order normative claim, drawn from the CA. While claiming authority from the constitutional text and the deliberative processes in the CA, the JPC prepared the ground for exceeding the scope of Article 11, justifying the fundamental changes that were being sought through the CAB in the 'principles' underlying citizenship in India. In the process, the JPC took recourse to a self-referential process, abrogating upon itself the responsibility of offering administrative and legal support for violation of constitutional norms. The reference to Article 11 of the Constitution as the source of legislative authority over all matters pertaining to citizenship, including its 'acquisition and termination', was presented in the report as an *unfettered power* of the Parliament to regulate the 'right to citizenship by law'.

The attribution of unrestrained legislative powers to the Parliament on matters concerning citizenship was derived from the expression 'nothing in the forgoing provisions of this Part of the Constitution shall derogate from the power of Parliament' in Article 11.[16] This position was buttressed with reference to the debate on the citizenship provisions in the CA, where Ambedkar, among other members, reported 'hardships' in drafting Article 5 of the Constitution of India. Ambedkar's statement that the citizenship provisions referred only to citizenship on the 'date of commencement' of the Constitution and did not intend to 'lay down a permanent law of citizenship for the country' which would be drafted by the Parliament in future, was cited by the JPC to affirm that the Parliament could, in the exercise of these powers make 'altogether a new law embodying new principles' (Report 2019, 9). While doing so, the JPC disregarded the fact that the Parliament's powers of regulating citizenship by law were not restrained by anything laid down in Part II of the Constitution on citizenship, but Article 11 did not exclude the constraints that other parts of the Constitution would continue to apply on the law-making powers of the Parliament, including, but not confined to, the Preamble and Fundamental Rights provisions.

Bounded Citizenship

While gravitating towards 'natural' citizenship congealing the relationship between legal status and blood ties, the JPC interpolated an idea of 'national' citizenship tied with what is called the 'right to vote' and 'run

---

[16] This refers to Articles 5 to 11 in Part II of the Constitution of India concerning citizenship.

for office'. These rights, it argued, are 'consequential' to the status of citizenship, since it allows for participation in the 'democratic process at the national level'. 'Eventual integration' of immigrants into the host society was seen by the JPC as a significant part of the 'resolution' of 'demographic problems', not only for a robust electoral democracy but also for 'the disbursement of welfare benefits' etc. This is where, the JPC, argued, liberal democracies balanced their commitment to 'the universal language' of 'fundamental human rights' along with 'the free association and participation of the people', with the enforcement of 'clear and enforceable boundaries', 'both in terms of territory and political membership'. The JPC termed this as the 'paradox' of 'liberal democracies' which are 'internally inclusive while remaining externally exclusive'.

The articulation of 'national' citizenship by the JPC expressed affinity to a bounded notion of citizenship. In this framework, the CAB was presented as an essential measure to resolve the 'crisis' generated by migrants and aliens by prescribing the terms on which migrants could be absorbed. The terms of absorption were premised in 'a thick and solidarity based model of citizenship', simultaneously marked by the logic of closure. Underlying this logic was the belief that it is desirable for states to 'allocate, distribute and manage national citizenship by setting up a wall between citizens and aliens' (Sadiq 2009, 7) to preserve national belonging and security. The CAB installed the wall of separation by identifying the solidarity of citizenship on the grounds of religion. At the same time, if the JPC report is an indication, the CAB served to bring in exclusionary nationhood hiding behind the veneer of liberal citizenship.

Protecting the Law from the Constitution

The JPC spoke to 'experts' from different ministries including law and home, apart from 'stakeholders' from different states. It is clear that the JPC was conscious that the CAB, when enacted into law, could face the charge of discrimination and judicial scrutiny could render the Act unconstitutional on the ground that it violated Articles 14 and 25 of the Constitution. The JPC considered the charge of a potential violation of Article 25 surmountable since the CAB in its opinion was not violating the right to freedom of religion. It devoted its efforts, therefore, towards preparing a defence against the charge of violation of Article 14, that is, equality before the law and equal protection of the law, guaranteed by the Constitution to all 'persons'—citizens and aliens. In this context, the JPC considered the suggestion given to it by constitutional experts that the category 'persecuted minorities' could be used in the Bill instead of identifying communities based on religion. It must be pointed out here that the category 'religious minorities' does not occur anywhere in the CAA. The text of the Act only refers to the Notifications dated 7 September 2015 and 18 July 2016 which mention the term 'religious persecution'. The text of the CAA uses the category 'minority communities' and proceeds to identify them on the ground of religion. The category 'persecuted minorities' was proposed by constitutional experts to deflect the charge that the word minority mentioned in the Bill was intended to be 'religious' minority only, and a further charge that it excluded some minorities in preference to others.

The JPC rejected this suggestion by constitutional experts in deference to the wishes of the 'legislative department', which advised it against the incorporation of a wider category of persecuted minorities, by arguing that this would 'negate the *objectives* of the Bill', and 'lose sight of' *religious* persecution as the *primary objective* of the amendment.[17] Indeed, the Department of Legal Affairs convinced the JPC that the CAB was sufficiently fortified against judicial scrutiny for violation of constitutional norms because it did not discriminate against persons on the ground of religion. Indeed, it was making distinction among persons on the ground of religion for the purpose of meeting the primary objective of the Bill, which was to extend the protection of citizenship to minority communities facing religious persecution in specified countries. The consideration of religious persecution for making distinction among persons for extending the protection of citizenship could not, in its opinion, be construed discriminatory, because the distinction was being made on the grounds of both *'intelligible' differentiation and 'reasonable' classification*.

---

[17] Emphasis added. The JPC noted that the Ministry of Home Affairs had informed them that 'migrants' who entered India due to persecution on account of race, religion, sex, nationality, ethnic identity, membership of a particular social group or political opinion, were treated under a Standard Operating Procedure (SOP) that had been in operation since 2011. This information convinced that JPC of the justification for 'specifying the six religious minorities in the proposed amendment'.

The JPC took recourse to these two standards of evaluation—of *intelligibility* and *reasonableness*—drawing from the Supreme Court judgment in 1952 in the case *State of West Bengal vs. Anwar Ali Sarkar*:

> The Legislative Department have clarified that the proposed Amendment Bill will not violate the spirit of Article 14 as it upholds the test of reasonable classification as propounded by a seven Judge Bench of the Supreme Court in the State of West Bengal vrs. Anwar Ali Sarkar case (AIR 1952 SC-75). The Department of Legal Affairs have submitted that differential treatment does not *per se* constitute violation of Article 14 of the Constitution. It has been very lucidly explained that any legislation may withstand challenge on the ground of discrimination and violation of Article 14 of the Constitution, in case the classification created by it is founded on an intelligible differentia which distinguishes persons or things that are grouped together from others left out of the group, and that differentia has a rational relation to the object sought to be achieved by the statute in question. The Department have further clarified that the positive concept of equality does not postulate equal treatment of all persons without distinction but rather stresses on equality of treatment in equal circumstances as to similarly situated persons and the Bill appears to have the object of facilitating all such members of minority communities without any discrimination. ….. Moreover, citing various Supreme Court judgements, the Department have emphasised that the Legislature is competent to exercise its discretion and make reasonable classification. In view of the above submissions and assurances of various arms of the Government including the Department of Legal Affairs, the Committee are convinced that mentioning the names of the six religious minority communities will not violate the spirit of Article 14 and Article 25 of the Constitution and the Bill will stand the scrutiny of Judiciary and vires of the Constitution. (JPC Report 2019, 50–51)

The Supreme Court judgment referred to by the JPC in the case *West Bengal vs. Anwar Ali Sarkar* (1952) had resulted in the dismissal of an appeal by the West Bengal government against a Calcutta High court judgment. The case involved the trial of Anwar Ali Sarkar under the West Bengal Special Courts Act (X of 1950). The objective of the West

Bengal Special Courts Act as declared in its preamble, was 'to provide for speedier trial' for certain 'cases' or 'offences' or 'classes of cases' or 'classes of offences' and to empower the state government to constitute special courts with procedures for trial, which were different from those laid down in the Criminal Procedure Code. The Court established the principles of 'intelligible differentia' and 'reasonable classification' as the only ground on which distinction could be made among 'classes of cases'.

Convincing itself that the CAB could be buttressed against constitutional scrutiny, the JPC relied selectively on that part of the Supreme Court judgement in Anwar Ali Sarkar case in which *intelligibility* of 'cases' or 'offences' selected for exception required that they must be clearly identifiable and distinguishable as a 'class' for exceptional treatment; *reasonableness* was satisfied by the fulfilment of the condition that the reason for making the distinction among cases corresponded to the 'object' of the Act. The JPC drew support from the Supreme Court judgement to argue that the classification of persons on the ground of religion in CAB would not constitute discrimination under Article 14 since these persons constituted a distinct group or class of persons requiring the protection of citizenship to escape religious persecution. The inability to get speedy admission into citizenship made their condition precarious, especially since they were likely to be slotted as illegal migrants. The CAB attempted to correct that anomaly, by inserting exemptions in the citizenship law. In the JPCs view, this constituted *both*—an intelligible differentia and reasonable classification. In other words, for the JPC, the test of reasonableness was primarily *procedural*, merely requiring correspondence between classification and the objectives of the law, which made different rather than equal treatment imperative.

In its judgement in Anwar Ali Sarkar case, however, the Supreme Court had gone beyond procedural requirements to lay down *substantive* conditions for fulfilling the criterion of reasonableness. The court did this by locating reasonableness in the stringent requirement of conformity to the equality provisions in Article 14 of the Constitution of India. This is evident in the explanation given by the Supreme Court for dismissing the appeal by the West Bengal government, stating emphatically that the West Bengal Special Courts Act violated Article 14 of the Constitution of India on two grounds: (i) for failing the test of 'equality before law' by discriminating among persons while conducting a trial, and; (ii) for removing the guarantee of 'equal protection of law' against the arbitrary power of the state. The dissenting judge Patanjali Shatri as well as CJI Harries who wrote the lead judgement agreed that the state had the power to distinguish and classify persons 'to be subjected to particular laws'. They also agreed that while the state government had discretionary powers which were plenary in nature, these powers *could not be arbitrary*. Thus, the criteria of intelligibility of the differentia and the reasonableness of classification foregrounded by the JPC as protection against judicial scrutiny could still be prised open for constitutional validation, to ask whether they satisfied **both** grounds of protection guaranteed by Article 14, that is, *protection against discrimination* (equality before the law) and *protection against the arbitrary exercise of state power* (equal protection of the law).

In 2009, the Delhi High Court judgement in Naz Foundation vs. Government of NCT of Delhi referred to the 'scope, content and meaning of Article 14' as elaborated in what it called 'a catena of decisions'. These decisions, the judgement stated, lay down that Article 14, while *forbidding* 'class legislation', allowed 'reasonable' classification for the purpose of legislation. The test of reasonableness and therefore 'permissible' classification required the fulfilment of two conditions:

> ... (i) that the classification must be founded on an intelligible differentia which distinguishes persons or things that are grouped together from those that are left out of the group; and (ii) that the differentia must have a rational relation to the objective sought to be achieved by the statute in question. The classification may be founded on differential basis according to objects sought to be achieved but what is implicit in it is that there ought to be a nexus, i.e., causal connection between the basis of classification and object of the statute under consideration. (Budhan Choudhry v. State of Bihar, AIR 1955 SC 191, cited in Naz Foundation vs. Government of NCT 2009, para. 88, 52)

The Naz Foundation judgment (2009), however, recommended *a further test of reasonableness*, requiring that the *objective* for such classification in the law must also be subjected to judicial scrutiny: 'If the objective be illogical, unfair and unjust, necessarily the classification will have to be held as unreasonable' (Deepak Sibal vs. Punjab University (1989) 2 SCC 145, cited in Naz Foundation 2009). Citing the judgement in Maneka Gandhi case, the Naz Foundation judgment augmented protection against state arbitrariness by stressing that the law should 'eschew arbitrariness in any form' since arbitrariness was antithetical to equality (E. P. Royappa vs. State of Tamil Nadu (1974) 4 SCC 3, cited in Naz Foundation, 2009), both according to political logic and constitutional law (Ajay Hasia vs. Khalid Mujib Sehravardi (1981) 1 SCC 722 cited in Naz Foundation, 2009).

While providing a test for reasonableness, the Naz Foundation judgement went beyond the procedural test of correspondence between an intelligible differentia and the objectives of law, by subjecting the objectives themselves to scrutiny. The judgement provided a substantive test for protection against exercise of arbitrary power by the state, to say that any violation of Article 14 is in fact a violation of equality provisions in the Constitution. The restraint on state arbitrariness was to come from constitutional morality, which as B. R. Ambedkar declared in the Constituent Assembly, was the responsibility of the state to protect (Naz Foundation Judgement 2009, 47). Upendra Baxi has read the Naz foundation judgement as a 'dignity plus' for enhancing the idea of constitutional morality through its 'scrupulous extension' by taking Parts IV and IV-A of the Constitution as constituting 'a nearly complete code of constitutional morality' (Baxi 2011, 235). Both these parts constitute for Baxi the 'thresholds of *critical morality* by which some actually existing standards of *positive morality* ought to be judged and where necessary further *constitutionally displaced*' (Baxi 2011). In this understanding 'constitutional morality must outweigh the argument of public morality, even if it be the majoritarian view' (Naz Judgement, para. 86, cited in Baxi 2011).

It may be argued then, that the Anwar Ali Sarkar judgement, the Naz Foundation judgement, and a series of judgements cited in the latter have built, incrementally and cumulatively, a set of substantive conditions that need to be satisfied to meet the test of reasonableness. While protection against the arbitrary power of the state is drawn directly from Article 14, the tests of equality and dignity are traced to the code of constitutional morality, which is to be found running through the constitution generally, but more specifically in the Preamble and Chapters III, IV, and IV-A of the Constitution relating to Fundamental Rights, Directive Principles of State Policy, and Fundamental Duties. The code of constitutional morality constitutes critical morality by putting in place evaluative frameworks for substituting those standards which may be acceptable to the 'majoritarian' public, but are against the norms of constitutional democracy.

The diffusion of constitutional morality, according to Ambedkar, was essential for the peaceful working and sustenance of a democratic constitution. Referring to constitutional morality as 'paramount reverence to the *form* of the Constitution', Ambedkar argued that there was a close connection between the form of the Constitution and the form of administration and emphasized that 'the form of the administration must be appropriate to and in the same sense as the form of the Constitution'.[18] He also warned that it was, 'perfectly possible to pervert the Constitution, without changing its form by merely changing the form of the administration and to make it inconsistent and opposed to the spirit of the constitution'.[19] Ambedkar's call for a firm adherence to constitutional morality reflected his apprehensions about the uncertainty of executive decisions and mistrust of legislative power, which could change the form of administration making it inconsonant with the spirit of the Constitution. Over the years judicial scrutiny of both has come to be seen as a legitimate component of judicial power. Successive decisions by the Supreme Court have enhanced judicial power to bring the legislative *as well as* constituent powers of the Parliament within the purview of judicial review, which is to say, they can both be tested for consistency with the Constitution.

In its attempt to 'protect' the CAB and buttress it against a possible charge of inconsistency with the Constitution, the JPC took recourse to precedent established through case law. Precedents articulate legal principles which are deployed by the courts in deciding later cases; but the authority of a precedent and the transferability of principles articulated in one case to another, depend on whether or not the issues and facts of the cases are consonant with each other. Writing on India's legal system, especially the possibilities and modalities of 'saving' it, Fali Nariman had lamented that the 'legal ethic of certainty' had become burdened by the 'rule of judicial precedent', the 'excessive burden of case law', and 'the lack of case law management' (Nariman 2006, 138–140).[20] It may be argued

---

[18] Speech in the Constituent Assembly, 4 November 1948, CAD, Vol. VII, Book no. 2, p. 38.
[19] Ibid.
[20] Nariman suggests a system akin to that in the United States. The relevance of specific case law and its retention for future usage as precedent for general applicability is decided in the United States periodically by body of 'learned' and 'wise' lawyers' who wade through the cases

that amidst the burden of (a messy) rule of judicial precedent, the legal ethic of certainty can be upheld by the judges themselves by exercising critical morality drawing from the Constitution. The deployment of critical morality provides the grounds for the substitution of public morality by constitutional morality, drawing from principles of equality laid down explicitly in the Constitution.

Constitutions embody popular sovereignty and affirm the principle that power in democracies lies with the people. As the source of law and the rules of recognition for all laws including statutes, case law, and customary law, constitutions ensure that power is not exercised arbitrarily and is bound by higher-order rules, norms, and principles. It is this restraint on power that protects democracy from the mercurial character of everyday politics driven by the political rationality of the ruling class, persuaded by the logic of maximization of power. The manner in which the NRC and later CAB/CAA were catapulted into the electoral domain through three elections in which the BJP successfully steered and consolidated its agenda of Hindutva, bolsters the argument that the CAA was propelled by the desire of larger electoral payoff as a strategy of political rationality. More specifically, the CAA ruptured the political consensus on the NRC in the Northeast, especially in Assam. The two tendencies that emerged out of the 2003 amendment as the hinge point—*hyphenated citizenship* associated with the NRC, which made citizenship contingent on conditions of descent, and *national citizenship* associated with the CAA, which made religion a principle of distinguishability in the creation of *bounded citizenship*—were subjected to debate in the Parliament in December 2019.

Constitutional and Normal Politics: CAB in the Parliament

CAB became an Act passing through significant signposts and critical intervals. The installation of the JPC in 2016 can be seen as a signpost which inserted a deferral in the life of the law, while tantalizing promises

---

reported in all decisions across United States and give a 'restatement of law' on all possible topics (2006, 144).

of elimination of 'infiltrators' and protection of those who had sought refuge in India were made in election campaigns in Assam preceding the introduction of the CAB in Lok Sabha. The JPC provided a critical 'interval' from August 2016 when it was set up to January 2019 when it submitted its report—a few months before Parliamentary elections were to take place. The JPC report on the CAB was a textual expression of the dominant ideological formation and political contestations which constitute the landscape of citizenship in contemporary India. The debates in the Lok Sabha in January 2019 before the Parliamentary election and then again in the Lok Sabha and Rajya Sabha in December 2019, each time towards the end of the Parliament session, served as decisive moments, opening up for debate the issues that the JPC report had brought to a resolution through a majority recommendation. Interestingly, the changes which were inserted in CAB 2019 exempting the 6th Schedule and Inner Line Permit states from CAA, to assuage the concerns raised by the states in North-East India, were independent of the recommendations made by the JPC. The debates in the Parliament revealed deep fault-lines along two mutually conflicting ideas of Indian citizenship: one which traced its pedigree to the founding moment of the Constitution and republican citizenship, and the other which situated itself in the idea of a Hindu nation that was interrupted by Partition. While the former found sustenance in an idea of a political community characterized by a constitutional identity embedded in equality and secularism, the latter dissociated itself from the constitutional moment to claim a pre-political identity of citizenship, embedded in an atavistic idea of the Indian nation.

The Parliamentary debates and their outcome served as another signpost, which assumed criticality. The resolution of the debate over the CAB in Parliament through a division in which the majority view prevailed became critical for its *potential* for instituting a new modality of political action. The constraint of parliamentary majorities under which the Bill was passed in Parliament and was subsequently approved by the President did not bring a closure to the questions that had been raised about the Bill in the Parliament. They found voice in two distinct sites. The 'urban street' became a powerful site where an unprecedented outrage against the CAA, perceived as a law against constitutional ethics and morality, was expressed in peaceful sit-ins and demonstrations. The Supreme Court of India was the other site where, in a manifestation of iterative practices in institutional spaces, 140 petitions were filed questioning the constitutional validity of the CAA.

Debates on the CAB in the Parliament were located in what Bruce Ackerman would call 'normal politics'. Ackerman makes a distinction between *constitutional politics*—characterized as politics of the highest order, which appeals to the common good, and makes itself manifest 'during rare periods of heightened political consciousness'—and *normal politics*, an inferior form of politics marked by narrow individual interests (Ackerman 1988, 162–163). Normal politics is sutured to the adversarial dimensions of electoral trials through which democracies take institutional form. The representative institutions of democracy become spaces for presenting competitive claims to speaking for the people. These claims are projected onto the realm of law making, where the authority to legislate for the people is drawn from electoral outcomes. Often lawmakers assume this function as an exercise of the sovereign power of the state, legitimated by discourses of securing the nation—its territory and people. The principle of 'rule of law' associated with liberal constitutionalism defines and limits state authority by bringing up the question of legitimate authority. The questions—who gives the law (a question of pedigree or source of law), why should people obey laws (a question of both source and content of law), and what are the means through which conformity to law may legitimately be achieved—become significant while responding to it. It is important that law-making functions be understood in relation to the Parliament's role and functions in a constitutional democracy. While Parliament enjoys enormous law-making powers, this power is coeval with other equally important roles that it performs—of representation and deliberation—and eliciting accountability from the executive. Indeed, its law-making function can be performed effectively only in tandem with its roles as a deliberative body and an institution of accountability. As a deliberative body, the Parliament can represent and encompass the diversity of interests, especially of the most vulnerable, and *not only* those of the majority. It is only through an effective performance of *both* these functions can it hold the executive accountable. Only when it reflects the synchronous performance of *all* these functions by the Parliament, can a law be truly democratic.

An examination of the debates on CAB 2019 in the Lok Sabha on 9 December and Rajya Sabha on 11 December 2019 show complex contestations surrounding the idea of the Indian nation and citizenship. Deep fissures were displayed on these fundamental questions along party lines. Significantly, the 'competence' of the Parliament to legislate on a subject within the purview of its law-making powers, was questioned by large sections of the legislators on moral grounds. It is significant that in his intervention in the debate in the Rajya Sabha to oppose the CAB, P. Chidambaram, who had served as a minister in the United Progressive Alliance (UPA) led by the Congress Party, warned against the pattern that had emerged in law-making 'in recent times', when laws made by the Parliament were invariably ending up before the Supreme Court. The reason for this, he averred, was the disregard shown by the Parliament while legislating, to its own role of being the judges in 'the first instance', of the constitutionality of the laws that were being passed:

> Sir, we have a Citizenship Act in this country. It recognizes citizenship by birth, citizenship by descent, citizenship by registration, citizenship by naturalization and citizenship by incorporation of territory ... Now, this Government is introducing a new category called 'citizenship by arbitrary executive fiat' and asking this Parliament to support the Government in passing what is patently an unconstitutional law. ... We are elected representatives of the people. *The Constitution has asked us, in the first instance, to judge the constitutionality of a Bill. We cannot pronounce on the constitutionality. But, we have a responsibility to pass what is constitutional.* Not all of us are lawyers. In fact, not all of us should be lawyers. We should be from every walk of life. And, from every walk of life, we must bring our collective wisdom and commonsense to say is this constitutional or not. What are we doing in this House? What we did in the other House and what we are doing in this House is abdicating our primary responsibility in favour of another of the three entities/organs of the Constitution. What we are doing is: You are pushing the issue to the lap of the Judges. Do you think it will stop here? It will not stop here. It will eventually go before the Judges. And, the Judges are respectable people. But, they are unelected Judges. Unelected Judges and unelected lawyers will ultimately decide what we do is constitutional or not! ... Knowing this is unconstitutional, I am afraid, this Government is ramming through this Bill in order to advance its Hindutva agenda. This is a sad day. Thankfully, we are not amending the Constitution; we

are only making a law. And I am absolutely confident and I am absolutely clear in my mind that this law will be struck off. (Rajya Sabha Debates, 11 December 2019, 127, emphasis added)

Paradoxically, both the detractors and supporters of the CAB, referred to the Constitution of India, the Preamble as a statement of its foundational principles, and secularism as its core value, for sustaining their arguments. While facts were contested and evidence questioned on both sides, legitimacy was drawn from claims to speaking for the 'vulnerable' people. In the course of the debate the legal category of 'illegal migrant', which was central to the CAB, became a fragmented category comprising the *sharanarthi* (refugee) and the *ghuspaithaiya* (infiltrator). The sharnarthi—the 'persecuted minority'—who the CAB sifted out for protection, became a figure burdened by antagonistic discursive formulations which made it simultaneously an object to be rescued *and* a threat to cultural identity and economic stability of the country. The ghuspaithiya was antithetical to the sharanarthi, a residual category—filtered out after the sharananarthi was brought within the purview of state protection—to be extracted and expelled since it constituted a threat to national security.

'Destroying the Soul of India': People, Political Leadership, and Constitutionalism Secularism

The CAB 2019 was introduced in the Lok Sabha on 9 December 2019 by the Home Minister (HM) Amit Shah. Several members of the Lok Sabha opposed the introduction of the CAB under Rule 72(1) of the rules of legislative procedure on the ground that the provisions of the Bill were unconstitutional. The HM resisted the objections saying that members could oppose the Bill at the stage of introduction, only if it was on a matter outside the 'competence' of the House—an interpretation which Saugata Roy of the TMC, among others, pointed out, was erroneous. 'He is giving a wrong interpretation to the rule—maybe, he is new to this House', asserted Roy. A brief discussion ensued on the Bill and the motion to introduce it was submitted to a vote. The tone and tenor of the debate on the Bill, which took place later in the afternoon that day was, however, set.

If the debate in the CA was on what should explicitly be stated in the Constitution as the organizing principle of citizenship, from which reasonable deviations could take place by future Parliaments, the debate in Parliament was fundamentally about *what* should have the *force* of law. In other words, the debates in the Parliament were animated by the question whether the assumption that the Parliament had the power/competence to make laws on a subject should be sufficient or the content of the law should be such that it inspired trust among the people.[21] In his opening statement in the Lok Sabha introducing the CAB, the HM called it a 'historic Bill' which would free 'lakhs and crores' of people from their tormented life [as refugees/illegal migrants] into a life of dignity as citizens. In the course of the debate, the claim that the Bill was 'historic' was disputed by those who saw it as a part of the BJP's political and ideological agenda to make India a Hindu nation. The Bill to them was no more than a continuation of the anti-Muslim agenda of the BJP, which had made itself manifest in various ways but especially in the Triple Talaq Act and the revocation of Article 370 of the Indian Constitution.

The HM, however, sought legitimacy for the Bill in the BJP's resounding victory in the recently concluded general election. The electoral verdict, he argued, was an endorsement of the BJP's manifesto in which the CAB figured prominently. Speaking in the Rajya Sabha later, Shah said that his party was committed to meeting its electoral promises and in bringing the Bill the government was only fulfilling the mandate (*janmat*) it had received in the election for its manifesto (*ghoshnapatra*). All parties and their candidates, he suggested *must* place their manifestoes before the people to mobilize a mandate—it was a constitutional process (*samvaidhanik prakriya*)—to contest elections on the basis of ideology and a manifesto which reflected the sentiments (*samvedna*) of the people (*jansamvedana*) (Rajya Sabha Debates, 11 December 2019, 25–26).

Research on election manifestoes and electoral mandates has found that the relationship between party manifestoes and electoral victories is ambiguous and not conclusive. Party manifestoes are often presented as policies that are submitted for the approval of the people in 'electoral trials' (Urbinati 2000). They are important for political parties to emphasize the distinctive elements of their party programmes and in ideal

---

[21] https://eparlib.nic.in/bitstream/123456789/788219/1/lsd_17_02_09-12-2019.pdf

conditions of political communication should serve as sites where the deliberative content of elections play out. Studies on policy-making by political parties that form governments after electoral victories have shown that 'partisan influence on policy' depends on both—'the capacity' of the office-holders for implementing policies evoked during their electoral campaigns and on the 'governing party's incentives to implement electoral promises' (Brouard et al. 2018, 1). It may be argued that 'frank and explicit declarations of principle' of government and a detailed official statement before elections covering economic policy, home and public affairs, and foreign relations elicit confidence for electoral candidates and political parties. It is believed that the party winning an election has a *democratic mandate* to implement the policies stated in its manifesto 'because they are assumed to have secured the imprimatur of democratic legitimacy' and an *obligation* to do so since their election was secured on the basis of the manifesto. This would serve as the standard against which the party can be held *accountable* in the next election (Quinn 2014, 6). The *mandate theory* of manifestoes, however, rests upon several contentious assumptions, argues Quinn (2014). The mandate theory assumes that most voters read the manifesto or are familiar with the main promises of the parties, even if they have not read it. A more powerful criticism of the theory refers to the disproportional effects of the FPTP electoral system in which parties that win parliamentary majorities often do so, on a plurality of the vote, and form governments without securing the majority of the votes. In a manifestation of what is called 'paradox of the platform', even those who vote for the party elected to power, do not vote for *all* the promises that are made in the manifesto. Yet, 'winning parties claim mandates to implement their entire manifestos' (Quinn 2014, 9). It is not surprising then, that in the debate on the CAA the opposition reminded the HM that his government was formed by securing less than 40 per cent of the votes cast. This would imply that the majority of voters rejected the manifesto of the party. Speaking in the Lok Sabha TMC MP Abhishek Banerjee declared: '65% of the country has voted for the Opposition and you should rightly know that the House belongs to the Opposition' (Lok Sabha Debates, 9 December 2019, 334).

In his statement in the Parliament, the HM described the government's efforts to legislate on citizenship 'constitutional', and not part of a political agenda. He drew a careful distinction between what is done merely for electoral gains and what emanated from a democratic mandate emerging from the electoral process. Members of the opposition refused to see a majoritarian electoral victory as the ground on which the government could claim constitutionality for the Bill or as a mandate of 'the people' for CAB. Indeed, the government was constantly reminded of the disgruntlement in Assam and other states in the North-East. Exhortations in the name of the people abounded on both sides—the government and the opposition—but took different forms. In what may be seen as the deployment of *populism as a political strategy*, distinct from its invocation as emancipatory politics, those who spoke in favour of the CAB from the BJP and the parties allied to it placed faith in Prime Minister (PM) Narendra Modi. The PM, they maintained, had 'authorised' the Bill in order to *emancipate* 'lakhs and crores' of people from their sufferings. The installation of the PM as the absolute referent for CAB was established by alluding to the extraordinariness of what CAB would accomplish, and related to this, a remarkable feat that only *he* could have achieved. The ascription of extraordinariness—in achieving what was described as historical and unprecedented and the unique prowess of the PM in accomplishing it— resonated the BJP's slogan in the 2019 Parliamentary elections: 'Modi hai to mumkin hai' (If Modi is there, anything is possible). Meenakshi Lekhi, BJP's Lok Sabha MP from New Delhi, took recourse to Ramdhari Singh Dinkar's celebrated poem 'Kisko Naman Karun Main?' (translated literally as, 'Who Should I Bow my Head to?'), in which the poet invokes the figure of the *braveheart* as one who is steadfast in his service to truth, and selflessly gives up his life to ensure justice for others. For Dinkar, the braveheart was the only worthy subject of his devotion. Lekhi raises the same question to identify the PM and HM as the worthy subjects for her 'naman' (devotion)—for showing the capacity to recognize the truth—of *ghuspaith* (infiltration)—'... migration without persecution is called a *silent invasion* and that is what is happening in this country.... This is an Act which is giving citizenship to those people who have been living in this country, just making their life a little easier, the ones who are persecuted' (Lok Sabha Debates, 9 December 2019, 384).

The authority to speak and act in the name of a 'vulnerable' and abject population was carefully crafted in a narrative where it was only the BJP which appeared to be speaking for, and on their behalf. In this narrative, the opposition, especially the Congress was doubly discredited—for their duplicity in going back on a commitment that they had made to the minorities left behind in Pakistan—and for being pro-Pakistan and anti-Hindu for *refusing* citizenship to *Hindu* refugees who had suffered religious persecution in Pakistan. Rajendra Agrawal of the BJP, who was the chairperson of the JPC, blamed the Congress for being 'selectively sensitive'—for being sensitive when 'Batla Kand'[22] happens but being apathetic when persecution of minorities took place in Pakistan and Bangladesh. The Congress Party, Agrawal believed, suffered from a 'flawed perspective' which was manifest in the positions they had taken on the NRC, Article 370, Ram Janma Bhoomi, surgical strike, Jawaharlal Nehru University, and the like (Lok Sabha Debates, 9 December 2019, 443). Agrawal cited the former Prime Minister Manmohan Singh's appeal to Lal Krishna Advani in 2003 when the NDA government amended the citizenship act to make provisions for persons of Indian origin, who were citizens of another country, to acquire 'overseas citizenship of India', as evidence of Congress's duplicity. Manmohan Singh, he said, had asked Advani to think about offering protection and citizenship to minorities who suffered after Partition due to persecution and sought refuge in India. Mocking the Congress for following 'vote bank ki rajneeti' (politics of the vote bank) which had long become redundant and given way to the BJP's 'vikas ki rajneeti' (politics based on development), he advised the party to correct its 'drishti-dosh' (flawed perspective).

Contrary to the repeated averments by MPs from the ruling NDA, no MP speaking against the Bill actually made a case for denying the protection of citizenship to the minority communities identified in the Bill who had suffered religious persecution. Almost all members opposing the Bill suggested modifications to make the ambit of protection inclusive. They also implored the government to evaluate the impact of the Bill on the demography and economic resources in the North-East, asking for adequate measures to protect indigenous people and their lifeworlds. In line with the submissions received by the JPC, opposition to the Bill came from a position of constitutional secularism grounded in the principle of equality. Making a case for the extension of citizenship to *all persecuted*

---

[22] Batla kand refers to the 'encounter' between police and suspected members of the extremist organization Indian Mujahiddin (IM), in Delhi in September 2008. The encounter resulted in the death of two members of the IM and an Inspector of the Delhi Police.

minorities so that religious identity did not constitute the principle for differentiation among persons or extend it to *persons of all religions* if persecution based on religion was to be retained as the principle for differentiation, the opposition parties referred repeatedly to the Constitution, especially the Preamble and Articles 14, 15, 21, and 25 in the chapter on Fundamental Rights. Reference to the Preamble and specific fundamental rights was made to affirm that principles of equality and non-discrimination were intrinsic to constitutional democracy and democratic citizenship. The reference to the Preamble with secularism as its inviolable component alluded to a constitutional identity that gave the Indian Constitution a distinctive character.

The literature on comparative constitutionalism speaks of the idea that constitutions have distinguishable salient features which give them a 'discernable identity' (Jacobsohn 2010, 3). Indeed, when the HM explained to the House, why only Pakistan, Bangladesh, and Afghanistan were specifically identified in the Bill—because all of them had a state religion and their constitutions declared them to be Islamic states—he inadvertently made a distinction between constitutions that professed a religion for the state and those like India which did not. The invocation of *secularism* by those who opposed the Bill drew attention to the inherently discriminatory nature of the Bill, which made it incommensurate with its stated objectives and the principles of *sarva dharma sambhava* (equal respect for all religions) which characterized Indian secularism. The various amendments that were proposed by those opposing the Bill in the Lok Sabha, some of which were put to vote and rejected, asked for the inclusion of Muslims among the communities identified for protection, the deployment of a more capacious category of persecuted minorities, and/or broadening the geographical ambit of the Bill to include all neighbouring countries including Sri Lanka from where large number of Tamil refugees had fled into India. Even though the BJP's allies in the NDA, including the Biju Janata Dal (BJD) and the Shiromani Akali Dal (SAD), voted for the CAB, they advised the HM to make the Bill inclusive. Sharmishtha Sethi, BJD MP from Jaipur in Odisha, for example, began her speech in the Lok Sabha confirming her party and her Chief Minister Naveen Patnaik's commitment to secularism. Her suggestions included adding Sri Lanka among the countries identified in the Bill, delinking the CAB from NRC, and a prayer to the government to dispel apprehensions regarding the CAB among Muslims. BJD member Sasmit Patra spoke in the Rajya Sabha, reiterating his colleagues points and expressing the hope that the government would be ready to discuss the NRC in future. Sukhbir Singh Badal from the SAD spoke 'as a Sikh'—a community especially impacted by the Partition—and welcomed the inclusion of Afghanistan, but also wondered why Muslims could not be added among the persecuted minorities mentioned in CAB. Members of the opposition exhorted members of the Janata Dal (United) (JD(U))—an NDA ally—to vote on the side of morality which lay with the Constitution.

The debate on the CAB so far as it referred to the relationship between religion and constitutionalism presents a moment of 'constitutional disharmony'. Such moments throw up challenges compelling the elaboration of the substance of the Constitution and are considered 'critical' for the development of constitutional identity (Jacobsohn 2010, 4). Ironically, even though the amendments suggested by opposition members were outvoted, the debates on CAB produced a site of contestation where secularism was reinforced as a distinguishing feature of the Indian Constitution. This was perhaps stated most forcefully by Javed Ali Khan from the Samjawadi Party (SP) who wanted an assurance from the Chairman of the Rajya Sabha that any advocacy by a political party, organization, or individual, to make India a 'dharmashasit rashtra' (a nation ruled by religion), whether Islamic, Khalistani, or Hindu, would be strongly rejected by the House. Javed Khan's appeal was flowing logically from the premise on which the CAB was based—that nations governed by religious laws—were likely to oppress religious minorities. Khan exhorted the BJP to openly declare that the House/nation will not endorse any kind of religious doctrine of the state and would actively thwart it (Rajya Sabha Debates, 11 December 2019, 84). He asserted the right of Muslims to protest against the CAB as 'citizens', rejecting the argument that the Muslim had nothing to do with the Bill and should therefore stay at home [and not protest in the streets]. In an emphatic statement of what would constitute a citizen's duty, he argued: 'if the Preamble was under attack and the secular foundation of the Constitution was being eroded then a Muslim could not sit at home' (Rajya Sabha Debates, 11 December 2019, 89).

Constitutionality of the CAB and Parliamentary Democracy

We have seen earlier that citizenship was a site of contestation in the Constituent Assembly (CA) where two diametrically different positions jostled for primacy. We also saw that the field of the debate was organized around a prior consensus on both norms and procedures. This made an agonistic expression of opposite positions possible and also enhanced the space for deliberative consensus not dependent on a decision through division/voting. The debates in the CA—a body agonistically arrayed in deliberating over a framework of citizenship appropriate for the context of Partition—worked towards a deliberative consensus. While this consensus was internally complex, it established two principles that were to serve as the foundation for the legal edifice of citizenship in India—Republican citizenship *and* the recognition of Parliament's preeminent role in making laws on citizenship. These principles were expected to unfold in tandem to remain consonant with the Constitution—after all, it was the Constitution that was the source of the Parliament's law-making powers. These powers were constrained by the essentials that the Constitution had put in place, which could not be subverted by any law made by parliament.

An integral aspect of the transition to constitutional democracy in India was the affirmation of popular sovereignty embodied in the 'people' who had agreed to live in the constitutional order that they had given to themselves. A constitutional order that obtains in a country can be understood best 'by reflecting on the course of its historical development' (Ackerman 1991). In this understanding, the 'real constitution' is not simply the constitutional text or its interpretation by judges but 'rediscovering' the set of principles that were adopted in 'extraordinary' moments of intense constitutional participation and deliberation, 'with or without changes in the constitutional text' (Ackerman 1991, 5). It is these extraordinary moments of creation and communication of constitutional symbols that install not just a constitutional order but a democratic order as well. Yet the relationship between a constitutional order and democracy is a fraught one. At the crux of this conflict is the irreconcilability between the institutional forms of democracy that claim to speak for the 'people'—and its sovereign form—'We the People', embodied in the Constitution. The debate in the Parliament on the constitutionality of CAB shows that the deliberative space of the Parliament was re-configured by majoritarian politics which supplanted democratic representation. In its substance, the debate in the Parliament on the constitutionality of CAB rehearsed the concerns that had already been *raised* and *resolved* by the JPC. The contours of the debate were, however, structured by the performance of contradictory narratives of citizenship that claimed reflexivity but were influenced by the logic of transaction intrinsic to the competitive party political-institutional space of the Parliament. Suggestions for deferral of the debate to allow for deliberation under conditions of repose were abandoned. The proposal for a more thorough discussion of the Bill in a Select Committee was moved and voted out in the Rajya Sabha, prompting questions on 'undue haste', while 'truth statements' were made, which were high on rhetoric and low on both fact and logic. BJP member of Rajya Sabha, Saroj Pandey claimed that the Bill was correcting the violence against Hindus during partition, which she argued was commensurate with the BJP government's commitment to 'harmonise' (*Samet kar*) India's culture, by bringing *both*—the culture of India and its Constitution—under its 'protection' (*sanrakshan*). Claiming that no one had the courage to speak when the breasts of thousands of Hindu women were cut off in the course of Partition; it was *only now* that a government had tried honestly to ensure that a person who is truly an Indian citizen, who was born in India, and is a Hindu—should be protected. It is for this reason, she argued, that CAB 2019 had been introduced by the government, for which the PM and HM must be welcomed and lauded (Rajya Sabha Debates, 9 December 2019, 177–178).

In a shift from the preoccupation with law as discourse or ideology, works on law have shown its relationship with affect and how different kinds of emotions are imbricated in law (Bandes 1999, Olson 2016, Naresh 2018). Emotionality in law is made palpable in different sites— in courtrooms, in police *thanas*, in detention centres, in the streets, etc. As the authoritative site of law making, the Parliament constitutes a space where passions flow from its structure as a differentiated space. The government and its opposition constitute this space of hierarchical and differential accumulation of power along party lines. Writing about constitution-making and emotions, Vatsal Naresh has noted that constitutions, more often than not are written during 'tumultuous times'. The

Indian CA, for example, held its meetings amidst communal violence, rapes, and murders, where hundreds of thousands of people lost their lives and millions were displaced:

> In addition, the fate of princely states, which constitute a significant portion of British India's population, was still unknown; and India and Pakistan became engaged in a war in Kashmir starting in October 1947; Gandhi's assassination in early 1948 only added to the tumult. Amid all this the Constituent Assembly met publicly in the British built Parliament House in central Delhi, a few miles from the refugee camps for those who had fled violence in Punjab and other parts of North India. The interim government declared curfew in Delhi on several occasions while the Assembly was in session. Members were given curfew passes, and some members asked for police protection. The events that shook the city also impacted the lives of the framers. Jawaharlal Nehru's official residence served as a makeshift refugee camp ... Muslim members of the government, and of the Assembly, felt a more immediate sense of danger. Mohd. Saadulla repeated his fear of rioters after his request for police protection was granted. (Naresh 2018, 64)

Amidst and despite this turmoil, the CA decided to make citizenship inclusionary based on the democratic principle of birth and decided to absorb all those who migrated to India to make it their home, as citizens, regardless of their religion. Indeed, religion was explicitly rejected as having any basis for Indian citizenship. Vatsal argues that 'hot emotions' like anger, fear and enthusiasm were mitigated by the CA through 'institutional arrangements' such as 'time delays' in discussion of drafts, further deliberations in committees, and the separation of legislative and executive powers (Naresh 2018). In 2019, while debating the CAB in the Parliament, a majoritarian view prevailed and was affirmed through a majority vote. Under these conditions where decision was to take place through a vote with the BJP/NDA having an overwhelming majority in the Lok Sabha and numerical advantage in the Rajya Sabha, it was clear that the Bill would become an Act through the force of numbers with the government.

Since its last appearance and passage in the sixteenth Lok Sabha before it lapsed in the beginning of 2019, the government had buttressed the Bill with special provisions pertaining to the North-East. In the course of the debate in both the Houses, regional identities were on display, with emotive evocation of literary icons, and accounts of heroic martyrdom. The representatives of various parties from the north-eastern states feared that their interests had been abandoned and pledged to take the struggle to the streets. Conflicting accounts of how many people the CAB was going to emancipate were communicated in exaggerated claims of lakhs and crores of persons, even as the naturalization of Adnan Sami, a case unrelated to the category the CAB was concerned with, was flagged as an example of how Muslims, even from Pakistan, could become citizens of India. In the Rajya Sabha, Ripun Bora, a Congress MP from Assam, spoke of the impact the passage of the CAB would have on Assam and the North-East:

> The whole country knows that Assam is burning, the North-Eastern Region is burning and lakhs of people are on the streets for days together. You have already finished Assam; you have finished the North-Eastern Region, but you have not learnt the lesson. Now, you are going to finish the entire country by the Citizenship (Amendment) Bill. It is not a question of Hindus. Are we not Hindus? Are the very people, who are agitating in Assam, not Hindus? They are all Hindus. It is a question of future and security of our country. (Rajya Sabha Debates, 11 December 2019, 204)

Bora's declamation in the Rajya Sabha was a pointer to the distinct premises on which Assam and the North-East were subsequently going to oppose the Act in the streets and the Supreme Court of India. It was not a question of religion alone, but the big price that was going to be paid by the country for those about whose numbers, despite its claims, the government was not clear. To substantiate this Bora referred to the series of questions he had posed to ministers since 2017:

> I want to draw your attention to my Question No. 2432, dated 23rd March, 2017, replied by the then External Affairs Minister in Rajya Sabha. I asked, "Whether it is a fact that there is a report of religious persecution taking place in Afghanistan and Pakistan after 1947 and in Bangladesh after 1971." What is the reply of the Government? The reply

is, "There are no authoritative statistics in this matter." Not only that, through my Question No. 875, dated 23rd November, 2016, I asked, "How many Hindus infiltrated from Bangladesh and Pakistan up to 31st December, 2014." What is the reply of the hon. Home Minister? He replied, "No record is maintained." The hon. Home Minister, in his introductory speech, said that crores and crores religiously persecuted people have come and are living in India, but they have not been given citizenship under the Citizenship Act, 1955 because there is no such provision in the Act and that is why this Amendment Bill is brought. In my Question No. 885, dated 25th July, 2018, I asked, "How many religiously persecuted people have applied for Indian citizenship?" What is the reply? Hon. Home Minister said, "Only 4044 applications are with the Government." ... when I asked about the country-wise detail, he replied, "687 from Afghanistan; 84 from Bangladesh and 2508 from Pakistan." And, when I asked the religion-wise break-up, he replied that religion-wise break-up is not maintained. If you do not have information and if you do not have data, on what basis are you going to give citizenship to these people? ... In my another question, I asked, post 1971 and pre-1971, how many people, how many Hindus migrated to Assam from Bangladesh? And, what is the reply? The Government said that there is no authentic figure available. (Rajya Sabha Debates, 11 December 2019, 205)

Raising the contentious issue of the relationship between the NRC and the CAA, which was at different points in time, either endorsed or rejected by the HM, Bora drew the attention of the House to the ramifications of CAA in Assam:

.... in NRC, Assam, names of 19.6 lakh people have been dropped. Now, the Home Minister is saying that these people will be given citizenship under CAB. But, how is it possible? These people are living in Assam for years together. They have been exercising their voting rights. They are doing Government jobs. They are holding lands. They are Indian citizens. In NRC applications, they have given documents as Indian citizens. And, in NRC hearing, they have given documents as Indian citizens. Now, how these people will say that they have come from Afghanistan; that they have come from Pakistan; that they have come from Bangladesh? That means by this CAB, you are going to force our Indians, our Hindu people to tell them as foreigners. You are going to do this. Not only that, you will be surprised to know in the Joint Parliamentary Committee meeting,—it is in para 2.14 of page no. 18 of the Report—, what the Director, IB submitted. The Director, IB said that it is not possible to verify that these persons have come due to religious persecution. ..... Not only that, Director, IB further said that those who have submitted any affidavit, those who have submitted any documents that they have come on religious persecution, that will have to be proved by Foreigners' Regional Registration Office. (Rajya Sabha Debates, 11 December 2019, 205–208)

The uncertainty about numbers pointed out by Bora was counterpointed by repeated assertions in both houses of Parliament by the HM and other members in favour of the Bill of the pervasive nature of repression of minorities in all three countries specified in the Bill—Afghanistan, Bangladesh, and Pakistan—which had reduced their numbers by 20 per cent in Pakistan and Bangladesh. What happened to them? Shah asks. They were either eliminated, or they converted, or they managed to flee, and seek shelter in India as refugees to save their dignity (Rajya Sabha Debates, 11 December 2019, 24).

The parliamentary debates were embedded in 'normal politics', distinct from 'constitutional politics', as the outcome of the vote on CAB rolled back the constitutional principles of citizenship that had prevailed at the constituent moment of the Republic. In this context, the *ghuspaithiya* or the infiltrator, a category extracted from the files of the Intelligence Bureau, became a ubiquitous label for justifying exclusion with religious belonging as an additional attribute of illegality. Locket Chatterjee, a BJP MP in the Lok Sabha from Hooghly, West Bengal, for example, stressed the urgency for the amendment to provide a 'lifeline' to 'thousands and thousands' of refugees coming to India from Islamic countries. The partition of India by Nehru, Chatterjee argued, had snatched large swathes of land away from Bengal overnight. This was compounded in contemporary India with West Bengal becoming averse to giving shelter to Hindus, while welcoming (Muslim) Rohingyas into the state, giving them land to settle, and voter ID cards—'indeed, West Bengal had 70 lakh ghuspaithiya votes and 120 seats which were entirely in their control. ... They (MPs from the opposition) are talking about NRC, when we are discussing the CAB' (Lok Sabha Debates, 9 December 2019, 428).

Reference to the NRC was made by most speakers, sometimes with an appeal to the HM to make the distinction clear to dispel apprehensions among the Muslims, but more often than not, to say that the two were related and any discussion on CAB could not be done without also discussing the NRC. Abhishek Banerjee, a TMC MP speaking in the Lok Sabha asserted: 'any decision on the Citizenship (Amendment) Bill cannot be had without understanding the context of NRC, and any attempt by the Government to make us believe that NRC and CAB are two different exercises is absolutely unconvincing. NRC was a trap and CAB which has been introduced today and considered for passing is even a bigger trap' (Lok Sabha Debates, 9 December 2019, 334). Calling the NRC a 'botched up exercise', Banerjee lamented that the government wanted to implement the NRC in the entire country. That the NRC and CAB had become the core points of contest between the TMC and the BJP, which locked horns in the political battleground of West Bengal, a state approaching assembly elections in April 2021, was evident in the Parliament. TMC leader and West Bengal Chief Minister Mamata Banerjee vowed not to implement the NRC in West Bengal. After the passage of the CAA, Banerjee led huge protests against the Act in the streets across the state, declaring that the CAA could be implemented in West Bengal only 'over her dead body'.[23] Playing upon the requirement of documents to prove citizenship under NRC, TMC MP Abhishek Banerjee informed the Lok Sabha that he had 'documented a list of people who lost their lives because of the ordeal of NRC and the panic caused because of NRC'. Claiming that the Bill was against the whole Bengali and Hindu community, which would rip apart the soul of Bengal, Banerjee reminded the House of the legacy of Bengal, which had experienced the pain of Partition:

> You did not heed our warning. You did not take our advice. Now, look where you have ended up. Out of 19 lakh people excluded from NRC, 11 lakh are Bengali Hindus, four lakh are Hindus from different States like Odisha, Bihar, Uttar Pradesh and Rajasthan, one lakh are Gorkhas,

[23] 'Over my Dead Body: Mamata Banerjee Leads Mega Rally Against Citizenship Bill', *Hindustan Times*, 16 December 2019.

and three lakh plus are Bengali Muslims; most importantly, each one of them, is an Indian citizen. The situation at the detention camp is even worse. It is a painful story. Estimates reveal that 60 per cent to 70 per cent of those held in detention camps are all Bengali Hindus. In our State of West Bengal, you would be happy to know, the refugees have all been given legal rights. We have regularised all refugees.... They are all proud Indian citizens, deemed citizens.... (Interruptions)... You do not understand the sentiments of ten crore Bengalis.... Sir, that we will fight to the last drop of our blood but will not allow NRC in Bengal. There will not be NRC in Bengal, not at any cost. *Bengaly NRC Hobe na! Jai Hind! Vande Mataram! Joy Bengali.* (Lok Sabha Debates, 9 December 2020, 345)

Gaurav Gogoi, Congress MP from Kaliabor in Assam, spoke in the Lok Sabha as 'as an Assamese', 'as a person from the North-East India', and as 'an Indian' to vehemently oppose the CAB. The CAB, he argued, was directly connected with the NRC and 'the politics of NRC which the BJP was doing in the country'. Indeed, he argued, it was to hide the failure of the NRC in Assam that the CAB was being brought by the party. Gogoi asked the HM to apologize to those who had been left out of the NRC in Assam—the Gurkhas, the migrants in Assam from Uttar Pradesh, Bihar, and Rajasthan—who suffered humiliation in being labelled 'infiltrators' (ghuspaithiyas) (Lok Sabha Debates, 9 December 2019, 412). Exhorting the government to address the real problems of the north-east, and refrain from scraping and opening up old wounds to disturb the peace in the region, Gogoi claimed a moral high ground in opposing the Bill: 'The North East opposes this Bill because we are not slaves. We will not slavishly agree to any Bill that you would choose to bring before the House. You may pass a Bill with the force of numbers, but we will fight from the streets' (Lok Sabha Debates, 9 December 2019, 412–416, translated from Hindi). Gogoi appealed to all 'North East regional parties' to vote with their 'conscience':'stand with your people and not vote with any political compulsions' (Lok Sabha Debates, 9 December 2019, 416). Yet, the North-East spoke in different voices. Speaking 'for' Sikkim, Indra Hang Subba, a member of the Sikkim Krantikari Morcha Party, regretted that Sikkim had somehow been 'left out' of the discussions on CAB and the North-Eastern Region, and did not figure in the 'exemptions' in CAB

2019. Opposing the Bill 'strongly', Subba recalled the different route that Sikkim had taken to citizenship:

> Sikkim was not there when India got its Independence. Sikkim merged into the Indian Union in 1975 with a special provision under Article 371 of the Constitution. Article 371(k) protects all the old laws of Sikkim. The citizenship of the Sikkimese Indians is defined by the Sikkim Subjects Regulation 1961. When the Citizenship Act, 1955 was enforced in Sikkim with Sikkim (Citizenship) Order, 1975, it is clearly specified that every person who immediately before 26th April, 1975 was a Sikkim subject under Sikkim Subjects Regulation 1961 shall be deemed to have become a citizen of India on that day. This means that the citizenship of Sikkimese Indians has been defined according to the Sikkim Subjects Regulation 1961. This brings up the point that Sikkim should be exempted from the Citizenship (Amendment) Bill which is under discussion today. (Lok Sabha Debates, 9 December 2019, 441–442)

The representative from Nagaland Tokheho Yepthomi, member of the National Democratic Progressive Party, part of the NDA alliance, referred to the discussions the government had with representatives of state governments, and civil society in supporting the Bill. Happy that Nagaland was kept out of the purview of the CAB, he felt optimistic that under the leadership of Narendra Modi as PM, the 'insurgency' problems in Nagaland would soon be solved. Yepthomi was happy that the army was stationed on the border with Myanmar to stall any conflict, and the Disturbed Areas Act which applied in Nagaland would not be required once the 'Naga solution' is reached in 'a few months time' (Lok Sabha Debates, 9 December 2019, 442–443) C. Lalrosanga of the Mizo National Front (MNF), part of the NDA, the 'lone representative' from Mizoram in the Lok Sabha, like Yepthomi was thankful to the HM for 'having listened to [their] fears and apprehensions' regarding the CAB, which was a major issue during the elections and threatened to disturb the peace that prevailed in the state. While appreciating that the fears of Mizoram had been alleviated, and protection had been promised to Manipur as well, he urged the Central and state governments to ensure that there would be no religious persecution in the country as it prepared to rehabilitate those who had suffered persecution abroad (Lok Sabha Debates, 9 December 2019, 444–445). Lorho S. Pfoze, member of the Naga People's Front, representing Outer Manipur in Lok Sabha, too expressed the 'fear and apprehension' experienced in Manipur since CAB was introduced. Like the speakers from Nagaland and Mizoram before him, Pfoze thanked the PM and HM for 'considering the points of peril in the State of Manipur', especially the impact on 'its demography after the implementation of this Bill. But since Manipur has now been brought within the purview of Inner Line Permit, I am sure the people of the State can now rest assured' (446–447). Agatha Sangma from the National People's Party from Meghalaya, spoke in support of the Bill, following the assurances that had emerged through the 'extensive consultation' on the Bill before it was tabled and all 'major issues' confronting the North-Eastern States had been put to rest. While her own state was exempted from the CAB, she hoped that similar protection would be given to the entire North-East 'and not just the Sixth Schedule areas and not just the ILP areas' (Lok Sabha Debates, 9 December 2019, 450–451). What must also be noted that in the course of the debate on the CAB one region that went unrepresented was Kashmir, with it MPs including Omar Abdullah and Farooq Abdullah detained under the Public Safety Act (PSA) following the dissolution of Article 370 of the Constitution in August 2019, which gave special status to Jammu & Kashmir.

Disputed Histories and Fragmented Citizenship

Citizenship in India was inextricably associated with the process of transition from colonial rule to a constitutional democracy founded on the premise of equality. The process of transition was marked by two different modalities and logics of transformation of power: the 'relocation' of power from the colonial state to the 'national' state and the cartographic 'reconfiguration' of power by crafting borders to carve out two nation-states out of a territory governed by the sovereign power of the colonial state and paramount power in the case of princely states (Dhabhai 2020); regardless of the legal frameworks that were inscribed in the constitutional text, in the historical moment of transformative constitutionalism (Baxi 2013), power came to reside in a sovereign people who would roll back colonial legacies of domestication (Mbembe 2001) and historical injustices (Bhatia 2019) that had an older pedigree, to craft a future consonant with the constitutional order. While the 'self definition' of the people as a nation was integral to anti-colonial movements and inspired the 'ideal of independence' (Smith 1983, 171), it was sovereignty implying freedom from external interference to frame one's own rules and set up institutions commensurate with one's needs and 'character' (Smith 1983) that became the basis of citizenship. The promise of constitutionalism in societies that were making this transition was one of self-rule—the 'democratisation' of power—through the installation of democratic government which derived its powers from the people, constrained by rule of law. The constituent moment was often also, as in the case of India, tied to the nation-building project, and the institution of republican citizenship and constitutional patriotism. While national liberation movements led to the installation of constitutional democracies, nationalism has not been seen as integral to constitutionalism. Even though nationalism performs the task of achieving the pre-political integration of the *demos*, there are other forms of solidarity, including constitutional patriotism, that have sustained democratic citizenship (Becker 2020).

The debates in Parliament show that three different trajectories of citizenship's troubled present were being traced. Each of these trajectories framed the present through an understanding of the past that was disputed by the other. For convenience, one could term the dominant frame which came from the ruling political formation of the BJP led NDA, and presented the CAA as a historical necessity because of the Partition—'communitarian majoritarianism'. A second strand represented by the Congress and other opposition parties which opposed the CAB on the basis of constitutional secularism foregrounding the constitutional moment while making a case for national citizenship may be termed 'deliberative constitutionalism'. A third strand was found dispersed among different opposition parties which found comparisons for the present, in laws of citizenship in the totalitarian and authoritarian pasts of contemporary democracies. Since they also called for resistance outside institutional spaces, this strand may be called 'citizen activist'. In a manifestation of the powerlessness produced by the manner in which the deliberative space of the Parliament is structured, they recalled plural idioms of dissidence, all of which lay claims to a higher ethics of political action—drawn from the different vocabularies of anti-national liberation struggle—civil disobedience of Gandhi and revolutionary patriotism of Bagha Jatin.

When Locket Chatterjee declared that Nehru partitioned India, she was only reiterating what the BJP's top leadership had professed inside and outside the Parliament. The JPC had concluded, citing different members of the CA including Nehru, and on other occasions, Gandhi and Shyama Prasad Mukherjee, that the sufferings of those who could not become part of independent India should be remembered and their return to India facilitated. In the BJP's formulation, however, the necessity of the CAA emerged from Nehru's 'mistake'. In his response to the speakers in the Rajya Sabha, Amit Shah pointed out that the biggest mistake had been Partition—not just Partition—but Partition on the basis of religion. Had there been no Partition, there would have been no need for an amendment in the Citizenship Act. The CAB had become necessary to address the conditions that emerged after Partition. Had subsequent governments solved these problems, he (HM) would not have had to bring a Bill to do so. The task of running a government demanded locking horns with problems (*do-do haath*), not just governance (*sarkar chalana*) but also reforming the nation, which is what the Narendra Modi government was doing. The government could have, like others before it, simply enjoyed power (*satta ka sukh*) but the CAB was not for political mileage or electoral gains, but for resolving problems. Shah asked those who were opposing the Bill to sit in their rooms in the dark of the night, and have a dialogue with their inner voice (*antaratma*)—had the Bill been brought fifty years back, the situation would not have been so serious. To those who traced the idea of Partition to Savarkar, Shah drew attention to the Liaquat–Nehru Pact of 1950, where an agreement had been made that both countries would extend equality to their minority communities and protect their freedom to practice any profession, faith, and worship. These promises were not kept by Pakistan and the percentage of minorities in that country came down from 22 per cent to 7 per cent. If those from the minority communities in these countries were now coming to India to protect the honour of their women, their religion, and their families, they must be protected. Where will they go now? Will we not give them citizenship, he asked (Rajya Sabha Debates, 11 December 2019, 275–276).

Meenakshi Lekhi had earlier in the Lok Sabha appealed to the members to 'know' the history of the nation *1930s onwards* before citing

Rabindranath Tagore, who belonged to 'a different nation'. The story of post-1930s nation was the story of persons like Jogendra Nath Mandal, an Ambedkarite from the SC community who chose to stay in Pakistan, whose history of religious oppression has remained hidden. The CAB was for people like Mandal who had no other place to go to escape oppressive regimes. Muslims could flee to 46 countries that professed to be Muslim, Christians to 40 countries which professed their faith, but for Hindus, there was none (Lok Sabha Debates, 9 December 2019). Speaking in the Rajya Sabha, Anand Sharma lamented that the present regime was attempting to disparage leaders who had spent years in prisons and sacrificed their lives for India's independence. Dispelling the charge that Nehru and the Congress were responsible for Partition, Sharma drew attention to the movement for constitutional citizenship and its inherently inclusionary nature: 'If this regime wants to deny that then it will be injustice and humiliation of history (*itihas ka apmaan*)'. Regimes that have tried to change history have not succeeded, he cautioned—when truth is sought to be erased, it re-emerges in a more vigorous (*prachand*) form. The idea of two nations based on religion was endorsed in 1937 by the Hindu Mahasabha in its meeting in Ahmedabad which was presided by Savarkar. A year later, the Muslim League too adopted a resolution for partition. When the Congress leadership was incarcerated during the Second World War, following the Quit India movement, it was Hindu Mahasabha and the Muslim League that committed to forming provincial governments which would be loyal to the British government (Rajya Sabha Debates, 11 December 2019, 44–45, translated from Hindi). Sharma promised to place authenticated copies of Savarkar's statement that he had no problem with Jinnah's proposal of two-nation theory before the House. Kapil Sibal reinforced Sharma's position and challenged the HM's contention that had the Congress not partitioned India on the basis of religion, the Bill would not have been required:

> I don't understand which history books the learned Home Minister has read and which authors he has consulted. But I would like to remind him of what Savarkar said. The two nation theory was not our theory. You are going to fulfil it today by passing this Bill if it is passed. Savarkar said and I quote, 'As it is, there are two antagonistic nations living side by side in India. Several infantile politicians commit the serious mistake

in supposing that India is already welded into a harmonious nation, or that it could be welded thus for the mere wish to do so. These, our well-meaning but unthinking friends, take their dreams for realities. That is why they are impatient of communal tangles and attribute them to communal organisations'. . . And this is what Ambedkar said. He said, 'Strange as it may appear, Mr. Savarkar and Mr. Jinnah, instead of being opposed to each other on the one nation versus two nations issue, are in complete agreement about it. Both agree, not only agree, but insist that there are two nations in India—one the Muslim nation and the other the Hindu nation'. I request the Home Minister to withdraw the allegation because we in the Congress believe in that one-nation theory. You don't believe in it. (Rajya Sabha Debates, 11 December 2019, 165–166)

The third strand looked for different sources of citizenship in regional traditions of martyrdom and in non-institutional spaces. Speaking in the Rajya Sabha, Derek O'Brien, who had earlier referred to his Irish roots and the dispersal of his family across the border and abroad, spoke first in Bengali and then switched to English. Asking the government not to teach patriotism to a Bengali, he traced the Bengali identity—the 'Bengali faith'—to its cultural legacy, reform movements, and revolutionary struggle for freedom:

My Ishwar is Vidyasagar, my Thakur is Rabindranath, my Ram is Rammohan, my Qazi is Nazrul, my Fakir is Lalon. Only a Bengali knows and follows a Bengali's faith. Sir, why am I saying this today? Because December is an auspicious month for the Bengalis. On 3rd December, Shahid Khudiram Bose was born. On 8th December, another auspicious day, the brave revolutionary Bagha Jotin was born. And who doesn't know about 8th December, 1930? Benoy-Badal-Dinesh, as you all know, attacked Writers' Building without caring about their own lives. This chapter of history is our pride. And what did the government do at a solemn time like this? They have brought in today an anti-Indian, anti-Bengali Bill. (Rajya Sabha Debates, 11 December 2019, 63–64)

Locating the CAB in the trajectory of India's transition to dictatorship, O'Brien drew correspondence between developments in citizenship laws in Germany under Hitler's Nazi regime eighty-four years back, and found 'an eerie similarity' between them and what the Parliament was likely to 'pass today':

> Basically, what I am trying to prove in the next three minutes or four minutes is how we, or the people who have drafted this Bill, have drawn from the Nazi Copybook. One, 1933— concentration camps; 2018— detention camps. By the way, sixty per cent of the people in those detention camps are Bengali Hindus. Two, 1935—the Reich Citizenship Law that protected those with German blood; ... Third, 1935—the focus back to the Nazis—you needed an identity to prove your lineage. So, what did you have? You were given an ancestral past. What is it today, in 2019? You rely on a piece of paper to prove your Indian citizenship, forget about deemed citizens. 1945 is very interesting. There was a plan to deport the Jews. What did they call it? They called it the Madagascar Plan. What do we have today? We have a *Mahaplan*, also known as the NRC. Number five, the Germans called it the große Lüge. It was a term coined by Hitler. And, in English, it meant 'big lie'. This is very interesting. This is very interesting, Sir, because if we keep saying lie, lie, lie, it will sound like a truth. What is the lie today? India is under threat. ... The sixth similarity, it was called the *Lügenpresse*. The *Lügenpresse* was lies and propaganda being pushed against the Jews. And, today, equivalent of the *Lügenpresse* is the fake news and media being pressurised to push the fake agenda. And, the last one, in the German Copybook they referred to a very interesting word 'Jews' as 'rats'. ... What are we talking about today—termites, cockroaches, vermin ...these words are being used by the Prime Minister and sometimes by the Home Minister. ... (Rajya Sabha Debates, 11 December 2019, 66–67)

Significantly, O'Brien referred simultaneously to the possibility of judicial scrutiny and the certainty of popular resistance—both essential to democracy: 'There is a view that the Bill from here will go 3.7 kms down to another domed building i.e., the Supreme Court. But, in between, we have a different view. In between, there will be people's movement. There will be *sangram*. ... Before it goes to Supreme Court—we respect it a lot—there will be people's movement against this' (Rajya Sabha Debates, 11 December 2019, 65). The faith in democratic forces and civil resistance was expressed by Assaduddin Owaisi who spoke earlier in the Lok Sabha.

Owaisi gave a strident critique of the Bill as discriminatory towards Muslims, but more specifically, for going against the commitment that was made in the Constitution towards equality of all religions. Owaisi lamented the decline in the democratic culture of the country, recalling H. V. Kamath's proposal that the Preamble should begin with the invocation of God, which was opposed by Rajendra Prasad, put to vote and rejected by the CA. It was this spirit of the constitutional moment which Owaisi claimed should be cherished, since it represented the rejection of 'Jinnah's paigam' (Jinnah's message) by his ancestors. Yet, the CAB was 'being brought for the five lakh forty thousand Hindus who had been left out of the NRC in Assam. The Bill was a conspiracy to make Muslims stateless . . . You are putting your feet on their chest and saying that you are not an honourable citizen of this country. Indeed, you are without a country. Which is why I am saying that this country is going through another partition . . .'. (Lok Sabha Debates, 9 December 2019, 494) Making a plea for democratic collective action, Owaisi exhorted the House to *condemn* the manner in which they had been consigned to a boat driven with communal and other divisions and *resolve* to democratically steer this boat to the shore and hold the irresponsible boatman to account (Lok Sabha Debates, 9 December 2019, 496). Owaisi made a call for civil disobedience to restore the dignity of the Constitution and those who had struggled for independence. While making this call, Owaisi placed the '1947 ki jange-Aazaadi' (1947 war of independence) at par with the civil disobedience movement launched by Gandhi in South Africa: 'Mahatma Gandhi Mahatma kaise bane? . . . Unhone South Africa ke national register card to phad diya tha, jala diya tha . . . [How did Gandhi become a Mahatma?... He had torn the national register card of South Africa, burnt it'.] (Lok Sabha Debates, 9 December 2019).

Vinay Sahasrabuddhe, BJP MP in the Rajya Sabha, claimed the opposite, declaring emphatically that the opposition was wrong in saying that the Muslims of India were unhappy. 'Why should they be unhappy?', he asked. 'They are nationalist Muslims (*Musalmaan Rashtrabhakt Musalmaan hai*)'. Inverting the arguments by those opposing the Bill and blaming them for being suspicious of Muslims, Sahasrabuddhe stated: '. . . the Muslims in India are nationalist Muslims, and they did not express any reaction when *we* revoked Article 370, when the triple talaq Act was passed, when *we* took a position on the Ram Mandir in the Supreme

Court—*kya Muslim Samaj me uska asantosh nirman hua? Kahi nahi hua... kya kahin Muslim samaj vichalit hua? Bilkul nahi hua. Musalman rashtrabhakt hai. Aapke mun me unke bare me sandeh hai, isliye aap ye rajneeti kar rahe hain. Aap unko vote bank ka khilona banate ho.* [Was the Muslim society disturbed by that? Not at all. The Muslim is nationalist. It is you [the Congress and other opposition parties] who harbour suspicion against them which is why you are engaging in this kind of politics. You treat them like toys in your vote bank' (Rajya Sabha Debates, 11 December 2019, 231–232).

Conclusion

While both the NRC and the CAA are part of the ideological landscape of citizenship in contemporary India, they emerged as specific tendencies out of the 2003 amendment in the Citizenship Act. The insertion of the category 'illegal migrant' through an amendment in 2003 became a hinge point in the trajectory of the law. Both the NRC and the CAA—one through the judicial route and the other through the legislative route—offered two distinct ways of identifying Indian citizens. Following the rules laid down in the Citizenship Act as amended in 2003, the NRC provides the modalities for the preparation of a register of Indian citizens through practices of identification and enumeration. In the case of Assam the procedures evolved under the direction of the Supreme Court by the NRC Commissioner for Assam, made citizenship contingent on conditions of descent, affirmed through papers that were considered valid by the state. Ironically, in the case of Assam the NRC became a register of citizens of Assamese origin, invoking a category of *hyphenated citizenship*, not part of the legal vocabulary of citizenship in India. At the same time, the process became one where the purpose of the NRC became one of sifting out 'illegal migrants'—an unfinished agenda in the promise made by the Assam Accord—rather than preparation of a register of citizens. Indeed, the discursive frameworks surrounding the NRC, the vocabulary of the debate around it, and the petitions before the Supreme Court in the course of its preparation in Assam, focused on the most effective way of identification of illegal migrants by strengthening the Foreigners Tribunals, and addressing the conundrum of putting those who were identified as such in detention camps. The NRC was thus simultaneously about affirming citizenship through descent and eliminating illegal migrants. The CAB is embedded in the idea of *national citizenship* with religion as the principle for making a distinction between those from among illegal migrants who could be exempted from penal action and made eligible for Indian citizenship through naturalization. These two principles defining citizenship have become conjoined in the contemporary context, in the citizenship practices of the BJP, which draws its provenance from the ideology of Hindutva.

Despite assertions by MPs supporting the CAB in the Parliament that the NRC and CAB were distinct, and statements by Ravi Shankar Prasad, Minister for Law and Justice that the NRC and CAB should not be conflated,[24] on several occasions—in April–May 2019 in his election campaigns in West Bengal, and in October–November 2019 before the CAB was discussed in Parliament—the HM spoke emphatically of the relationship between the two. He spoke of both in the same breath, sometimes as the same law, at other times as linked to each other in an indispensable chronological sequence. Indeed, 'aap chronology samajhiye' (You must understand the chronology), became a popular theme for irreverent memes on Twitter during the protests against the CAA. On 11 April 2019 speaking in an election rally in Raigang in West Bengal, Shah promised his audience that he would ensure the implementation of the NRC in West Bengal and expel all illegal migrants from Bangladesh—who he called 'termites'—after coming to power. He assured, however, that citizenship would be granted to Hindu and Buddhist refugees. A tweet on the BJP handle the same day, quoted Amit Shah as saying that the BJP would ensure the implementation of the NRC in the *entire country* 'to remove every single infiltrator, except Buddha [*sic*], Hindus and Sikhs'.[25] In a YouTube video uploaded by the BJP's official channel on 23 April 2019, Shah explained the 'chronology' to the people: 'First the CAB will come. All refugees will get citizenship. Then NRC will come. This is why refugees should not worry, but infiltrators

---

[24] https://www.indiatoday.in/india/story/no-question-of-linking-caa-to-nrc-union-minister-ravi-shankar-prasad-1629020-2019-12-17 (accessed 19 June 2020).
[25] https://indianexpress.com/elections/will-remove-every-single-infiltrator-except-buddhists-hindus-and-sikhs-amit-shah/ (accessed 19 June 2020).

should. Understand the chronology'.[26] On 1 May in an election rally in Bongaon, in West Bengal, home to large number of Matua refugees who had fled to India from Bangladesh in 1950 to escape religious persecution, he explained the chronology once again: 'It is our commitment to implement National Register of Citizens (NRC) across the country to weed out the infiltrators. First, we will bring the Citizenship (Amendment) Bill to ensure that eligible refugees get citizenship, and then we will introduce NRC to throw out the infiltrators'.[27] 'They are termites, they are eating into the country's resources', he asserted.[28]

A speech uploaded on the BJP's official Twitter handle, apparently given in 24 Parganas, was replete with eloquent claims to the same effect—drawing applause from the audience. In an interview with ABP news channel telecast on 2 October 2019, Shah blamed the TMC for deceiving the people on the NRC by saying that the BJP wanted to remove Bengalis from Bengal by compelling them to show papers. To dispel the apprehensions of the people he emphasized that the 'imagination' of NRC was linked to the CAB: 'No Bengali will have to fear. They will not be asked to show papers'.[29]

On 20 November 2019, in the course of responding to a series of questions on the NRC, Shah confirmed that faith-differentiated citizenship in the CAB had been approved by the JPC, and passed by the earlier Lok Sabha. He was responding to a question by Syed Nasir Hussain on the confusion that Shah's speech in West Bengal that non-Muslims had nothing to fear from the NRC, had raised among Muslims: 'I just want to ask the Government and the Home Minister whether the NRC can give citizenship to any immigrant belonging to these communities, leaving out Muslims alone' (Rajya Sabha, 20 November 2019, 59). Swapan Dasgupta asked the HM whether the gazette notification of 7 September 2015 under which exemptions to illegal migrants had been provided, was

---

[26] https://www.youtube.com/watch?time_continue=18&v=Z__6E5hPbHg&feature=emb_title; also https://scroll.in/article/947436/who-is-linking-citizenship-act-to-nrc-here-are-five-times-amit-shah-did-so (accessed 19 June 2020).
[27] https://www.ndtv.com/india-news/lok-sabha-elections-2019-amit-shah-says-mamata-banerjee-extending-support-to-those-who-wish-to-divid-2031385 (accessed 19 June 2020).
[28] https://www.deccanchronicle.com/nation/politics/010519/mamata-supporting-those-who-wish-to-divide-country-amit-shah.html
[29] Intruders Will Be Shown The Door: Amit Shah | Exclusive Interview | *ABP News*, 2 October 2019, https://www.youtube.com/watch?v=k8-R4DOze_g (accessed 19 June 2020).

applicable to the whole of India and whether the NRC in Assam made a 'fundamental distinction between those who are illegal immigrants and those who are non-citizens'. 'Has that distinction actually been made?', he asked, and 'if it has been made, why various people, who are categorized in the notification, are being incarcerated?' (Rajya Sabha, 20 November 2019, 60). Shah responded that the NRC in Assam was prepared under the directions of the Supreme Court under a separate Act. When he referred to a separate Act, Shah was probably alluding to the exception laid down in 2009 to the Citizenship Rules of 2003, laying down a separate procedure for the preparation of the NRC in Assam. Shah further explained that a nationwide NRC, whenever that is conducted, would most likely also cover Assam. Agreeing with Dasgupta that a distinction needs to be made between illegal migrants (probably ghuspaithiya) and non-citizens (foreigners, also those exempted from the category of illegal migrant under the Gazzette notification): 'But, this is true and the government acknowledges that Hindu refugees, Buddhist, Jain, Sikh, Christian, Parsi refugees should get citizenship, and this is exactly why we have brought the Citizenship Amendment Bill' (Rajya Sabha, 20 November 2019, 60).

Dominating the landscape of citizenship in India, the CAB and NRC induced tensions in what Baruah has called 'non-national spaces' (Baruah 2009) and precipitated anxieties regarding the changes that were being sought in the 'national order of citizenship' (Baruah 2009). Unlike Baruah's argument that the tensions between the 'national order of things' and the realities of 'non-national spaces' (Baruah 2009) would adversely affect governmental legitimacy, the NRC and CAB converged in their articulation of exclusionary citizenship, to help the BJP reap electoral advantage in successive elections. The convergence is not only because of the shared anxiety for preserving historical legacies of culture, and access to land, livelihood, and resources, but a larger spectre of (in)security—of the territory and the people—that both the NRC and the CAB claim to be addressing. Indeed, considering that the most vociferous opposition to the CAB came from the northeastern states of India, it is ironic that the JPC raised concerns of security associated with the fear of loss of territory in lower Assam due to 'indiscriminate influx of illegal migrants' from Bangladesh. Citing from the judgement in *Sarbananda Sonowal vs Union of India & Anr* (2005), the JPC warned against the 'dangerous consequences of large-scale illegal migration' from Bangladesh for people of Assam and the nation as a whole. Arguing against 'misconceived and mistaken notions of secularism' coming in the way of stopping this influx, the JPC raised the spectre of the indigenous people of Assam being 'reduced to a minority', rendering 'their cultural survival' in jeopardy, weakening their political control, and undermining employment opportunities (JPC Report 2019, 12).

In his remarks as the leader of the opposition in the Rajya Sabha, Ghulam Nabi Azaad referred to the exaggerated numbers being presented by the government in whose name the Bill was being brought and the small numbers who had actually applied for citizenship. While the government had no figures for persons who would actually benefit from the law, large numbers of people were protesting against the Bill in the country, he argued. Citing the army's flag march in Dibrugarh while the Bill was being discussed in Parliament, to quell mobilization against the CAB, and the use of *lathis*, tear gas, and rubber bullets against protesters on the national highway in Dibrugarh, protests in Arunachal Pradesh, Manipur, Meghalya, in Tinsukiya, and Guwahati in Assam, Azaad sought to dispel the notion that there was a public consensus on the CAB. Supriya Sule of the NCP had earlier pointed out in the Lok Sabha that several members of the JPC had dissented against its recommendation. In an attempt to assuage the north-eastern states, the CAB 2019 provided special exemptions for the ILP states and Sixth Schedule regions. To specifically address the turmoil in Assam, the Clause 6 Committee was expected to communicate to the Assamese people that the government was serious about protecting their cultural identity. Yet, in the months after the passage of the CAA 2019, unprecedented protests were witnessed across the country, and not just in Assam. The protests were peaceful and socially diverse. In some pockets the protesters were predominantly Muslim, but in most cases, they were young college and university students, a large number of them were women, all of whom believed that they were defending the Constitution by resisting the implementation of the CAA with NRC. The apprehension that the NRC was an exercise *intended* to deprive poor Muslims, who may not be able to show appropriate papers, and ran the risk of being labelled illegal, propelled the mobilization. The government attempted to alleviate these apprehensions with the PM taking the lead to say that there were no plans for initiating the preparation of a nation-wide NRC.[30] Yet, towards the end of December, a day after the PM gave the assurance, the government announced the approval of 3900 Crores Rupees to fund the preparation of a National Population Register (NPR). The government presented the NPR as a routine and, therefore, an innocuous exercise, to be carried out along with the census household enumeration, beginning from 1 April 2020, and as the continuation of an exercise that had been underway since 2010 when the UPA was in power. It is, however, difficult to separate the NPR from NRC and several states, including Kerala, Punjab, and West Bengal passed resolutions in their assemblies that they would not participate in the preparation of the NPR, for asking questions pertaining to the date and place of birth of parents.[31] It must be noted that Section 14A of the CAA empowers the Central government to prepare the NRC and issue national identity cards to Indian citizens. Sections 3 and 4 of the Citizenship (Registration of Citizens and Issue of National Identity Cards) Rules 2003, lay down the procedure for the preparation of NRC. The NPR is listed as an initial and indispensable step in Rule 3(4) and Rule 4(3) under which the Central government issues an order regarding the date by which the population register would be prepared by collecting information of persons residing within the jurisdiction of local registrar; Rule 4(3) empowers the local registrar to verify and scrutinize the particulars collected of every family and individual in the Population Register; Rule 4(4) states that 'particulars of such individuals whose Citizenship is doubtful, shall be entered by the Local Registrar with an appropriate remark in the Population Register for further enquiry'. Gautam Bhatia argues that it is here that the NPR and the NRC processes blur into each other: 'the Citizenship Rules essentially give local government officials the power to ascertain if a person is a 'Doubtful Citizen', based on information they glean during the NPR process. As was evident during the NRC process in Assam, lakhs of these 'doubtful' citizens were forced to 'prove' their citizenship to hard-nosed and often unsympathetic government officials'.[32] It was this uncertainty that the NRC had spun and

---

[30] https://www.indiatoday.in/india/story/no-talks-on-nationwide-nrc-now-amit-shah-interview-1631224-2019-12-24 (accessed 20 June 2020).
[31] Deeptiman Tiwari, 'At Meeting on NPR, Opposition States Object to Question on Place and Birth of Parents', *The Indian Express* 18 January 2020.
[32] Gautam Bhatia, 'NPR, NRC: 2 Sides of the Same Coin', *Mumbai Mirror* 27 December 2019.

CAB only appeared to confirm that large numbers of Indian citizens were protesting by invoking the Constitution. The portraits of two icons of the national and constitutional movements—Gandhi and Ambedkar—peppered the spaces of protests as powerful reminders of the constituent moment of the transformative.

3
Liminal Citizenship
The 'Returnees' and 'New' Citizens

On 6 June 2015, the governments of India and Bangladesh entered into an agreement to resolve long-standing disputes pertaining to demarcation of boundary and the exchange of enclaves, and land in adverse possession of the two countries along the border states of West Bengal, Assam, and Tripura. The agreement was a culmination of previous efforts by the governments of the two countries, which included a Land Border Agreement Treaty (LBAT) signed in 1974 a few years after the creation of Bangladesh, followed by the signing of a Protocol in 2011. The 1974 LBAT proposed exchange of territory and land held in adverse possession. Consultations with enclave residents suggested the need for a more flexible understanding of exchange to prevent displacement of people. The 2011 Protocol showed deference to the wishes of those who wanted to continue living on the land they had inhabited for generations. Signed between the prime ministers of India and Bangladesh, the Protocol reflected the need to maintain the status quo as far as land held in adverse possession was concerned. It was agreed that India would receive 2777.038 acres of land from Bangladesh and transfer 2267.682 acres of land to it. The protocol could not be implemented due to opposition by some political parties including the BJP, which saw it as a loss of territory for India. Till the summer of 2015, when another LBAT was signed, this time by a BJP led government, residents of enclaves were citizens of the country to which the enclave belonged, but governmental machinery had meagre or no access to the enclaves since its legal-juridical sovereignty over them was interrupted by the territorial sovereignty of another state. Enclaved citizens did not reside within the contiguous nation-state boundaries of either country, and for all practical purposes they were displaced persons with ambivalent citizenship. Denied political rights and constitutional protections, they led a precarious life of perpetual liminality.

This chapter is based on fieldwork conducted at five sites in Cooch Behar district in West Bengal—in three transit camps for Indian 'returnees' in Dinhata, Mekhliganj, and Haldibari, and two chhits with 'new citizens', Balipukhuri and Dhabalsati Mirgipur. Unlike the category 'returnees' in the Constituent Assembly Debates and the citizenship provisions in the Constitution of India, where it connoted persons who *left* India in the course of Partition and subsequently *decided to return* on permits issued by the government of India, the enclave dwellers were Indian citizens under the Indian Constitution because they were 'found living' in Indian territory. With the exchange of territory in 2015, they were pushed into a position to make the decision, quite like the 'Partition returnees', to move to India from what had now become 'foreign' territory or stay on and become citizens of Bangladesh. In making the decision to move to India, the enclave dwellers would displace themselves from their land, to continue being Indian citizens. The fieldwork was conducted in December 2016, more than a year after the LBAT 2015 was signed and the exchange of land and population had taken place, and about six months after the state assembly elections were held in West Bengal, in which both the returnees and the new citizens voted for the first time. The camps in Dinhata, Mekhliganj, and Haldibari were set up as transit accommodation for two years for Indian citizens 'returning' from Indian enclaves. Balipukhuri and Dhabalsati Mirgipur were Bangladeshi enclaves that had become part of the Indian territory. All its inhabitants consequently became 'new' Indian citizens. The LBAT 2015 is largely considered a moment of closure in the history of contests over territory along the border with Bangladesh by ensuring correspondence/alignment between territorial boundaries and political sovereignty. In the context of the preparation of the National Register of Citizens (NRC) in Assam around the same time and subsequently the CAA, this chapter examines the 'land' exchange as a political resolution of a festering conflict over territorial borders and citizenship. This chapter seeks insights from the field to argue that the administrative measures of relocation and rehabilitation generated experiences of *split-citizenship* among both the returnees and the new citizens, which they expressed through idioms of loss and betrayal. The purpose of this chapter is to explore the polyrhythms of citizenship by relocating the contemporary debate on citizenship in India into an anthropological terrain. By invoking 'polyrhythms' (Barkley-Brown 1991) as an analytical lens, one can see the contemporary landscape of citizenship as one which is composed of multiple, dispersed, disparate, and often dissonant rhythms. The idea is to 'isolate' specific rhythms or strands to see how they stand apart, and at the same time are shaped in conversation with others.

Enclaves are pockets of land located inside the territory of another nation-state. They are islands of sovereignty surrounded by the sovereign territorial jurisdiction of another state. Often located deep inside the territory of an alien state, the residents of enclaves remain ambivalent citizens. Distanced from effective citizenship of their country, as 'nowhere people' (Philipose 2009), they are perilously on the verge of becoming stateless and illegal aliens. Until 6 June 2015, when an agreement to exchange enclaves was reached between the governments of India and Bangladesh, there were 111 Indian enclaves in Bangladesh and 51 Bangladeshi enclaves in India, accounting for 17,160.60 acres and 7110.02 acres of land, respectively.[1] According to *kimvadanti* (folklore) enclaves or *chhitmahals*—as the enclave dwellers call them in local Bangla—were created as *chhits* or stakes which the Raja of Cooch Behar and the Maharaja of Rangpur lost to each other in a game of chess. The haphazard distribution of the enclaves along the border region, in this rendition, displays the randomness of the stakes lost and won. The *chhits* may also be seen as a product of the manner in which the 'national' boundaries were drawn in straight lines along areas where land was intersected by a web of water bodies on the eastern borders, and as a peculiar legacy of state accession in the context of Partition of India. While Rangpur assimilated with East Pakistan, the Maharajah of Cooch Behar—a native state—exercised the option of merging with India.

The 'haphazard' border produced contests that played out in *two different ways* corresponding to the manner in which the association

---

[1] See Annexure I and II of the publication 'Land Border Agreement Treaty between India and Bangladesh', published by Ministry of External Affairs for maps of the region. https://mea.gov.in/Uploads/PublicationDocs/24529_LBA_MEA_Booklet_final.pdf

between territoriality and state sovereignty unfolded. On the one hand, land was construed as territory over which the nation could affirm exclusive sovereignty through proprietary control, and on the other hand, land needed to be abandoned to ensure the integrity of national territorial borders. Underlying both was the concern over the dissociation between cartography and territory and the dilution of state sovereignty because of territorial fragmentation. These concerns manifested themselves at different points of time in the relationship between India and Pakistan and between India and Bangladesh from 1971. Citizenship correspondingly vacillated between its association with territory as the source of national and political identity, and territory becoming aligned with livelihood practices and lifeworld. In its association with livelihood, territory invoked a sense of belonging to the geographically contiguous area of the other nation-state, which then became a source of effective identity, substituting the physically distant mother country as the source of affective belonging and political identity. Between the two, the people residing in the enclaves experienced fragmented citizenship, where the quest for belonging led to an aporetic existence, alternating between illegality, displacement, and legal citizenship. To leave the enclave and enter Bangladeshi territory, for example, the resident of an Indian enclave needed a passport and visa issued from mainland India—and that required crossing Bangladeshi territory. A news report described their predicament as follows:

> Indian citizens in Bangladesh are often forced to provide false information to Bangladeshi officials to conduct business, send their children to school or receive medical care nearby, said Mizanur Rahman, a 34-year-old farmer from Dashiar Chara and a father of two. *Duplicity is at the core of an enclave-dweller's existence*, he said.[2]

The LBAT 2015 marked the moment when not just territory but also the citizenship of those inhabiting the exchanged territory had to be 'fixed'. The LBAT recognized the right of more than 50000 enclave dwellers in

---

[2] Bangladesh: 'Enclave' residents campaign for citizenship, IRIN News, https://www.thenewhumanitarian.org/feature/2011/11/23/enclave-residents-campaign-citizenship (accessed 15 June 2019).

India and Bangladesh to *choose* their citizenship. Only about 990 of those residing in Indian enclaves in Bangladesh decided to leave their homes to retain their Indian citizenship. These persons were, as the Standing Committee on External Affairs termed it—*returning to India*—and should be welcomed. The rest stayed back on the land they had inhabited for generations and became citizens of Bangladesh. On 16 November 2015, *The Hindu* reported that the 'new Indians' who made their passage to India from the Indian enclaves in Bangladesh reported to be 'torn between their love for their land in Bangladesh and the promise of a new beginning in India'.[3] As far as those who resided in the Bangladeshi enclaves in India were concerned, no one left for Bangladesh and continued to live on the land of their forefathers. Forty-year-old Jyotsnarani Barman had been living in one such enclave in India after her marriage twenty years ago: 'They signed on a paper, and my country changed', she said, 'Never knew I could weep so much for Bangladesh'. The chhits, it was reported, were 'filled with grief' as dwellers thought of their separation from their motherland, which they would need a passport to visit. These too were 'new citizens', but unlike the returnees, these erstwhile Bangladeshi *chhit* dwellers would become Indian citizens under Section 7 of the Citizenship Act of India 1955, which permits the conferment of citizenship on those people who become part of the India *through acquisition of foreign territory*.

The redrawing of boundaries between the two countries had ramifications for those residing in the enclaves who experienced the change in political jurisdiction which occurred with the exchange of land, with an offer/opportunity to choose their citizenship. Choosing one's citizenship was, however, a fraught process. Bangladeshi citizens residing in enclaves in Indian territory had the choice *to keep their land and home* but *lose their identification* with a *homeland* to become Indian citizens—a choice precipitated by the absorption of their enclave in the political boundaries of India. Indian citizens residing in enclaves in Bangladesh could retain their citizenship only by leaving their land and homes as 'displaced persons' to reside in camps in Cooch Behar awaiting 'rehabilitation'. Both groups experienced liminality marked by distinctive

---

[3] Suvojit Bagchi, '990 "new Indians" to Make Their Passage from Enclaves', *The Hindu*, 16 November 2015, 13.

experiences of precarity, generated by their association or dissociation with land in a condition of what I call *split citizenship*. I use the word split in two senses: as a way of pulling apart or breaking asunder, suggesting a spatial separation which is implicitly violent; and, as a division or separation of a whole into its constituent parts, which co-exist in a disorderly fashion as they seek to congeal together in a hyphenated relationship. I argue that while the transition to a legally stable citizenship through the swapping of territory brought closure to the ambivalence and often illegality of enclave dwellers, it ruptured their relationship with 'land' and 'homeland' in peculiar ways, depending on whether or not they 'migrated'. The experience of rupture was tied to experiences of 'mobility' and 'immobility' in relationship to land and was at variance with the governmental process of demarcation of boundaries which identified land with territory.

Borders, Territory, and Citizenship

The conflict over demarcation of territorial boundaries and competing cartographic claims that unfolded through distinctive signposts along India's eastern borders was propelled by the imperative of installing uninterrupted political and territorial sovereignty. Enclaves emerged worldwide when the sovereign state political system was implemented or reorganized in a particular region (Jones 2009). Cartographic precision was integral to the emergence of 'fully demarcated territorial states' (Akerman 1984). In the course of decolonization, the process of mapping created morphological models for states that imparted cultural attributes to spatial structures such as core regions and frontiers. Paula Banerjee has argued that these models provided the 'basis for theorisation for both the morphology of states and the spatial processes connected with it', leading also to the redefinition of territoriality as the means to achieve material survival and political control (Banerjee 2010, xxxi). The acquisition of political control over mapped territories has been seen variously as 'justification for claims against occupation' (Sack 1980) as well as the ruling elite's desire to establish their domination over a bounded geographical space and beyond (Parker 1988, Saco 1991). In the context of transition to sovereignty from colonial rule, the process of 'negotiation' of and over borders shows the complex ways in which the phenomenon of state sovereignty itself unfolded. Integral to state formation, borders both buttress, and circumscribe sovereignty. They also reflect the transition from frontiers in the colonial context to border regions, which are subject to special forms of administrative control. Mapping of border lines across these regions becomes imbricated in the histories of contestations over the division and control of power over territory. While much of this history is traced to the state formative practices that accompanied decolonization and the political contexts in which the parcelling of territory occurred in the wake of the Partition, the histories of borders are also 'continuing histories' that remain live through conflict. The history of the enclaves may be seen in contemporary border making and border managing practices but can also be traced to the ways in which political power was organized historically amidst war-making in the region.[4]

The contemporary history of this contest traversed two distinct phases, with the creation of Bangladesh in 1971 as the point of demarcation. The first phase was marked by the Nehru-Noon agreement over the 'disputed' territory of the Berubari Union and the exchange of enclaves, and the Supreme Court decision turning it down. Beruberi Union No. 12 was an area of 8.75 square miles in the Jalpaiguri district. The dispute over Berubari Union arose because of the discrepancy in the award made by the Radcliff Commission entrusted with the responsibility of demarcating the boundary between the two newly created provinces of West and East Bengal. In the narrative text of the award, the Commission described Berubari Union as part of West Bengal. But the map annexed to the narrative text, showed it as part of East Bengal. In 1958, the governments of India and Pakistan signed an agreement to resolve boundary disputes. According to the Nehru-Noon agreement, as it was called, the government of India would cede the southern part of the Beruberi Union

---

[4] The treaty of 1713 by which the Maharaja of Cooch Behar and the Mughuls agreed on cessation of conflict resulted in the practices of revenue collection and taxation whereby Cooch Behar and Rangapur obtained the right to collect taxes from people conquered by the respective armies. When the Mughals ceded power to the British, the system of tax collection in the enclaves was left intact (Jones 2009). The boundary commission set up after partition did not concern itself with the enclaves which were not directly under British control and the princely states were given the option of joining either of the new sovereign states. On 20 August 1949, the Maharaja of Cooch Behar opted to join India marking the date of the official creation of enclaves (Jones 2009).

to East Pakistan and exchange all the enclaves created by the Radcliff line, whereby both the countries would acquire the enclaves located in their territory. The agreement thus sought to alleviate cartographic anxieties of the new nation-states and ensure the correspondence between territorial borders and territorial sovereignty. The agreement precipitated outrage in West Bengal and elsewhere in India over what was seen as loss of territory for India, and compelled the President of India to seek a reference from the Supreme Court to ascertain the constitutional validity of the agreement. On 14 March 1968, an eight-member bench of the Supreme Court decided that the agreement did not amount to mere determination of boundaries which was within the purview of the powers of the government, but involved cessation or alienation of a part of India's territory. The power to cede territory, the judges concluded, rested only with the Parliament, and could become effective only through a constitutional amendment which required political consensus. The Constitution (Ninth Amendment) Act (December 1960) was subsequently passed to amend the First Schedule of the Constitution to give effect to the transfer of territories.

The legal wrangles and political turmoil, which followed prevented immediate transfer. It was ultimately in 1974, following the creation of Bangladesh in 1971, that an accord was signed between the prime ministers of the two countries, Indira Gandhi and Mujib-ur-Rehman. The two countries agreed that Berubari would remain with India in exchange for the Bangladeshi enclave of Dahagram and Angarpota, with access to a tract of land, the Tinbigha Corridor, providing the link to mainland Bangladesh. The accord also repeated the earlier agreement on the exchange of all enclaves, with ramifications for the states of Assam, West Bengal, Meghalaya, and Tripura, in which the enclaves existed. The agreement remained unimplemented, however.

The Constitution 119th Amendment Act, 2015 sought to give closure to the long-standing dispute. Amidst the long-drawn process of settlement of dispute over territory, the effectively stateless residents of the enclaves had for an equally long period remained in a state of ambivalent citizenship. In 2011, when then Indian Prime Minister Manmohan Singh visited Bangladesh to sign a protocol, the residents of Indian enclaves kept their homes in darkness to press their demand for Bangladeshi citizenship, which would entitle them to welfare programmes and employment opportunities. One such resident of an Indian enclave, Biplob Hossain, whose father had fought for Bangladesh's liberation in 1971, was an Indian citizen in an enclave inside Bangladesh. The exchange of enclaves, Hossain believed, would allow him to spend his remaining days as a Bangladeshi citizen. Hossain lived in Garholjorha-2 enclave, also known as Elengbarhi enclave, in Kurhigram with his wife and three children (Niloy 2015).

The LBAT 2015 promised that the exchange of enclaves would not involve displacement of population and that the territories of the enclaves would be absorbed by the two countries along with their residents, who would henceforth become legal citizens of the country of absorption, with the assurance that they could exercise choice in citizenship. The question, *how* those who left their enclaves of residence and chose the citizenship of the country to which the enclave originally belonged would be rehabilitated as *citizens*, remained contentious. The removal of 'border anomalies' became yet again a process of aligning national cartographies and citizenship.

'We were *Bharat Panthi*, pro-India'

The precise figures of those who came to India following the exchange of enclaves and those who were absorbed along with the Bangladeshi enclaves in the Indian territory is difficult to ascertain. In her report on the LBAT, Prachi Lohia (2019) points out that in the first census of the enclaves conducted in July 2011, the total number of persons residing in enclaves in both countries was placed at 51,549 with 37,334 Indian residents in Bangladeshi enclaves and 14,215 Bangladeshi residents in Indian enclaves.[5] Following the LBAT in 2015, a second survey was conducted which was, as the Ministry of External Affairs was to report in response to a question in the Parliament, 'an option taking survey', 'conducted solely to record the number of persons who wanted either Indian or Bangladeshi citizenship; the number of persons who wanted to stay on their land and renounce their former citizenship; and the ones who wanted to relocate

---

[5] Ministry of External Affairs, Government of India, 'India and Bangladesh Land Boundary Agreement', *Public Diplomacy Division*, 18, https://www.mea.gov.in/Uploads/PublicationDocs/24529_LBA_MEA_Booklet_final.pdf

to their home country.[6] Lohia notes that in this survey 979 Indians who were residing in Indian enclaves in Bangladesh chose to return to India, while all the Bangladeshi residents in Bangladeshi enclaves in India chose to stay on. Significantly, the option taking survey was done only among those whose names were part of the 2011 survey. Both the surveys—2011 and 2015—had discrepancies, owing to the manner in which the headcount was done: 'The most banal and yet important fact to note here is that the number of persons—in Indian enclaves, in Bangladeshi enclaves and the ones who decided to relocate—has not remained constant in any of the documents, including the data provided by the Government itself' (Lohia 2019, 24).[7] Tables 3.1 and 3.2 below, show the statistics available with the Office of the District Magistrate of Cooch Behar, as collated by Banerjee et al. The Camp dwellers, however, reported their own estimates of the numbers to me when I visited the camps.

In Dinhata camp, Abdul Rehman,[8] assumes the role of a leader, giving information, and guiding us through the different lanes along which the camp dwellings had been set up.[9] A cluster of people accompany us, participating in the conversation, when instructed by Rehman but often also on their own. Rehman informs us that the Dinhata Camp provides transit dwellings to 222 people from 58 families who came from two Indian enclaves—Phulbari/Dasiachara and Gurungabari in three batches on 22 November, 24 November, and 29 November 2015—198 came from Phulbari enclave and 24 from Gurungabari enclave. Two of those who came died and 6 children were born in the camp. Four members were added through marriage. While all the 24 who came from Gurungabari

---

[6] As answered in the Lok Sabha by the Ministry of External Affairs on May 4, 2016. http://loksabhaph.nic.in/Questions/QResult15.aspx?qref=34008&lsno=16, cited in Lohia (2019, 24).

[7] Lohia notes that the LBAT text shows the Bangladeshi residents in Indian enclaves to be 14,215 while the MHA notification places the number of Bangladeshis who were given citizenship at 14,864. Similarly, the number of Indian citizens who came back to India have also varied: It was 979 in an answer in the Lok Sabha, 989 in a Press Release by the MEA on 20 November 2015 (https://www.mea.gov.in/press-releases.htm?dtl/26048/Exchange+of+enclaves+between+India+and+Bangladesh) and 922 in a RTI response from the District Magistrate of Cooch Behar on 5 June 2017 (2019, 23).

[8] All names have been changed to protect the identities of the people we met. A pseudonym has been allocated to each person in accordance with regional and religion-specific naming conventions.

[9] The field visit was conducted with the help of funds provided by JNU under the UPOE-II scheme. I was assisted in the field by Shreya Ghosh who also helped with transcribing the interviews.

Table 3.1 New Entrants by Religion from Indian Enclaves in Bangladesh

Entry Point	Hindus	Muslims	Christians
Sahebganj-Bagbandar	159	146	-
Changrabandha-Burimari	191	4	1
Haldibari-Chilahati	466	-	21
Total	816	150	21

Column group header: Religious Communities

Source: Banerjee (2017, 8). Report on Entry and Settlement of People from erstwhile Indian Enclave, Government of West Bengal, Office of the District Magistrate of Cooch Behar, West Bengal.

Table 3.2 Transit Camps in Cooch Behar

Camp	Family	Male (Persons)	Female (Persons)	Total (Persons)	Male (Children)	Female (Children)	Total (Children)	Children Below 5 Years
Dinhata	58	127	118	245	12	16	28	28
Mekhliganj	47	97	100	197	29	39	68	18
Haldibari	96	247	231	478	64	73	137	58
Total	201	471	449	920	105	128	233	104

Source: Banerjee (2017, 17). Report on Entry and Settlement of People from erstwhile Indian Enclave, Government of West Bengal, Office of the District Magistrate of Cooch Behar, West Bengal.

enclave were Bhatia Muslims, about fifty per cent of those who came from Phulbari enclave were Hindus.

The conversations with Rehman and other camp dwellers gave us insights into their perceptions and experience of the processes of 'exchange', in particular how 'India' and 'Bangladesh' figured in the transition as competing sources of belonging and allegiance. Rehman's account of the process suggests a rift between those who wanted to retain both—their land *and* Indian citizenship—and those who wanted the exchange, which would involve giving up their land to 'migrate' to 'India'. Almost all of the nine thousand residents in Dasiachara enclave did not want an exchange of territory and wanted a corridor to be built from Dasiachara to

Kushirhaat, Shaoti border, where the fencing was—a distance of about one and a half kilometres. They had made this proposal during the first survey conducted in 2011 jointly by India and Bangladesh. The *Vinimaya Committee* (exchange committee) set up by Bangladesh was, according to Rehman, 'complicit' with the Bangladeshi administration and misinformed the Indian officials that the corridor they were proposing would be twenty kilometres long. There were others in the enclave working in tandem with the exchange committee and the Bangladeshi administration: 'We were, however, "pro India"', clarified Rehman.

Dasiachara was under Phulbari thana, but the residents of Dasiachara enclave had their own local committee and lived separately. All the nine thousand enclave dwellers had constituted a panchayat and possessed identity cards that enabled them to travel to India and back, through a gate in the fence which was installed in 1991. They used the travel cards till 2007 after which 'few people from Bangladesh and India, some self-interested vested people formed a committee—the *vinimaya* committee. Bangladesh's Jamaat Shibir, along with Jatiyo Party and the BNP (Bangladesh Nationalist Party), formed an organization, and contacted some people from this (Indian) side, who went there and hoisted the Bangladeshi flag. The flag was hosted in Dasiachara enclave, in front of the Chhitmahal United Council office. They hosted Bangladesh flag in an Indian enclave, where we always hoisted the Indian flag. Our group decided to hoist the Indian flag in response. A conflict broke out'. The Chhitmahal United Council (CUC) was a central committee that consisted of representatives of committees that existed in each enclave. Rehman represented his committee in the CUC. Competitive claims to the enclave and disagreements around the process of exchange were expressed through commemorative events and observation of 'national' days. The hoisting of national flag became a 'movement'—not only to mark 'independence day'—but events such as cricket matches were organized as occasions when the flag could be hoisted: 'Whatever used to happen, we hoisted the Indian flag':

> We celebrated 15th August in 2014. They wanted to observe the death anniversary of Sheikh Mujibur Rahman [which falls on the same day]. Our people were also ready. We raised the Indian flag in front of our office. They raised the Bangladeshi flag next to it. We called a meeting

on September 14th. They came with lathis, with some Bangladeshis—members of the Bangladesh *Vinimaya* Committee and Bangladesh *prashasan* [administration]. My younger brother was injured in the violence. We could not go to Bangladesh from the enclaves for treatment, so we came to border gate no. 22 on the fencing and spoke to the Cooch Behar district administration. BSF gave medical aid to the injured. After crossing six rivers, we got the injured to Assam border and kept them there for 15–20 days for medical treatment. Then on 21 February, they again hoisted Bangladesh flag and disrupted things. Till then there was no exchange. We raised the Indian flag and went around singing our national anthem. They said we were campaigning around *jana gana mana*. The Bangladesh Police came and stopped everyone from singing. After few days, Bangladesh-India bilateral talks reached its final stages. The Indian Chief Minister and Prime Minister went to Dhaka and it was announced that there would be an exchange of enclaves.[10]

The announcement of exchange, according to Rehman exacerbated the differences between the *Bharat panthis* and Bangladeshis and the Bangladeshi government started using coercion to stop people from listing themselves to leave for India. Rehman himself was framed in 'false cases', making it difficult for him to move out of his house. Amidst this, it was declared that the headcount and enrolment of names by the joint survey committee would take place from 6 to 16 July 2015. Rehman recalls: 'After receiving this news, around 1500–2000 people from various enclaves came to my house. It was good news, and we welcomed the initiative'. But on 6 July—the day the enrolment began—the *Daroga* and the Phulbari thana Station Officer came to his house where about 200 people were present discussing the exchange: 'Bangladesh Vinimaya committee had informed them that if people were not stopped, then 3000 people would leave for India immediately. It is then that the police and administration came and directly threatened me saying, if within one minute everyone does not disperse from here, your skin will be ripped off and if anyone goes and enrols his/her name in the Indian list, we will bury you under seven layers of soil'.[11] Rehman recounts contacting authorities

---

[10] Conversation with Abdul Rehman, Dinhata Camp, Cooch Behar, 15 December 2016.
[11] Ibid.

in India including Debababrata Chaki, the Councillor of Chhitmahal units in Cooch Behar, Member of Parliament—Renuka Sinha, the BSF, and the District Magistrate's office in Cooch Behar. The people who had gathered in Rehman's house had fled and no one could enrol on the first day as the Vinimaya Committee patrolled the entire area on bikes: '15–20 bikes—their bike bahini was everywhere'. Rehman alleged that the Indian members of the Vinimaya Committee too did not want them to go to India: 'They got favours from Bangladesh. The bike bahini of the Vinimaya Committee intimidated the enclave dwellers to prevent them from speaking to the survey team that came from India. The Indian team went to the house of those from the Vinimaya Committee and made the lists there. The counting was done in this manner'. This was the experience, he said, in other Chhitmahals too. Earlier in November 2014 members of the CUC, representing six chhitmahals including Lalmonirhaat, Baskatha chhitmahal, and Enclave number 10, Desiachara, where Rehman resided, attempted to give a 'prayer' to Mamata Banerjee, the Chief Minister of West Bengal. Rehman remembers these representatives having gathered in his house the night before, but when the news spread, on the morning of 4 November Bangladesh Rifles (BDR) personnel blocked all the border exits to stop the delegation. Unable to meet the Chief Minister, the representatives left for their respective villages but on their way back, when they crossed Phulbari, the police beat them up and 'parceled them to the Bangladesh thana jail accusing them of being members of the Jamaat Shibir'. When the exchange process started, and they were not able to enrol due to intimidation by the bike bahini, they tried contacting ministers from the TMC and BJP. On 8 July, an 'observer' arrived from Delhi, who was, however, put up in the house of Altaf, Sabhapati (Chairperson) of the Vinimaya Committee, who was a resident of the Indian enclave but had procured papers of Bangladesh and had been working for the Bangladesh administration. This was the reason, according to Rehman that he was made part of the Exchange Committee. Encouraged by the presence of the observer, Rehman and about 200–250 other enclave dwellers decided to go to the Sabhapati's house and get their names enroled:

> On 8th, when we got to know that an Observer has come, we decided, that we all would definitely go and enrol our names now, not thinking

anymore whether we will end up beaten up, thrashed or dead. Two hundred people went to Altaf's house where the observer was staying. When we reached the house, we found at the least a hundred Bangladeshi policemen there. We went and spoke to the observer and told him about the situation. People from the Bangladesh administration, who were also there, threatened us in front of the observer. An officer of Phulbari Thana, equivalent to the rank of the Sub Divisional Officer (SDO) in India, directly threatened us there itself, saying why do we need to write your name. Earlier, the Sabhapati threatened to chop off the legs of an elderly enclave dweller, it he registered to go to India. Yet he did not listen and went and spoke to the observer.[12]

Sajid Ali and eighteen members of his family wanted to go to India. Ali was among those who went and spoke to the observer. The observer asked members of the Vinimaya Committee to remain silent so that he could listen to the people who had come to meet him and assured them that they would begin listing the names the next morning. As a result of the intervention of the observer, three additional booths were set up. The existing booths were in the houses of the members of the Vinimaya Committee, which deterred people from approaching them. The additional booths were set up in the schoolteacher, Mahanand Master's house and in the Mosque next to Sajid Ali's house enabling eighty-eight people to enrol. Since intimidation was not possible anymore, people were *persuaded* not to get enroled:

> They started going to all houses and started asking us not to go. They said that if you go to India, your wives will be taken away and men in India will put *sindoor* (vermillion) on the foreheads of Muslim women. Yet some people still got enrolled. From our enclave, Dashiyachora, 305 people could register their names.[13]

Rehman explains why of the 9000 residents in the enclave only a small number 'returned' to India: 'They wanted to enrol. If you come with me to the border today, I can call up people. If an announcement for fresh

---

[12] Ibid.
[13] Conversation with Sajid Ali, Dinhata Camp, 15 December 2016.

enrolment is made with the assurance that there will be no police interference, I can guarantee that five hundred people will enrol themselves within three hours. It was the intimidation by the police which prevented the enrolment of many people, in the Indian list as well as the Bangladeshi list'. A week after the enrolment, 20 names were withdrawn: 'For instance, there was this old lady, the day we were coming, she caught hold of us on the road and held our feet asking that we take her family too. It was the Bangladesh administration which forced her to withdraw their names promising her this and that if she stayed'.[14]

Several residents in the camp, when they were residents of Indian enclaves in Bangladesh, had been travelling to India for work on the basis of an enclave dweller's card. These residents had come back to their homes in the enclaves during the 2015 survey to enrol their names but were not able to do so. Moinuddin, a resident in the transit camp, had been working in Delhi for 18 years and his four children were born in Delhi. It took Three Thousand Rupees for one person to cross the border to go to Delhi and then return to the enclave. Moinuddin did not have the money for the entire family to travel. He, therefore, travelled from Delhi alone, assuming that he could enter his as well as the names of his family members in the list. Upon reaching the enclave, he found that his name was listed under the column 'BD' (Bangladesh) and not 'IN' (India):

> I do not know how to read, they forcefully got my name in the 'BD' column. I knew that I wanted to go to India, and I thought I had enroled for the exchange to India. Later I got to know that my name was in the 'BD' list. I came to know about it around two days after I enroled. My name and thumb sign was in the 'BD' column. I was enroled in the 'BD' list.[15]

A BBC journalist interviewed Moinuddin. The interview was circulated widely. As a consequence the bike bahini started looking for him. Rehman took Moinuddin to the border and intimated the DC office Cooch Behar about the threat to Moinuddin's life. Newspapers and news

---

[14] Conversation with Abdul Rehman, Dinhata Camp, 15 December 2016.
[15] Conversation with Moinuddin, Dinhata Camp, 15 December 2016.

channels in India also covered his story. Moinuddin narrated his experience of enrolment as follows:

> For two months, we were running around. I was travelling constantly between Delhi and Cooch Behar. Then, sir [DM Cooch Behar] called me and said that my travel card is ready and I came here. The DM told me the BSF car is there and my family and I could go and collect my travel card from Rajshahi, Bangladesh. But the cost of travelling to Rajshahi with family, staying in a hotel, food etc, could take around 10–15 thousand and more. This was very expensive. I was then told that the High Commissioner had announced that those who have still not got their travel card would get it soon, so there was no need to spend money. Around 2nd November, I got my card. Before that, those conspirators, who favoured the Bangladesh administration, followed me. But I spoke to everyone and I got a lot of attention. The High Commissioner assured me that there was no need for tension, the officials are working and would call you. You can come and take the card. Before this, the Bangladeshi side was giving my son such allurements: "We will give you cycle, food etc., call your father". I was asked to give a statement that I was being bribed to go to India. The SDO there himself called me and said this. I told them that why 20 lakh, even if you give me 20 crore, I will not unnecessarily take anyone's name like that. As it is my family was in Delhi, my children were born in Delhi, my home was in the Indian enclave, and my name was written in Bangladesh list by force. Whether we go to India or Bangladesh, it is my wish. They were saying *sindoor* will be put on the forehead of the wife, they will give you house along the rail-tracks in the desert, they will beat you. I have been living in India for 18 years. Am I mad? Will I not know what happens and what does not? I was given documents the day 20 delegates from India and 20 from Bangladesh were there, in the presence of Renuka Sinha and Sheikh Hasina. My family lives in India and works in India. Why will I not opt for India? How did my name happen to be in the Bangladesh list? It was done by force. I proved it alone to everyone.[16]

[16] Ibid.

One of the residents of the Dinhata camp suggested that had the BSF and the Indian administration gone to the Indian enclaves, more people would have felt emboldened to register. The officials who did go from the Indian side in 2011 and 2015 to do the survey, they claimed, were corrupt:

> Between all the 111 enclaves, only 2000 might have stayed back. It was the fault of the Indian government. Those who went there to do the survey in 2011, and later the 11 people who went there, most of them were corrupt, which is why most of our people could not enrol their names and could not come. These 11 people went on the 6th, why did they go? To enrol the names of all those who wanted to come, right. The idea was that everyone would exercise their choice, but our 11 people did not do anything towards it, they agreed to all that Bangladesh said. The representatives from Bangladesh constantly asked every person why they wanted to go. What was the need? When the people from the enclaves asked the Indian representatives what would happen [when they reached India], the Indian representatives responded saying they did not know anything. Bangladeshi representatives seemed to know a lot. They would constantly say, don't go, no one should go. The Police was constantly patrolling, the SDO, when I was standing to enrol my name, had personally held my hand and asked—tell me what you require, I will ensure that you are provided for; he said to me, just spell it out, and I will arrange for it, do not enrol your name.[17]

Indeed, it appeared that the persuasion continued even after the transfer of people from the enclaves had taken place. The residents of Dinhata camp claimed that on 27 January 2016, a member of Jamaat Shibir came to the camp: 'He roamed around the entire camp, and told people that if they wanted to go back to Bangladesh, he could help us'. The camp dwellers reported him to the police for engaging in 'anti-India activities'. Before that they locked the gates of the camp. Rehman, who appeared to have been active in this episode, claimed that the member of Jamaat Shibir filed a case of harassment against him and two other camp residents:

---

[17] Conversation with Imtiaz, Dinhata Camp, 15 December 2016.

I am still fighting this false case. As a result my passport is also stuck and I am not able to travel across the border. Otherwise I would have at least gone and done something about my land there. There were some enclaves from which people could not come at all. For example, in enclave number 121, no head count was done in 2011, and no one came to India from it. They went especially to the Muslim households—went door to door and convinced them to not to go to India. *I was always an Indian follower, bharat panthi.* If I had refused to come, no Muslim would have come from my enclave. As it is very few Muslim families came, they had intimidated them so much.

Rehman's enclave Dasaichara, according to him, was the only enclave from which Muslim families came because he was able to persuade them to resist intimidation. Only two Muslim families came from other enclaves, who were now residing in Mekhliganj camp. Dinhata camp residents believed that several more would have come to India had the promised central team from Delhi had gone to the enclaves. Like Moinuddin, there were others who were issued travel cards by the government but could not travel to the enclaves from Delhi and other parts of India where they were working to enrol themselves. There could be several such people in India who were Indian citizens but not enroled as 'returnees'.

'Caged Like Birds'

Arrangements were made by the Indian High Commission in Bangladesh to transport the 'returnees' to settlement camps in India in buses under security. They were provided with temporary travel cards and identity cards and were welcomed with 'much fanfare' at each entry point by MPs, MLAs, the DM, and SP, Cooch Behar, who received the new entrants (Banerjee et al. 2017, 13). For the new entrants into the Indian territory, their reasons for choosing to migrate were many. Mrs Burman, who left half her family in Bangladesh to move to West Bengal, was happy to be moving closer to her daughter in Siliguri. Osman Gani was hopeful of finding new opportunities for work in 'fresh' brick kilns. For a large number of those who migrated, of whom 20 per cent were Muslims, moving out of their 'homeland', was expected to 'end routine crossing of the border for work'. For others like Jayaprakash Roy, a medium farmer of chhit number 42 in Panchagarh district, the decision to shift was determined by the desire to escape into a system where they would receive equal protection of law. Roy and his family changed their 'homeland' since condition in Bangladesh had 'worsened': 'we had about 900 bighas (360 acres). Half of it has gone under a river and the other half was encroached upon after my father was murdered in 1985'. There had never been a proper investigation into the murder because he was in an 'Indian territory', a problem that had always hounded enclave dwellers. 'The body was taken to India, and we never saw him ... only the shirt arrived' (Bagchi 2015, 13).

Abdul Rehman in the Dinhata camp has to take care of his four children. He left behind a small plot of land and a pond in Bangladesh. He does not possess any papers related to his land and is still running around to procure them. Another Dinhata resident with 14.5 bighas of land and a pond in Bangladesh laments: 'Here there is no food, which country, which government have we come to? Here we have been caged like a bird. We have not got any work, any place to labour, nothing'. Look at this old man, Rehman points at a person among those who have gathered around us in Dinhata camp:

> He had land there, now there is nothing. Now he, in this age, is thinking of going to Delhi to find work. He has taken a loan of 1000–1500. Where will he repay it from? Look at him. Is he of an age when he should work to feed himself? There are 4–5 members in his family, and no one to earn. How will this old man earn? Will the government not think about this? When will they think? We have been here for a year and a half. Neither have we got land and electricity nor do we get ration properly. They are giving only 30 kilos of rice for 5 people, how will we manage?[18]

The returnees in the camp were given papers by the Bangladesh government when they left for India as proof of ownership of the land that they had left behind in Bangladesh. They were assured that both the governments would decide the modalities through which their land would be

---

[18] Conversation with Abdul Rehman, Dinhata Camp, 15 December 2016.

sold and the money transferred to them: 'All these matters were supposed to be dealt with by the two governments and we were supposed to get money in lieu of the land we left there ... When we were there, we were told not to sell land for minimum/compromised price. But it has been one and a half years, and the government has not done anything. Neither are we getting proper food nor are our children getting proper education'.[19]

One of the residents claimed that 9 bighas of his land in Bangladesh had been sold for sixteen lakhs, while he received only two thousand rupees: 'Others have occupied it in Bangladesh. We have one thing to say whether it is Central government or state, Modi or Mamata—justice should be done'. Narratives of loss of land and discontent over their predicament as camp dwellers abounded—the story of a mother who died of a heart attack, worrying about their land, a father suffering a brain stroke, longing for what they had left behind—'supari bagaan, paan bagaan, a concrete house' and discontent over the uncertainties of the present—jostled to be told and heard. There was a palpable sentiment of disappointment and a repeated call for 'justice' from 'Mamata and Modi'. A resident expressed his disheartenment:

> All the land papers have been given to the government. Their offices are full of our papers. We have become tired of giving them documents. We have given so many papers and documents to the DM, Cooch Behar. When we came here, they asked us to submit all documents, saying that our claims will be settled immediately. It has now been one and half years, nothing has moved. We keep going to the DM's office. It takes 100 Rupees to travel every time to go to the DM's office. But we have received no money. What do we do with our family? We have not got any justice—justice for our land. We have to hang ourselves with our family. We have to die.

An officer in the Block Development Office disagrees with the claims made by the camp residents. Those who owned land decided not to come to India, he asserts: 'Actually those who were landless are the only ones who came here. For instance, Upen Barman, who had 1200 bighas of land, did not come to India. The 300 Muslim families that came from

[19] Ibid.

Dinhata, were landless'. The camp residents claimed, however, that a list was prepared by the Bangladesh government: 'See this document. This was done by the Bangladesh government. This is the list of our enclave, listing all the landholding with details of us all. This document belongs to one family. Every family has such a document showing the land they have left behind in the enclave'. The camp dwellers resented being compared with the chhit dwellers, 'the new citizens':

> They cannot compare us with those who are living in Bangladesh enclaves inside India because we have come here leaving all our land and belonging there. Those who are here, they are here with all their belongings. What is the comparison of us with them? We have come here, leaving everything behind.

A resident, Suvajit Rai lamented:

> A camp was set up to submit all papers. There is proof and acknowledgement of it. We were asked to submit all documents related to land and compensation. They told us that matters will be taken care of. We photocopied documents for compensation and submitted. But till now, nothing has been done. It has been one and half years. If we do not get anything, what do we do? My mother died of brain broke, thinking that there is not going to be any justice. In Bangladesh my mother cultivated and sold *begun*, *patol* and *aloo* and always had 5000–10000 Rupees in her hand. Here she did not even have 10 paise. When she asked an officer about the compensation for her land, he said it would take ten years or so. Hearing that, my mother had a stroke and died. In Bangladesh my father did farming but here there is no work. My mother died in Cooch Behar MGM hospital. After completing the last rites of my mother, after the 13 day rituals followed by Hindus, I gave an application to the SDO and BDO, for some support. I have the receipt. Where else do we go? We have access only to SDO, BDO, other than that where do we go?[20]

---

[20] Conversation with Suvajit Rai, Dinhata Camp, 15 December 2016.

The Haldibari camp consisted of two settlements—A and B. It housed the 700 people from 96 families that came from different enclaves in Bangladesh—Doikhata, Dhohlakhagrabari, Bharjini, Devigunj, Natoktoka—on 22 November 2015. All camp residents received Aadhaar cards, ration cards, and MNREGA job cards upon their arrival. Bashir Ahmed, the officer-in-charge of Enclave Settlements in the BDO office, informed us that all settlements in Dinhata, Haldibari, and Mekhliganj were completed before 31 July 2015 when the enclave exchange happened: 'The day these people came, that day itself Aadhaar cards were prepared for them. Bank accounts were also allotted to them that very day. Job cards were given within one month. Voter IDs were given before the election. For two months they were given cooked food. After that, till today, ration is distributed'. The distribution of these documents was in keeping with the Home Ministry's policy that the 'returnees' when they arrived in India, would furnish their biometric details to enable keeping track of all those who came.[21]

Sujit Dev and his six-member family came from Doikhata enclave in Panchagarh district in Bangladesh under the administrative control of Haldibari *thana* in Cooch Behar. Dev informed us that of the 250–300 families in the enclave, only five families came to India. As was the case in Dinhata camp, these families expressed their choice to come to India in July 2015 and the survey to take a headcount of enclave residents was taken in 2011. Dev finds it difficult to tell us the reason why he chose to come with his family to India: 'It is difficult to give a *reason*'. While there were problems in the enclave, 'there was no injustice'. Was there any particular reason why the other families did not come? Dev is reticent. They just did not come. Land was not the reason, which more or less everybody had. They did not have any facilities there: '*They simply did not come*'. While coming to India, some families sold their land, but Dev's family did not. He left his land in the care of his brother, who had stayed on in Doikhata. Dev does not tell us why his brother decided to stay: 'He stayed back for whatever reason'. As to the life in the enclave which they left behind, 'a lot could be said':

---

[21] Conversation with Bashir Ahmed at the BDO officer, Haldibari, 15 December 2016.

I will tell you one thing. No one leaves their birthplace easily. My father left 99 bighas of land for his three sons. He died before his retirement—killed by a dacoit. At that time, there were thefts almost thrice a month and dacoity twice a month. That was how life was in those days. Father was a master (school teacher). When father died, one of us was entitled to get the job. But the Bangladesh administration resisted saying that we are from the enclaves and cannot be given work. This was around 1982. In the absence of a job, our property got expended. I had to sell my inheritance. To fill the stomach, I started making furniture. This is how life went on. Then there was the survey in 2011 and again in 2015. We were asked to choose where to go. I decided to come to India. Others stayed back. After coming here, we voted. Then they gave us job card, Aadhaar card. The day we came, they gave us an 'agreement' that we will stay in this non-permanent place. Within two years they will give us a permanent place to live. We will be transferred there—when, where, and how—we do not know.[22]

Dev now makes masks and wooden toys which he sells in the locality: 'Who will take my furniture here? I make masks. Some people buy them. In Bangladesh, there is a lot of demand of such masks, but here it is not much'. The decision to leave the enclave to come to India was a 'risk' that people had taken, compelled by their socio-economic conditions. For a lot of people, it was a decision to 'migrate' to escape the uncertainty of being an enclave dweller, and the promise of new opportunities. Unlike the strong sentiments around being 'bharat panthi' that Abdul Rehman and some other Dinhata residents expressed as being the driving force behind their coming to India, Rinita Roy, a resident of Haldibari camp, decided to come because others were coming too. Roy has two sons—the older son was a farmer and the younger, a mason, in the erstwhile enclave. When asked why and how they decided to come to India, whether or not there was a discussion following which a decision was taken, Roy says that she saw some people coming and she joined them. Those who did not come were also thinking of coming, but did not take the risk: 'Some of us, did not think so much, we thought whatever happens, let that be,

---

[22] Conversation with Sujit Dev, Dinhata Camp, 16 December 2016.

we came, took the risk. Those who did not come were worried about what would happen afterwards. There was no clarity'.[23] Roy had given an application in the BDO office appealing to allow her other relatives to join them—her daughter, nephew, and other family members whose names were in the 2011 headcount, but were not able to exercise their choice in 2015. The problem of family members left behind was a common one, voiced by residents in other camps as well. Shubhranshu, a resident of Mekhliganj camp informed us that while some of his family members were able to come, others were 'stuck' in Bangladesh. In Shubhranshu's case, the separation of family members was largely because of the problems in the way the surveys took place:

> We are four brothers, of whom only two could enrol. My mother could not enrol either. Both the enrolments were done wrongly. In the 2011 enrolment, two brothers were counted and the other two and my mother were not. In fact in 2011, someone else wrote our names in the survey. We did not even know that there was a survey in 2011. We got to know about it only in 2015, when the survey for choice happened. That is the reason my two brothers could not come. Had we known about the survey, all of us would have registered our names.[24]

Shubhranshu had constructed a house in Bangladesh, just next to the enclave in which he resided and possessed another house. When the 'oppression increased in the enclaves', his family would go to their house in Bangladesh: 'If you did not have a house in Bangladesh, you cannot even sell a cow'.[25] Jagat Ray, who too came to Mekhliganj camp in November 2015, expressed similar views about the 2011 survey: 'Those doing the survey did not even come to our houses. It was supposed to be a survey. I got to know about it only when the discussions around it started happening. That is when we got to know something. Even then we did not have a clear idea'.[26]

---

[23] Conversation with Rinita Roy, Haldibari Camp, 15 December 2016.
[24] Conversation with Shubhranshu, Mekhliganj Camp, 16 December 2016.
[25] Ibid.
[26] Conversation with Jagat Ray, Mekhliganj Camp, 16 December 2016.

Bashir Ahmed at the BDO office disagreed with this version of what happened during the survey. Ahmed was part of the 62 members Indian delegation that went to the Indian enclaves in 2011 to conduct the survey. The Bangladesh government gave them administrative support:

> The survey happened—that much they knew. They perhaps did not know that the exchange pact was signed, or that there will be exchange. When the team went there, they enroled those who came. How could they have enroled those who did not come to them? The fact is that many of these people got Bangladesh border ID cards to take advantage of services. They sent their children to schools in Bangladesh. Since I deal with these matters, I know. Entire families have taken services; even elderly people of the families have signed receiving rations that they have taken from Bangladesh government. Most of them can sign. [They have] good handwriting. Many of them have typewritten-like handwriting. In the Indian enclaves there were no schools, but they all went to schools [in Bangladesh].

The response to why they decided to come to India elicited interesting insights. While the Dinhata camp residents appeared to be more vocal in expressing their choice of coming to India as a reflection of their pro-India disposition amidst the conflict in the Indian enclave, and the Haldibari camp residents remained reticent, the residents in Mekhliganj expressed it in terms of 'return': 'We lived in the Indian enclaves for so long, thought of going back to actual soil'. They had heard that there is 'some land across the river and that they would get something there'. They would have preferred something close by, having now become familiar with their new surroundings. Sujit Roy mused: 'It would be good if we get something here. I have become adjusted to this place. One does not know what this land across the river is, and going there with kids will be difficult'. While coming to India, Sujit Roy gave part of his land to his sister and sold the rest. When he exchanged the money obtained through purchase for Indian currency, it was insubstantial. He kept the money in a bank.

Rehabilitation, Franchise, and Family

A salient feature of the new political order that was installed in India after independence was 'a deliberate and successful dispersal and democratisation of power' alongside the expansion of governmental institutions and activities (Weiner 1965, 199). In such a framework, universal adult franchise played an important role in political socialization, generating the belief that institutions can be subjected to popular control through the power of the vote—a power which resided with every individual. The state assembly elections were conducted in West Bengal in April-May 2016—a few months after the exchange took place. Political parties came to the camps to campaign and the 'returnees', as well as the 'new citizens', voted in the election. The meaning they attributed to the vote is important. It was not simply an affirmation of their citizenship, but a promise that they had extracted from the state through their vote, and subsequently found themselves betrayed:

A Dinhata resident, Shabir Ali describes this sentiment as follows:

> All candidates who were contesting the elections came and campaigned in the camp. They said, you have come from the enclaves, you must support us. Vote for us and we will do your work. Till today nothing has been done. Where is the MLA? He came every day asking for vote. And after taking our vote, the MLA hasn't come a single day, we have not even seen the feet of the MLA since then. He is not bothered about what the people are eating, whether or not they have work. The kids don't have much to wear and winters have come. Eid went by and so did Durga Puja. We did not get anything. What law is this? In which country have I come, leaving behind all land and property? We hired labourers to work on our land. But after coming here we have gone about asking people to hire us as labourers. We go 5 to 10 kilometers on our cycle, searching for work. Before we came here, the government was ready to pay us 5 lakh rupees. This was printed in the 'Pratidin' newspaper. What happened to that money? We were supposed to get 88 rupees per head (per day).[27]

---

[27] Conversation with Shabir Ali, Dinhata Camp, 15 December 2016.

The residents in the camp voted for the first time in India. Sujit Dev, a Haldibari resident recalls that he had voted once in Bangladesh, in the time of President Zia: 'There was no mention of enclaves. This was 20–25 years back. I voted as a Bangladeshi. No documents were required. My name was in the electoral roll. Everyone had their names. We were in Indian enclave, but we voted as Bangladeshi nationals. But after Zia, came Khalida, and since then we did not vote'. As far as the promises by politicians are concerned, there is an element of resignation and disappointment that having been brought to India the government seems to have given up its responsibility towards them: 'The government has brought us here, we are interested in what the government does, they are responsible for us. Who is the opposition here, who is not, we do not want to know, we listen to everyone'.

The Dinhata residents had been informally communicated that 16 bigha land had been kept aside for them in Dinhata subdivision. They were not sure if they would be given land or houses. In the absence of any official communication, they could only surmise. They understood that they would be allotted flats in two-storied houses, in which several families could reside. They had information that the government had only marked out the space for construction but had not acquired the land yet. The residents were keen that the flats should be allotted in a way where each family lived on a separate floor to prevent quarrels and acrimony. To have eight families staying in flats on a single floor would be very difficult, they said. Fights would ensue if they lived in close proximity with each other. It is interesting to see how the 'family' figured in the survey for identification of 'returnees' and in the subsequent rehabilitation process. We may recall that while updating the NRC in Assam, the 'family' became *simultaneously* an *object* of scrutiny for affirmation of legacy and *subject* to individuation through the extraction of suspect members. In the survey of the returnees from enclaves, their accommodation in camps and their eventual rehabilitation, the family became a unit for allocation of sustenance for disbursement of food and accommodation. In some cases this assumed the form of an aggregate unit where a number of nuclear families were treated for convenience as a cumulative singular unit.

In one such cumulated family in Dinhata camp, a 'single' 'undivided' family consisted of 9 to 10 members. This family consisted of two married and one unmarried brothers. There were other families with up to

14 members. These families, the residents said, needed to be split. When such aggregate families were registered as a single-family they were given a 'two room quarter', which is normally allotted to a family and 'one ration'. If the bigger families were counted as separate family units, they would become entitled to more ration—sufficient for their needs. A big family with three married brothers would be entitled to 90 Kilograms of ration rather than the 40 Kilograms they were presently receiving. Shabir Ali's family and his brother's family resided in two separate houses located at some distance from each other in the enclave. In the 2011 survey, they were listed as a 'single' family by the officials. Ali talks about their predicament:

> Bangladesh gave them some list of who was where, and the Indian part accepted it without cross checking the lists handed over to them. Whatever bluff Bangladesh wrote and provided to the Indian side, they accepted. Mezanul's son is now one and half years old, how did the list have the son's name in 2011? Mezanul and his brother had distant houses, Krishnam Adhikari and Sitam Adhikari had different households. How were they made one family. Here is this Mullah. Their family has a lot of members, but they ate separately, stayed separately—they were converted into one family.[28]

The enclave settlement in-charge explained the principle of distribution to us: Up to five members of a family would get ration of 30 kilograms of rice for one month, 5 kilograms of dal, mustard oil, one and a half kilograms of salt, one kilogram of milk powder, and 5 litres kerosene. A family of more than five members would get more, depending on the number of members in each family.

Mekhliganj camp residents too had voted on 27 May 2016 to elect their representative in the state assembly. For them too, this was not the first time they had voted. They had voted in Bangladesh. A camp resident told us: 'We did this cleverly. We were in Indian enclaves in Bangladesh. Our name fell under the Mekhligunj thana, India, booth number 147. Instead of voting there, we voted in our Dhapra side, in Chandrabhanga'. Residents complain about the shortage of space: 'We have not got rooms.

---

[28] Ibid.

We are a family of nine', says one resident. The family had been given only one room: 'Can that suffice? I have a father-in-law, sister-in-law, brother-in-law. My father-in-law is ill. Where do I keep my things, keep the kid, where do I dry the clothes of the kids. It is very difficult'.

The 'New' Citizens

With the LBAT 2015, it was agreed that when the exchange of enclaves took place, the people residing there shall have the right to continue staying if they desired and obtain the citizenship of the country to which the enclave had been transferred (Article 3 LBAT 1974). In preparation for the LBAT 2015, the Constitution 119th Amendment Bill 2013 was referred to a Standing Committee on External Affairs, which submitted its report on 21 December 2014. Among its various recommendations were those that pertained to the citizenship of persons who were impacted by exchange of enclaves:

> As per the Ministry, the inhabitants of the Bangladeshi Enclaves in India, which will be transferred to India under the Protocol, can be granted Indian citizenship under Section 7 of the Indian Citizenship Act, 1955 (by incorporation of territory). As per this provision, if any territory becomes part of India, the Central Government may by order notified in the Official Gazette, specify the persons who shall be citizens of India with effect from the date to be specified in the order.[29]

This procedure of conferment of citizenship under the provisions of the Citizenship Act of India was different from those who were 'returning' to India from the enclaves in Bangladesh, who were Indian citizens with the right to return. While explaining this position, the Home Secretary also informed that when these 'returnees' arrived in India, the government intended to take their biometric details:

---

[29] Standing Committee on External Affairs (2014–2015), 'First Report: The Constitution (One Hundred and Nineteenth Amendment) Bill, 2013', Lok Sabha Secretariat, New Delhi, 2014. http://www.prsindia.org/sites/default/files/bill_files/SCR-_119th_%28A%29_Bill_0.pdf, p. 15, cited in Lohia (2019, 18).

But when they come back, we intend to take the biometric details of all of them and carry out the entire exercise to ensure that we know who all are coming. Then in close cooperation and consultation with the Government of West Bengal, they will be taken to the respective places where they are proposed to be settled and there we will keep a close watch for some time.[30]

It is interesting that the 'mobile' Indian citizens were rendered suspect because of their former location within Bangladesh. As far as the Bangladeshi enclave dwellers located in the Indian territory were concerned, it was the district administration of Cooch Behar that was given the responsibility of eliciting their choice of citizenship and send the list to the Central government. In a 2019 report prepared for Forum Asia with Masum, Prachi Lohia points out that on 2 July 2015, directions were issued to the DM of Cooch Behar by the Central Government to record the names of Bangladeshi citizens who wished to acquire Indian citizenship and of Indian citizens who wished to renounce Indian citizenship.[31] A Ministry of Home Affairs notification dated 12 October 2015 stated that all the 14,864 Bangladeshi citizens residing in enclaves within Indian territory would be considered citizens of India from 1 August 2015. The enclave dwellers remained sedentary on their land to become the 'new' citizens of India. Yet, they had to wait for their formal absorption as citizens through documentation of their new identities even as they continued with their lives in which they had become informally integrated into the larger community. Lohia states that till 2019, when she completed her report, the District Magistrate of Cooch Behar had not 'notified the recipients of their citizenship' and they had not 'received any documents that explicitly confirmed their Indian nationality' (Lohia 2019, 19).

The *chhit* dwellers in Balipukhuri who made the transition to Indian citizenship felt that the Indian government had taken their votes but did not give them anything in return. There appeared to be a lack of trust of a different kind from what was witnessed among the camp residents in Dinhata, Haldibari, and Mekhliganj camps. While the camp residents had

---

[30] Ibid.
[31] The number of returnees as answered in the Lok Sabha by the Ministry of External Affairs on 4 May 2016. http://loksabhaph.nic.in/Questions/QResult15.aspx?qref=34008&lsno=16.

expressed their distrust of the survey, the chhit dwellers lamented that the funds given by the government for the development of the 'Chhitmahals' were being underutilized due to what they termed 'corruption'. A resident pointed out to a 2 km road which was being made with a fund of 2 crores and 67 lakh rupees, most of which he said would be diverted and laundered.

The biggest change that the transition to Indian citizenship brought to the lives of the former chhit dwellers was a re-articulation of their relationship with the Chhitmahals, especially with the land on which they had been living for generations. This re-articulation was not only because the land was designated Indian territory but the demand this designation placed on them to prove their relationship with their land with evidence of ownership: 'Our parents lived in the 'chhit' and we have spent half of our lives in the 'chhit' and now we have become 'Indians'. Previously, the land used to be in the name of our parents. We can show the documents. The land belonged to our fathers and forefathers. The land is still in the name of our parents. The ownership has not been still transferred to us'. Their parents had rights over the land and paid taxes to the jotedar in Patagram. 'But that was a different nation, then':

> Earlier also we had land. From our birth we have been living in the enclave, now also we live here. Now it is India, but we have been living here for ages. My parents have been living here too. Much of my life was in Bangladesh but now it is in India. But we have been living in the same place. We did not have citizenship then, but we had land of our fathers and forefathers who had been paying taxes to the jotedars in Patgram. Earlier the border was open. Now the land has not been transferred to us. The officials say land will be transferred and land deeds will be given to those who have control over land. We have said we have the documents and we have been paying taxes.[32]

The angst over dissociation from land in the case of the 'returnees' and the desire to confirm their association with land under the new legal regime brought by the transition to Indian citizenship for the enclave dwellers, was an enduring narrative. The fact that what they had always owned had

---

[32] Conversation with Hiren, erstwhile chhit dweller in Balipukhuri, 17 December 2016.

to now be 'transferred' to them was tantamount to estrangement. Despite possessing documents proving that they had paid taxes, the DM's Office, the chhit dwellers said, had not given them any assurance of transferring ownership. Indeed, in their verbal communications, the office considered their land 'khas jameen' or land which is owned by the government. With the exchange of territory, those that had been tilling the land of their 'forefathers' were asked to prove ownership. Others had to cut their trees or shift their houses to allow the government to build new roads and build a bridge to connect one chhit with another. The compensation which was promised was not given to them, they complained: 'It is because of our tenacity that we have been able to sustain ourselves here. In the past, many people have left the land due to the difficulties they have faced. But where will we go leaving our lands here? The remaining people stayed on, especially after 2015'.

An erstwhile chhit dweller in Balipukhuri tells us that almost 300 people belonging to 61 families in the chhit stayed on. The residents hoped that the change in the status of the chhit would help them surmount problems pertaining to admission in schools and getting jobs. Asha was visiting her maternal uncle's home in Balipukhuri chhit, from the adjoining Khuchlibari chhit. Born and brought up in the 'Chhitmahal', she recounted the disadvantages they had experienced in their daily lives because of the ambiguity of their status as a chhit dweller:

> Our life was difficult. It is very difficult to speak of those days. While remembering and talking about them, our eyes well with tears! Let us not go back to those days. Nowadays we are better—at least, we are fine for now. We have faced and tolerated all those things with utmost patience. We never disclosed our identities as residents of 'chhitmahal'! You can guess why. If people had come to know that we were from 'chhitmahal', we would have been denied every opportunity and not allowed in any sphere.[33]

Asha's eighty-year-old uncle had obtained 'higher education' but was compelled to do agricultural work for livelihood because he could not get a job. Asha was studying Bengali for her Master's degree in a college in Jalpaiguri. She did not disclose her identity as a resident of Chhitmahal to obtain admission:

---

[33] Conversation with Asha in Balipukhuri chhit, 17 December 2016.

Since they know the names of our parents, we have to change our parents' names and give names of some other persons impersonating as our parents. Now, after the exchange, those who are young can change the names of their parents yet again. But, for people like us who are older, it will be more difficult. I don't know if at all I will be able to change the names written in our graduation, secondary (madhaymik) and higher secondary (uccha madhyamik) examination. With much difficulty we were able to send our children to other people's homes in Jalpaiguri or Mekhligunj to study.[34]

Asha had given the address of an adjoining village to enrol for studies: 'I could not even give the name of my motherland!' After she completes her Master's degree, Asha wants to teach in a primary school, if one was set up in her village:

But as of now, I can't see anything coming up. Besides, there is also an ICDS (Integrated Child Development Scheme) centre. But, given the present situation, it is uncertain whether we will get an opportunity. Being resident of chhitmahal we are entitled to receive some facilities now. But, I am not sure whether we will get them. We should get some facilities, like people belonging to the Scheduled Castes.

Pulin Barman from Dhabalsuti Mirgipur chhit recalls that despite some problems, there was generally cooperation among 'the enclave and non-enclave people'. This was because we were 'living side by side'—there was 'consideration and also affection'.[35] The chhit dwellers were always conscious of their 'precarious status' and did not get involved in 'any tussle'. In Asha's village—Kuchlibari chhitmahal—57 families had been residing continuously since 'colonial times' on 700 acres of land which they tilled for subsistence. Balipukhuri village did not have electricity yet, but the process of electrification had begun with the installation of poles for supply. There was no supply of electricity in Kuchlibari. When Kuchlibari was still a Bangladeshi enclave, electricity supply lines were installed through it to supply electricity to an adjoining village in India:

[34] Ibid.
[35] Conversation with Pulin Barman, Mirgipur chhit, 17 December 2016.

They got electricity supply but we were deprived because we lived in chhitmahal. So, we had to take our own electricity supply forcefully. This happened around two years back. We were adamant that if electricity lines go through our village, we must have our share of electricity. Otherwise, no line could go through our village.[36]

The chhit residents received a Voter ID card, an Aadhaar card and digital ration cards when the chhits became part of the Indian territory. The state assembly election had concluded only recently in West Bengal—in May 2016—five months after the absorption of the chhit. Asha claimed that no political party and candidate came to them for their votes. The middlemen (*dalals*) came, however, in large numbers, with promises to get their work done. These middlemen, she alleged, forged their signatures, and claimed money from agencies. When asked who these middleman were, Asha could not tell, but she was sure they were 'outsiders' who came with a lot of 'information', and cheated the gullible elderly people in the village with assurances of money, jobs, public transport, and bus stands for their village. At the time of the field visit, the residents had still not received their MNREGA job cards, and the promised 100 days of work for each household. The idea that the land belonged to their forefathers recurred in our conversations with Asha. She complained that the road for which their land was taken was now being diverted to a different direction: 'Just a 2 km road will cost around 2 crores and 67 lakhs of rupees. The road was already present, but now they will just put sand and soil over it':

> The government is doing what it has to. The Prime Minister has given some crores of money for the enclaves. Someone said a small part of the land will be taken to build a road there. But no survey of land has taken place. They were supposed to build a bridge. But now they are only doing a bit of expansion of the earlier road itself. That road was always there, for decades. Now they will spread some mud around on two sides, and take away all the 2 crores rupees.[37]

---

[36] Conversation with Asha in Balipukuri chhit, 17 December 2016.
[37] Ibid.

Asha desists from blaming the political leadership in the Centre and the state and believes that the funds allocated for the 'chhitmahal', if utilized properly, would lead to the improvement of their condition. She believed that the compensation for the land acquired from them to build the road had been sanctioned by the Prime Minister, but had not reached them. The Chief Minister had also assured them that the people living in the 51 'chhitmahals' would receive electricity supply, roads, primary schools, anganwadi centres, and much more, and those who lost their land would be compensated adequately. These promises, she said were made because 'we, the people of 'chhitmahal' had organized protests and movements for quite a long time'. Asha refers in this context to the Chhitmahal Movement started by Dipak Sengupta in Dinhata in 1992, and steered by his son after Sengupta's death in 2009. This was also the year when Asha joined the movement. The main slogan of the movement was: 'Start exchange of chhitmahal immediately'. Sengupta went to Kolkata and Bangladesh to campaign for the cause: 'Dipak started the movement and we just helped him. We went to the protests, whether in the DM's office or in Kolkata to submit the deputation letters'. It was through channels that the movement had access to, that they came to know that the total money allocated for the 51 'chhitmahals' was 1500 crores of rupees. Their source of information was not the DM's office, but 'other channels': 'A schedule for the government's work comes out. If someone with appropriate knowledge goes through the schedule, one can know this. However, this is official—bound by secrecy, and cannot be made public. ... We know. We know how to get information and from where. The person, who has given us the leadership, goes to different places to get relevant news'. When the exchange happened in 2015, the residents of the chhits did not face any coercion or persuasion from the Bangladesh government to cross over to Bangladesh: 'Many of them, even, the DM had come from Bangladesh. They did not directly request us to remain with Bangladesh. They told us that it was entirely our choice. If we wanted to go, we could go, otherwise, we could stay'.[38]

In the erstwhile Dhabalsati Mirgipur enclave, Rohtas, a farmer like most residents of the enclave, tells us that his life was the same as before. Did the fact that he is now a citizen of India make any difference, we ask

[38] Ibid.

him. 'We continue to work and live the same way that our parents did. Some work on the land they own, and some on land owned by others'. The only difference was that they cast their vote in the state assembly elections, the first time in their life. The voter ID card and the Aadhaar cards were the first identity documents they received. A bank account with passbook was opened subsequently and ration cards were given to them—both after the election—informs Devyani Rai, a student. According to another resident, Pulin Barman, the distribution of ration on the ration card had begun a month back. Barman informs us: 'We had demanded the voter photo ID card first, and then the ration card. Bank accounts have been given. Now we have voted once. Some enclave dwellers had used Indian currency before, and some, who had school passing certificates, already had bank accounts'. In the sequencing of demands the prioritization of the voter ID card is indicative of not just the completion of their absorption that the voter ID signified by enabling them to exercise their political right to vote, it also suggests the effectiveness, in their perception, the demands would assume if they could collectively present themselves as a voting group. At another level, it also points at the various degrees of absorption that had already taken place for most enclave residents who had been residing there for generations. The compulsion to access schools and hospitals surreptitiously or through deception would no longer be there. Devyani Rai continued to study in the same school after the absorption of the enclave in India. What difference then had the transition to Indian citizenship made? To her, the possession of a ration card and the ease of access to hospitals was a major difference. Earlier, they 'managed' by concealing that they were from the enclaves, and gave the address of an Indian village upon hospitalization.

They all voted—all the 38 families in Mirgipur chhit with the cumulative vote of 112. Pulin Barman recalls that their leader Diptiman (name changed) had been saying for a long time that enclave exchange would happen: 'We were also hoping for a long time that the exchange will happen, since that would make things much easier'. A team from Bangladesh visited them and asked whether they wished to go to Bangladesh: 'We said we will stay here. We were born and brought up here, so why should we go'. The officers from India did not insist that they should stay here. While most residents of the chhits are farmers, around 50 of them, including Barman go to the city to work. Barman worked in

Pitam Pura in Delhi in a fibre plate manufacturing company. He confirms the problems people have faced with respect to getting papers to show land ownership:

> We have small bits of land, but we never had papers. The selling and buying happened by signing 10 rupee stamp papers. We are all poor. We sold our land to meet the expenses of our daughters' wedding. Now even that is becoming a problem since no one is buying our land. They are saying that the status of this land is unclear. It has become India's land and the government might take it over. There is no ownership document for us. Everyone knows who owns which land. Whoever is in possession of the land, it is their land. Now we are demanding that we should be given documents for our land as soon as possible. The DM's office has ordered that if anyone wants to buy or sell land immediately, they should apply to the DM's office to get an order. Since 2015, no one has been able to sell land. If we get our land papers, we won't have to look for people to buy our land. They will all come to buy. The district administration has been conducting a survey of land. They come once in three months, stay for a couple of hours and the *babus* then go away. They ask which land is whose. They have asked everyone. They have noted which land is under whose possession. But nothing has happened. They assured us that they will give us the land deeds after the survey is completed. This might take 3 years.[39]

Conclusion

In an official Press Information Bureau (PIB) release dated 15 March 2017 the Ministry of Home Affairs, probably for the first time in the various official texts pertaining to the LBAT, used the expression 're-turnees' to refer to those inhabitants of the erstwhile Indian enclaves in Bangladesh who chose to come to India when the exchange of territory happened in 2015.[40] The release was based on a response given by the

---

[39] Conversation with Pulin Barman, Mirgipur chhit, 17 December 2016.
[40] 'India Bangladesh Land Boundary Agreement (LBA)', Ministry of Home Affairs, Government of India, Press Information Bureau, Release dated 15 March 2017.

Minister of State for Home to a question in the Rajya Sabha.[41] Stating that the LBAT had 'necessitated development and integration of Bangladeshi enclaves in India and addressing issues of rehabilitation of returnees from Indian enclaves in Bangladesh', the Minister disclosed that the government had sanctioned 1005.99 crores of Rupees on 2 December 2015 'for the rehabilitation and up-gradation of infrastructure'. Out of this 898.50 crores had been allotted for creation and up-gradation of infrastructure and 107.49 crores for 'rehabilitation and construction of pucca houses for Indian returnees'. My visit to Cooch Behar had taken place almost a year after the allocation of funds had been made for the purposes indicated in the Minister's response. These funds were allotted to the state government for implementing the rehabilitation plan for a period of five years. Alongside the rehabilitation programme, the government had sanctioned barbed wire fencing to the extent of 3326.14 kilometres along the India-Bangladesh border. The fencing of 2731 kilometres had already been completed when the Minister made the statement in the Rajya Sabha. In November 2018, the West Bengal Assembly passed a Bill giving land rights to enclave dwellers. The West Bengal Chief Minister, Mamata Banerjee described the West Bengal Land Reforms (Amendment) Bill 2018 as a 'historic Bill' which would enable the enclave dwellers to acquire 'full-fledged status as citizens of India'. The process of allocation of land rights, Banerjee said, would lead to the creation of new administrative districts, while giving ownership of land to the dwellers, who were now 'residing on khas land'. While stating that this would require additional funds that would have to be put in by the state government, Banerjee made a distinction between the ease with which the process of integration of enclave dwellers as citizens had taken place and the exclusionary NRC in Assam which had produced statelessness among those left out.[42]

In 2016, Banglar Manabadhikar Surakhsa Manch commonly known as MASUM—an organization of social activists engaged in the protection of rights of the marginalized sections—filed a writ petition in Calcutta High

---

[41] The statement was made by the Minister of State for Home Affairs, Hansraj Gangaram Ahir in a written reply to a question by Shri Vivek Gupta in the Rajya Sabha on 15 March 2017.
[42] 'Bill to Give Land Rights to Enclave Dwellers in Bengal Passed', *The Indian Express*, 19 November 2018.

court pointing at the contradiction in the status of the 'new citizen' of the erstwhile chhits who did not have official documents confirming citizenship, but possessed identification documents such as the Aadhaar card and the voter ID card which had enabled them to vote in the Assembly election. MASUM filed a writ petition in the Calcutta High court in 2016 pointing at the anomalous situation where a person could be registered to vote without having become a citizen of the country. In its judgement dismissing the petition, the court appeared to suggest that the extension of citizenship to the enclave dwellers would be an outcome of scrutiny of applications for citizenship 'with reference to various aspects' that would have to be considered for its 'issuance'. Applicants may have different backgrounds, and facts pertaining to the date of residence in India would have to be ascertained—which would require each applicant to show 'when he came to this country, how he has come, from where he comes and through whom he has come. Unless these facts are analysed after due enquiry, citizenship cannot be considered'.[43] It is significant that the High Court appeared to be endorsing a process of identification for citizenship akin to the NRC process in Assam, which would require enclave residents to show documentary proof. Our conversations with the camp residents and enclave dwellers showed how in the perception of both the 'returnees' and the 'new citizens', citizenship was a spectrum on which narratives of loss and hope jostled for space. The choice of a political identity of citizenship was offered as a possibility of new life, which was experienced by the old and the new citizens differently. The mobility of the old citizens and the immobility of the new led in different ways for both, to processes of estrangement from land and identity. The experiences of estrangement and the legal resolution of citizenship presented a site of entangled possibilities, where notions of family, borders and belonging, and state and identity, assumed unfamiliar forms.

---

[43] W.P. No. 5859(W) of 2016, See Lohia (2019).

4
Recalling Citizenship
The Constitutional Ethic

On 21 December 2019, Varun Grover, a writer-poet-lyricist and stand-up comedian, posted a video on his Twitter handle. In this video, Grover had recited a poem titled 'Hum Kagaz Nahin Dikhayenge' ('We will not show our papers'). The video became viral and quickly assumed the status of an anti-NRC anthem for Indians protesting against CAA/NPR/NRC. Following Grover's declaration that he claimed no copyright to his creation, protestors modified its words, adapted it to different genres, and made it the rousing slogan of their movement. The refusal to show papers was presented in the poem as the culmination of several acts of defiance through which citizens would resist coercion by the state. All these acts were envisaged as exemplary display of civil disobedience in the face of the force that the state could unleash, and as faith in the power of peaceful resistance in a country which had come together to 'save the Constitution'.

The *Constitution*—as a performative text, as a historical legacy of ideas and icons integral to the national imagination, and as a source of consciousness of democratic citizenship—became a powerful idiom of protests that proliferated across the country after the enactment of the CAA in December 2019. As people read out the Preamble and held up its copies in sit-ins and rallies or displayed posters with the text of the Preamble inscribed on them, the Constitution became the most visible symbol of people's disquiet and popular churning. Two months into the protests, the Constitution also became a 'best seller'. A publisher, who earlier sold only a thousand copies of the Bare Act of the Constitution in a month, reported five-fold increase in sales. The paperback edition of the Constitution in Hindi became the 'number one best-seller' in the constitutional law category on Amazon. The owner of the publishing house which had been printing the Constitution of India in different sizes and updated versions for years, attributed the enhanced sales to the *universalization* of the Constitution's appeal. Whereas earlier it was 'the most popular book among the Dalits', 'people from all sections of society' were buying it now—they wanted to make sense of the removal of Article 370 and CAA—he explained in an interview.[1] It was not clear from the interview whether the publisher established the popularity of the Constitution among Dalits *empirically*, or inferred it from its association with B. R. Ambedkar. Yet, the allusion to its universalization in the present context was revealing since it pointed to the fact that people were buying *physical* copies of the Constitution and not just reading it online. Evidently, the popularity of the Constitution was not simply because people wanted to make sense of executive decisions and legislative processes, but also as a text which could be lobbed into the public space as an expression of fraternity and empathy—the core components of Ambedkar's idea of democratic citizenship. The installation of public spaces of protest through 'insurgent'[2] reading, 'postering', and 'posting' of the Constitution, produced a vocabulary of citizenship interlaced with the constitutional ethic, which persisted until Covid-19 became a pandemic. The 'pandemic effect' imposed a different order of public life and political practice, as the state acquired 'necessary' powers to put the people under a state of lockdown, and the protests folded up into the virtual space of political communication.

Interestingly, examples of the Constitution becoming an insurgent text abound and have resonated with people's resistance in other parts of the contemporary world. In June 2019, Olga Misik, a schoolgirl in Russia read out the constitutional rights of the Russian people listed in the Constitution in a pro-democracy rally in Moscow. Called to protest

---

[1] Manoj Sharma, 'CAA Stir Spurs Demands for Copies of Constitution', *Hindustan Times*, 10 December 2020.

[2] In his book *Insurgent Citizenship* (2010), James Holston uses the category 'insurgent' to refer to the relationship of entanglement between two kinds of citizenship in the urban peripheries of Sao Paolo—entrenched and insurgent. Insurgent citizenship is 'conjoined with the entrenched', but it also disrupts it as a counter politics, that destabilizes the present, and renders it fragile. While borrowing the idea of counter politics from Holston's framework, I use insurgent in the normative sense, whereby 'insurgent' as counter politics must be anchored in the appraisive content of democracy.

the suspension of freedom of association in the context of the deferral of the opposition's right to contest the upcoming Moscow City Duma elections, the 'lone figure' of Misik sitting cross-legged in front of a heavily armed, and 'notoriously brutal' Russian riot police, reading out from the Constitution, became almost as iconic as the figure of the 'lone man' facing a line of tanks in the Tiananmen Square in Beijing in the summer of 1989. Misik told newspapers that her intention was to communicate to the policemen that what they were doing was illegal, and it did not occur to her then that 'someone other than them would hear it'. Misik was detained soon afterwards—not from the protest site—but from a subway station close by, where there was no rally or crowds to witness it.[3] The protests around the CAA/NPR/NRC in India similarly reclaimed the Constitution. This reclamation took diverse forms which remained united in their recourse to the Constitution as a text through which the constituent moment could be recalled. This process was sutured to constitutional politics and resurrection of the promise of democracy embodied in the transformative moment of the constitution giving process.

The Constitution as an Insurgent Text: The 'People's Constitution'

The Constituent Assembly (CA) of India articulated the principle of popular sovereignty in the Objectives Resolution moved by Jawaharlal Nehru on 13 December 1946 in the claim that it 'derived from the people ... all power and authority'. The concept of the 'people' is central to the universalist imaginings of modernity. 'The people' is abstract but also historically specific and can be traced through diverse genealogies. In the transition to constitutional democracy in India, the *people* were constituted as the repository of sovereign power when they gave to themselves the Constitution on 26 November 1949—a Constitution that they had enacted through the Constituent Assembly. That the people also held constituent power was established emphatically through Article 395

---

[3] Colin Drury, 'Olga Misik: Teenage Girl Reads Constitution in Front of Putin's Riot Police During Moscow Protests', *The Independent*, 31 July 2019, https://www.independent.co.uk/news/world/europe/olga-misik-russia-protests-constitution-moscow-riot-police-putin-a9029816.html (accessed on 26 June 2020).

of the Constitution which repealed the Indian Independence Act (1947), severed all relations with colonial authority, and rejected the chain of validation which required that the Indian Constitution be placed before the Crown-in-Parliament for its approval (Swaminathan 2013). The electoral domain was another space where the *people* acquired meaning and form—constituted through a collective act of voting. The electoral domain made manifest the unfettered sovereign power of the people, achieved through the deferral of political authority concentrated in the state apparatus, to install a *constitutional* democracy (Gilmartin 2009).

The constitution was made 'popular' through different modalities which were part of the process of structuration of the state and the democratization of state power. In her work on the preparation of the electoral roll for the first general election in India on the basis of *universal* adult franchise, Ornit Shani suggests that the electoral roll became part of the 'popular narrative' connecting people to a democratic imagination of the state constrained by the Constitution. Shani argues that through a process of consultation, the Constituent Assembly Secretariat engaged public officials, people, and citizens association in the details of voter registration and citizenship, *mentoring* them into *both*—the abstract principle *and* practices of electoral democracy—so that 'people and administrators began using the draft constitution to pursue their citizenship and voting rights, and they linked its abstract text to their everyday lives' (Shani 2018, 252–253).

In a different formulation, Rohit De explores the relationship between 'the people' and the constitutional order and the nature of the social contract that validated this order, given that the people had only a 'limited role' to play in what was a largely oligarchic process of framing the Constitution (De 2018). De argues that rather than looking for the people in the Constitution or even in the modes through which the people were represented in the Constitution-making process, and its subsequent validation through elections, it would be more effective to see how people *looked at* the Constitution. This shift in vantage point enables one to understand the crucial ways in which the Constitution became *intelligible* to the people as a part of their daily lives. Quite like Shani's study of the conversations spun among people around a governmental activity of identification and enumeration of the voting population, which made the draft Constitution accessible to the people, De looks at specific instances where ordinary people invoked the Constitution to claim their fundamental rights. In one such instance, Mohammed Yasin, a vegetable vendor in a small town, who would otherwise have remained 'a nondescript bystander' witnessing the 'grand narratives of Indian history', became one of the first Indians to present himself before the Indian Supreme Court as a 'rights bearing citizen', to appeal to the court to issue an order to the local governmental authority to perform their functions properly (De 2018).

The Constitution has been archived in different forms and narrativized in different genres of art. Indeed, the constitutional text, as conserved in its original textual rendition, is both calligraphic and pictorial—a product of the combined labour of artists and calligraphers. Calligraphed by Prem Behari Narain Raizada and illustrated by Nandalal Bose and his students from Shantiniketan's Kala Bhavana, the handcrafting of the Constitution began when the draft Constitution was ready for printing. It took six months for the artists to complete the two copies of the handcrafted Constitution—in Hindi and English—which are preserved in a helium case in the Parliament Library in New Delhi.[4] Naman Ahuja (2020) argues that the illustrations in the Constitution preserved as a historical artefact, coalesce the historical people in a harmonious representation of the country's diversity, with the help of motifs from its mythical and textual past.[5] The juxtaposition of myth and history in a linear narrative of the past, argues Ahuja, may appear problematic to a modern reader of the Constitution but it generates 'productive tensions', which when inserted into the present, offer scope for 'succour and hope' (Ahuja 2020).

The 'original' Constitution has been resurrected in installations and live art performances in which the Constitution as a 'body of law' has found expression in spatial and embodied experience. Summoning the historical form of the Constitution in installation art to recall it in a contemporary space replete with 'vulnerabilities', Riyaz Komu's art exhibition 'Holy Shivers' gave form to emotions—of *fear*—of the violent present and uncertain future, and of *hope*—in the weight of the promises made in

---

[4] https://indianexpress.com/article/express-sunday-eye/handcrafted-constitution-india-6233517/; https://www.theheritagelab.in/constitution-india-art/; https://transfin.in/constitution-of-india-body-of-law-a-work-of-art#:~:text=Constitution%20as%20Work%20of%20Art,Survey%20of%20India%20in%20Dehradun (accessed 28 June 2020).

[5] Naman Ahuja, 'Can the Historic Art of Our Constitution Look to the Future', *Live Mint*, 20 January 2020, https://www.livemint.com/mint-lounge/features/can-the-historic-art-of-our-constitution-look-to-the-future-11579885322689.html (accessed on 28 June 2020).

the past. By invoking symbols from constitutional calligraphy and those that have become part of the narrative of India's constitutional democracy, Komu's installations took the form of a political critique of human aggression. Komu termed this aggression, 'militant enthusiasm'—an instinctive component of human psychology—to wreak destruction for a fictional cause.[6] In an innovative use of *mirror imaging* as a concept—to represent 'reflections/images' as an aspect of reflexivity—Komu set up digitally scanned original pages of the Constitution in collocation with x-rayed images receding into darkness, to evoke an imagery of what was being lost amidst the violence. In an evocative framing of 'Dhamma-Swaraj' through the juxtaposition of Ambedkar and Gandhi's portraits in successive panels which blend into each other and eventually appear inseparable, Komu suggested the relevance of both *in tandem* instead of unbridgeable binaries. Komu explained the juxtaposition as follows: '"Dhamma Swaraj", is an overlapping triptych portrait of Gandhi and Ambedkar that explores the interaction between two apparently disparate ideologies in the scope of a single frame.'[7] The figure of Ambedkar on a pedestal supported by iron legs, unusual for Ambedkar's figures that have taken a modular form , is without a copy of the Constitution in his hand, and not instructing nor showing the way forward, but raising both his hands in a gesture of reasoned argument.[8] The representation presents the possibility of a dialogic space around the Constitution, which produces communities driven by a different moral order, that is, of public conscience bound by empathy that makes the alleviation of human suffering its primary concern.

---

[6] Rahul Kumar, 'In Artist Riyas Komu's New Work, You Can See How Far India Has Drifted from Its Founding Ideals', *Scroll.in*, 8 February 2018, https://scroll.in/magazine/867176/in-artist-riyas-kumos-new-work-you-can-see-how-far-india-has-drifted-from-its-founding-ideals (accessed on 24 June 2020). Kumar writes: 'The title of the show references a theory of Austrian zoologist and ethologist, Konrad Lorenz, which is shared in his book *On Aggression*. According to Lorenz, the tendency or willingness to kill or be killed in defense of one's community physically manifests in the tingling sensation in the spine or the raising of hair on an animal's back as the first step in a fight with an enemy. Lorenz's idea of "militant enthusiasm" refers to the act of eliciting participation for destruction for a fictional yet ideal cause in the service of the contriver's aims.'

[7] Ashlin Mathew, 'Silence is a Powerful Enemy of Social Justice', *National Herald*, 11 March 2018, https://www.nationalheraldindia.com/art/silence-is-a-powerful-enemy-of-social-justice (accessed on 28 June 2020).

[8] See for a discussion on Dalit symbolism and caste icons, especially the portrayal of Gandhi as a national and Ambedkar as a 'particular' icon Wankhede (2010).

The reproduction of the Constitutional text as images arranged in a visual constellation produces different effects. The *re-cognition* of the text from a 'distant' legal text to 'text image' configured in a familiar space, the Constitution acquires new relationships with those who look at the images, and evokes sensory experiences different from its 'legal/textual' form. The passage from the cognitive to the somatic makes way for a different universe of the representation of law. Writing about the 'pictorial turn' or visualization of communication, Boechme-Neßler (2011) argues that the relationship between law and art is reciprocal—it is not just images *in* the law which change the law, but images which society makes *of* the law, which also change its meanings. The cultural environment in which these meanings take effect play an important part in shaping 'the people' (Boechme-Neßler 2011, 51, 119). Public performances, whether or not the spectator is invited to participate, produce a 'visceral somatic' effect—producing tangible resonances—shaping an emotional citizenship. Empathetic citizenship generated through an act of seeing as a participant in the affective public space is bound by emotion that produces appraisive political engagement (Miller 2011) and relational experiences of being citizens (Wood 2013). The geographies of affect imbricated in emotional citizenship have the property of reproducing beyond the proximate physical space. 'The Walk'—a performance by Maya Rao[9] on the Delhi gang rape, for example, became the inspiration for an installation performance—'The Walk'—created in South Africa in 2013, as a response to the gang-rape and murder of a young black woman. The play followed the performance by Maya Rao and took the form of a series of performed installations, which involved the audience walking among them, and combined live and recorded performance and sound.[10] Sara Matchett, Senior Lecturer in the Drama Department of the University of Cape Town, South Africa, and Artistic Director of The Mother Tongue Project, a women's arts collective, wrote of her experience of Rao's performance:

---

[9] Maya Rao is a Kathakali dance exponent, theatre performer, and street theatre activist, engaged in theatre in education campaign. See also Dutt (2015) for an analysis of Rao's performance as protest.
[10] http://www.mothertongue.co.za/index.php/productions/past-productions/walk

It's hard to articulate what was evoked in me.... It was most definitely not a cognitive experience, but rather a visceral somatic one.... I feel very tearful, deeply moved and somewhat internal. Words are unable to express this felt sense. It's like you pulled me inside you, into your core. And from this place your call placed itself in me, to continue and extend the call ... I realised, viscerally, how through the performance we have made in South Africa, we carry your legacy. I realised how big the work is. I've always known how important it is, but somehow yesterday I was struck differently. These works in conversation make somatic sense. The resonances are palpable.[11]

On 3 January 2020, a march in Jantar Mantar in Delhi against the CAA organized by LGBTQI groups brought together women's organizations, women trade unions, autonomous groups, and women not associated with any group, in the streets of Delhi.[12] Maya Rao read out the Preamble of the Constitution while draping the sari, presenting 'an aesthetics' of protest which she said 'derived from the urgency of the moment' (Sahai 2020). Rao explained her performance: 'Every time one can approach the Preamble from a different lens. In the context of the women's march, I wanted to create devices that speak to women, and can be read with ease. The sari is not just a garment, it is layered socially and culturally. Many women wear the sari from girlhood till the day they die, and for an Indian woman, it is often a layering of her own skin'. While the sari in its multiple modes of draping and textures represents the diversity inherent in 'Indian tradition', it also manifests the trope of unity in the seamlessness of the garment itself. Significantly, this seamlessness expressed itself in the powerful display of unity 'spoken' through women's garments by the women of Shaheen Bagh, who had been agitating against the CAA and were also part of this protest. The women strung their *dupattas* together, and passed them around, with the participants and the performing artists 'adding to them and holding them tightly as a rope, creating a motif of collective expression' (Sahai 2020). Viewing the performance from the perspective of artistic aesthetics and method of 'making art', this was an

[11] http://mayakrishnarao.blogspot.in/p/street-theatre.html (accessed 30 May 2018).
[12] https://www.thehindu.com/entertainment/art/maya-rao-leads-the-way-in-art-uprising/article30521874.ece https://www.shethepeople.tv/news/women-trans-queer-citizens-march-caa/ (accessed 27 June 2020).

exemplary moment where art was made extemporaneously, 'almost in a folk form manner' (Rao in Sahai 2020). Yet, 'art making' was also special as a 'protest event'—where the high passion of large numbers present was channelled into what Rao called 'uplifting, thought-provoking collaborative art' (Sahai 2020).

Citizen Democracy

The movement against the CAA/NPR/NRC rallied around the symbols of the Republic to protest against the politics of Hindutva for the elaboration of democratic citizenship. The centrality of the Constitution of India in this elaboration made the movement around the CAA a 'critical' event. An event, according to Veena Das becomes critical if it holds out the possibility of a 'new modality of historical action' (Das 1995, 5). As a 'critical event' the movement against the CAA elaborated an ethics of political action, in which the constraints of the present were alleviated though an accumulation and aggregation of practices of signification. In such practices, the Constitution became a trope and a metaphor invoked in different sites in spectacular and quotidian ways to invoke democratic citizenship.

In the literature on transformative constitutionalism (Baxi 2013, Vilhena et al. 2013, Bhatia 2019), constituent moments are seen as both events and processes, prompting us to look at the constitution-giving, and if one may add, constitution-claiming processes as a deeply moral experience. The literature on comparative constitutionalism locates the constituent moment in countries that emerged out of a struggle against colonialism and authoritarianism in their histories of transition to the 'magnificent goal' of democracy (Baxi 2013). The central motif of transformative constitutionalism is a conscious and meticulous re-figuration of the relationship with the past (Mehta 2010). In this framework, constitutions embody the momentous present from where a vision of a democratic future could be professed. This vision aimed specifically to repudiate and transform 'legacies of injustice' (Bhatia 2019); passage through the constituent moment ensured that the atavistic bonds of 'blood, territory, and historical hurt' were replaced by bonds of fraternity as a defining feature of citizenship. Yet, the transformative is a continuous process. The Preamble of the interim Constitution of South Africa characterized the transition to constitutional democracy in terms of the 'traditional metaphor of a bridge' (Langa 2006, 353). The metaphor suggested that the Constitution was not a terminal point in the journey towards democracy. The bridge as 'a space between an unstable past and an uncertain future' was continually created by 'remaining on it, crossing it over and over to remember, change and imagine new and better ways of being'. In this perspective, transformation was 'a permanent ideal':' ... a way of looking at the world that creates a space in which dialogue and contestation are truly possible, in which new ways of being are constantly explored and created, accepted and rejected and in which change is unpredictable but the idea of change is constant' (Langa 2006, 354).

In their distinctive ways the diverse strands in the movement against the CAA/NPR/NRC were opening up the spaces for both 'dialogue and contestation' (Langa 2006) summoning popular sovereignty for the reconstruction of democratic politics. Through these modalities, they sought to go beyond the conception of 'public reason' found in John Rawls (1993) who emphasized the importance of dialogue among citizens over a 'constitutional consensus' on democratic procedures and institutions to be secured by a civic political culture. The protestors invoked the idea of 'public conscience' found in B. R. Ambedkar. Public conscience for Ambedkar meant 'a conscience which becomes agitated at every wrong, no matter who is the sufferer', and that 'everybody, whether he suffers that particular wrong or not, is prepared to join him in order to get him relieved' (Ambedkar 1952). With the elaboration of an idea of public conscience, Ambedkar's notion of constitutional morality characterized by the habit of 'pacific criticism' of the state under conditions of self-restraint, met a different ethic of public action and principle of social solidarity, which was based on trust and empathy. This ethic of public action guided by empathy was displayed when the women of Shaheen Bagh sat in a dharna on 15 December 2019 following the forced entry and subsequent violence by the Delhi police in Jamia Millia Islamia University campus in Delhi in pursuit of students protesting against the CAA. The women of Shaheen Bagh set in motion a process whereby 'the city street' assumed ubiquity as the space where 'new forms of the social and political [could] be *made*' (Sassen 2011, 574). Writing about the importance of 'public space' for giving 'rhetorical and operational openings' to the 'powerless', Sassen sees the city as the critical space where the powerless can make history. By becoming present and visible to each other, the powerless, alter the character of powerlessness: 'Powerlessness is not simply an absolute condition that can be flattened into the absence of power. Under certain conditions, powerlessness can become complex, by which I mean that it contains the possibility of making the political, or making the civic, or making history' (Sassen 2011).

In December of another year—2012 to be precise—protests over the rape of a young woman in Delhi surged in the city. After their sudden appearance in the high security Raisina Hill, the protestors moved to Rajpath at the India Gate. Known as the King's Way when India was a colony, the Rajpath is a site where an annual display of military power and the cultural heritage of India, takes place on 26 January, the day the Constitution of India came into force in 1950. The Boat Club and India Gate lawns along the Rajpath, where people watch the spectacle of the Republic, were also often sites embodying the 'sphere of appearance' (Arendt as quoted by D'Entreves 1994, 104), where the people claimed the Rajpath to express their discontent through speech and persuasion. In the early 1990s, a government order made Rajpath out of bounds for political rallies and demonstrations in the interest of national security and public order. Rajpath was purged of the people and restored to the state. The people and their tents were shifted to Jantar Mantar, adjoining the Connaught Place, and then again to a more constrained space at the Mandir Marg-Shankar Road crossing, where people could sit in after obtaining permission from the local police station. The progressive constraining and confinement of public dissent to designated spaces—to a virtually five and a half yards of democracy from the mammoth possibilities offered by the vast stretches of the India Gate lawns and Boat Club—is symptomatic of the manner in which a security state reinforces itself through the affirmation of power by force (Roy 2014). Following the protests around the gang rape, the government invoked section 144 of CrPC, which restricts public gathering, making the region around India Gate and Rajpath out of bounds for the people.

If the December 2012 protests were about claims to public places to make them visible through public presence, the protests associated with the anti-CAA movement were more about making *public*, spaces that were familiar in the lives of the local people. The *chowks, chaurahas, baghs,* and significant signposts of old city scape, such as the *ghantaghar* (clock tower) from which a chowk would get its name, became spheres of appearance. Shaheen Bagh was one such familiar place—a neighbourhood—in the proximity of Jamia Millia Isamia, close to the border of Delhi with NOIDA in Uttar Pradesh. Over the course of the protests, Shaheen Bagh, a place name, became a metaphor for citizen democracy. Drawing from the idioms of Gandhian satyagraha as voluntary suffering, local Muslim women gathered in the street on 15 December 2019—where they stayed till the pandemic lockdown began in the last week of March in 2020—to 'protect the future of their children'. Rajvi Desai described the sit-in as follows:

> On a silent, empty street in Delhi, straddling the boundary between the capital and its suburb of Noida, past numerous police barricades and amid small, winding alleys, lies a phenomenon never before seen in Indian society. Within an almost impenetrable wall of men, thousands of Muslim women, some as old as 82, sit underneath a makeshift tent, often with their children cradled in their laps, one eye on a wandering toddler and the other toward a stage on which activists deliver battle cries of the impending revolution. They sit in protest, most of them seven days a week, 24 hours a day, because the BJP-led government has compelled them to sleep on the streets, they say; because there's nothing else left to do, they lament; because their children need them and because they'd rather die than be anywhere else, they proclaim. *This is Shaheen Bagh.* (Desai 2020, emphasis added)

The deployment of motherhood as a trope to 'shame' the state resonates the invocation of political motherhood in other contexts—largely authoritarian regimes where enforced disappearances were used as a mode of regime sustenance. The mothers' movement launched by fourteen Argentinian women in April 1977 is one such example. The mothers' march to the Plaza de Mayo in front of the Presidential Palace in Buenos Aires in Argentina demanding information about their sons who had 'disappeared' under the authoritarian military regime since 1975, continued unabated as a weekly march till 2006. The movement inspired the song 'Mothers of the Disappeared' by the Irish Rock band U2. Part of their 1987 album *The Joshua Tree,* the song was a tribute to the disappeared persons under dictatorships in Argentina and Chile, but was also a critique of the support Ronald Regan's administration gave to these regimes. While the slogan *nunca mas* (never again) reflected the mothers' resolute defiance of a powerful state through peaceful protest, it also opened up a register of emotional citizenship along an axis of affect.

The performance of affect by the local Muslim women in Shaheen Bagh, hitherto considered politically disengaged, became encompassing to bring into its fold broader solidarities to speak a shared language of *empathy as citizenship*. The wooden stage set up in the enclosure where the women sat, displayed portraits of B. R. Ambedkar, Bhagat Singh, and M. K. Gandhi, resonating the Dhamma-Swaraj invocation in Komu's art installation. Amidst allegations that the women were being paid by the opposition parties and petitions in courts for the removal of the sit-in for blocking the road and causing hardships to commuters and businesses, Shaheen Bagh became *the* public stage of appearance where ordinary people and political leaders flocked to identify with the cause. In January 2020, almost a month after he was arrested and subsequently released on conditional bail for leading an anti-CAA protest in Jama Masjid in Delhi, the Bhim Army chief Chandrashekhar Azad spoke from the 'rickety stage' of Shaheen Bagh holding a copy of the Constitution in his hand. Before ending his speech with a stanza from the revolutionary poem 'Sarfaroshi ki Tamanna', Azad reminded the gathering that they had the right to protest peacefully. In this protest, it was the Constitution which would be their protective armour, their *suraksha kavach*. On one side was the entire might of the state; and on the other, the Constitution—*Ek taraf poori hukumat, puri takat aur ek taraf yeh Constitution.*[13] Shaheen Bagh as an idea and idiom of protest proliferated in other parts of the country—from Sabzzi Bagh, Phulwari Sharif, and Mangal Talab in Patna, through Shanti Bagh in Gaya, Hussainabad Clock Tower in Lucknow to Park Circus Maidan in Kolkata, the protests were replicated all over the country. In Ahmedabad a woman held a placard that expressed the anxieties of those who had gathered in the protest as follows: 'My documents were burned in 2002 riots, *ab kagaz kahan se laaye* (where do we get our papers from)'.[14]

---

[13] Somya Lakhani, 'Rickety Stage, Faulty Mike, but Chandrashekar Azad's Loud and Clear at Shaheen Bagh', *Indian Express*, 23 January 2020.
[14] 'Ahmedabad: Inspired by Shaheen Bagh, Rakhiyal Area Stages CAA Protest', *The Wire*, 17 January 2020.

This animation of constitutional we-ness was not confined to the Muslims of India who expressed both anxiety and anger at the articulation of faith-based citizenship which departed from republican citizenship of the foundational moment. Broad alliances and solidarities were evident in unprecedented 'irruptions' (Holston 2007) across the country that sought to consciously reject religious identification as the basis of belonging. These irruptions recalled the constitutional ethics for generating a 'we-consciousness' through democratic dialogue and participation and also for instilling a 'sense of belonging' that bind people in a shared life.

'Have you read the Constitution?'

On 20 December 2019, Chandrashekhar Azad of the Bhim Army was arrested by Delhi Police for leading and organizing an 'unauthorised' protest at Jama Masjid. In this protest, Azad read out the Preamble of the Constitution and criticized the Prime Minister for not listening to the voices of the women in Shaheen Bagh. While delivering his speech Azad also recited lines from Rahat Indori's sher/poem: '. . . sabhi ka khoon shaamil hai yahan ki mitti mein, kisi ke baapka Hindustan thodi hai' (this land has witnessed sacrifices from everyone/Hindustan is not anyone's ancestral property), invoking we-consciousness based on shared history of sacrifices made by the people. This was the second time in the recent past that Indori's sher/poem was read out as an indictment of the BJP regime, the other being Mohua Moitra's inaugural speech as an MP in the Lok Sabha in July 2019. Azad's bail petition heard by Justice Kamini Lau at the Tees Hazari Court in Delhi was opposed by Delhi Police on the ground that he had organized a protest from Jama Masjid to Jantar Mantar for which the Delhi Police had denied permission. The judge granted bail to Azad referring to the Supreme Court's order whereby repeated use of Section 144 of CrPC was construed as abuse of law. The judge was reported in newspapers as having asked the public prosecutor to show her the law which prohibited someone from protesting outside religious places. In what was construed as a firm indictment of the police, Justice Kamini Lau finally asked the public prosecutor, 'Have you read the constitution?': 'In the colonial era, the protests were out on the roads. But your protest can be legal, inside the courts. Inside the Parliament, things that should have been said were not said, and that is why people are out on the streets. We have full right to express our views but we cannot destroy our country', she said.[15] Azad was given conditional bail the following day. A few days before the order in Azad's bail petition, a Delhi High Court bench of Chief Justice D. N. Patel and Justice C. Hari Shankar had refused a plea which had asked the court to issue directions for the removal of the Shaheen Bagh sit-in to a designated place to alleviate the inconvenience it was causing to large numbers of people, especially those who wished to access hospitals in NOIDA and Delhi.[16]

Amidst police crackdown, another judgment, this time by the Aurangabad Bench of the High Court of Bombay upheld the constitutional right of the people to protest against the CAA. The order came in response to a petition by residents of Majalgaon in Beed district in Maharashtra to be allowed to 'hold peaceful demonstrations and agitations' at old Idgah Maidan for an 'indefinite period' in the evening from 6 pm to 10 pm. On 31 January 2020, the Additional Magistrate of Beed issued orders to address apprehensions pertaining to 'law and order' problems emerging due to agitations by political parties and associations that had resorted to 'blockade of roads, taking out morchas, etc., for many causes including protest against the Citizenship Amendment Act (CAA)'. The Additional Magistrate's order mentioned the following 'specific possible agitations': (a) Farmers who had suffered damage to their crops due to excessive rains were 'likely to start agitations' through their associations; (b) Political parties and social organizations could start an agitation because of an increase in the prices of essential commodities; (c) Persons belonging to Dhangar, Muslim, Bhoi, and other communities 'were likely to start agitation for getting some social protection'; (d) 'The people of *all religions* were likely to start agitations to show protest against CAA'. In order to prevent these agitations that were 'likely' to take place, the district administration disallowed 'carrying arms', 'sloganeering, singing [and] beating drums'.

The judges noted that although the district administration's order was of a general nature, it appeared to be specifically against those who wanted

---

[15] 'Have You Read the Constitution?' Asks Judge as Delhi Police Oppose Bail for Aazad', *The Wire*, 14 January 2020.
[16] 'Delhi HC Dismisses Plea Seeking Removal of Anti-CAA Protestors at Shaheen Bagh', *The Hindu*, 10 January 2020.

to agitate against the CAA, since these agitations were already happening everywhere, and there was not even a 'whisper' of agitations of any other nature in the region. The judges concluded 'that there was no fairness and the order was not made honestly'. Taking note of the fact that the constitutionality of the CAA had been challenged in the Supreme Court, the Judges stated that they were not concerned about the content of CAA, but only the question of permissibility of agitations against the CAA. Holding the 'main order' of the Additional District Magistrate illegal, the judges 'quashed and set [it] aside' along with the order subsequently made by the police station of Majalgaon. The court instructed the district authorities to give the 'necessary protection' to those who wanted to agitate, who the judges stated would be permitted to do so. While giving permission to the agitators to sit on an indefinite *dharna* in the Old Idgah Maidan, the court noted the undertaking that had been given by them that 'no slogans will be raised against the country, against any religion, against the unity and integrity of the country'.[17]

In 1952 in the case *West Bengal vs. Anwar Ali Sarkar*, in which a constitution bench went into the question of 'constitutional prohibitions' contained in Article 14 of the Constitution, Justice Vivian Bose opined that a judge must 'look straight into the heart of things'. Justice Bose found it 'impossible' to read the provisions of liberty, freedom, and equality in the Constitution, 'without regard to the background out of which they arose'.[18] He stressed:

> I cannot blot out their history and omit from consideration the brooding spirit of the times. (T)hese portions of the Constitution ... are not just dull, lifeless words static and hide-bound ... but, living flames intended to give life to a great nation and order its being, tongues of dynamic fire, potent to mould the future as well as guide the present. (The State of West Bengal vs Anwar All Sarkarhabib 1952 AIR 75, 1952 SCR 284, paragraph 98)

---

[17] Order delivered by Justice M. G. Sewlikar and Justice T. V. Nalawade on 13 February 2020 in writ petition no. 903 cri wp 223.20 brought by Iftekhar Zakee Shaikh, a resident of Majalgaon against the state of Maharashtra and the civil and police administration of Beed district.

[18] Supreme Court of India, *The State of West Bengal vs Anwar Ali Sarkar*, judgement delivered on 11 January 1952, AIR 1952 SC 75.

The Aurangabad bench of the Bombay High Court too, while setting aside the ADM's order, invoked constitutional prohibitions to constrain arbitrary power. Justice Bose was scrutinizing the West Bengal Special Court Act 1950 against the provisions of Article 14 of the Constitution and differed from other judges on the bench on the modalities and grounds on which the prohibitions would apply. While doing so he put his confidence in the 'collective conscience' of the Republic and its representation in 'fair-minded' and 'reasonable men' who would protect the liberties of people without any 'prejudice':

> The test under Art. 14 is neither classification nor whether there is absolute equality in any academical sense of the term but whether the collective conscience of a sovereign democratic republic as reflected in the views of fair-minded, reasonable, unbiased men, who are not swayed by emotion or prejudice, can consider the impugned laws as reasonable, just and fair and regard them as that equal treatment and protection in the defence of liberties which is expected of a sovereign democratic republic in the conditions which obtain in India to-day. (Judgement, Anwar Ali Sarkar 1952)

Writing about court judgements as a 'compelling genre', Kalyani Ramnath speaks of the importance of 'judicial observations' in judgements which may not be part of the operative order, but leave a legacy which becomes 'instrumental in the shaping of public discourse'. Through these observations, judgements speak to 'multiple audiences' and 'maybe read not merely as judicial orders directed at the parties in the case but as writing that inspires, creates and shapes textual and actual realities' (Ramnath 2011, 3). While judicial observations may often be seen as 'unnecessarily verbose' and 'runaway', they articulate 'constitutional visions at a particular point in the Court's history, its place and importance vis-à-vis its public', and also 'create possibilities to formulate strategies by which laws and courts can be a site for resistance and empowerment' (Ramnath 2011). The judicial observations made by Justice M. G. Sewlikar and Justice T. V. Nalawade of the Aurangabad bench of Bombay High Court, while operatively quashing the ADM's order denying permission for protests, looked for reasons in constitutionalism and the rule of law, and the legacy of the freedom movement that made the Republic intelligible to the people. The judges started from the premise that the Constitution gave the 'rule of law' and not 'rule of majority' to acknowledge the possibility that any law may be perceived by 'a particular religion', in this case 'Muslims', to be 'against their interest'. While the Court could not go into the merits of that perception, it was 'bound to see whether these persons have right to agitate' and 'oppose the law'. Once the court 'finds' that agitating is 'part of their fundamental right', it was not its responsibility to 'ascertain whether the exercise of such right will create law and order problem': 'That is the problem of a political government. In such cases, it is the duty of the Government to approach such persons, have talk with them and try to convince them'. Significantly, in an order delivered on 17 February 2020, the Supreme Court had also emphasized the need for communication with the protestors in Shaheen Bagh and appointed a three-member committee to act as 'interlocutors' to help lift the impasse. In the Idgah case too, the judges reminded the government of its responsibility to convince the people. Importantly, however, the judges also felt, that it would be wrong to presume that it was 'only a particular community or religion' that was interested in opposing the CAA, especially since the ADM's order had mentioned that 'persons of all religions' had started the agitation. The possibility that 'many persons of all the communities' may feel that the law is 'against the interest of mankind, humanity or the basic human values', persuaded the judges to locate the sentiment in 'the history of the constitution', and sense of *fraternity* that 'the freedom struggle' had instilled in the journey towards the Republic:

> In preamble, there is a mention of fraternity. *The circumstance that the persons of other communities, religions are supporting the minority community show that we have achieved fraternity to great extent.* Doing something against this will hurt the fraternity and will create danger to the unity of the country. (Order dated 13 February 2020, petition no. 903 Cri WP 223.20, emphasis added)

In addition, the court acknowledged the right of the people to 'express their feelings' as provided under Article 19 of the Constitution if they felt that the Act was against 'equality' assured by Article 14 of the Constitution and prevented their enjoyment of 'life' under Article 21 of the Constitution. The ADM's order could be construed as a 'breach' of fundamental rights. Locating the agitations again in the history of the freedom struggle, the judges held the view that 'non-violent and peaceful protests' were 'not against the constitution', and were the way India had 'won her freedom'. The agitators could not be called 'traitors' and 'anti-nationals' for opposing the law:

> We are fortunate that most of the people of this country still believe in non-violence. In the present matter also the petitioners and companions want to agitate peacefully to show their protest. In British period our ancestors fought for freedom and also for the human rights and due to the philosophy behind the agitations, we created our constitution. It can be said that it is unfortunate but the people are required to agitate against their own Government now but only on that ground the agitation cannot be suppressed.... *This Court wants to express that such persons cannot be called as traitors, anti-nationals only because they want to oppose one law. It will be act of protest and only against the Government for the reason of CAA.* (Order dated 13 February 2020, petition no. 903 Cri WP 223.20, emphasis added)

Elaborating on the importance of 'dissent of the people', the judges reminded the government that it needed to be 'sensitive when it exercises powers given by law':

> Unfortunately, many laws which ought to have been scrapped after getting freedom [have] continued and the bureaucracy is exercising the powers given under those laws and now against the citizens of free India. The bureaucracy needs to keep in mind that when the citizens who believe that [a] particular act is an attack on their rights which were achieved by freedom struggle and when it is against the provisions of constitution which people have given to themselves, they are bound to defend that right. If they are not allowed to do so, the possibility of use of force is always there and the result will be violence, chaos, disorder and ultimately the danger to the unity of this country. That seriousness needs to be kept in mind by the bureaucracy while making such orders. This Court is observing with all possible seriousness that officers from bureaucracy who are vested with powers of aforesaid nature need to be sensitized by giving them proper training on human rights which are

incorporated as fundamental rights in the constitution. (Order dated 13 February 2020, petition no. 903 Cri WP 223.20)

Among the protections afforded by the courts to anti-CAA 'agitators' was the Rajasthan High Court's order in a petition against an FIR filed by the Rajasthan Police against protestors in Udaipur on 29 January 2020. In its order of 12 February, the court issued a notice to the state government and restrained the police from taking any action against the petitioners till the next hearing. The protest had been organized by what the petition described as 'practicing advocates, retired police officers, and social activists, among others', under the aegis of Bahujan Kranti Morcha, for which permission had been obtained from the administration. Yet, the petitioners alleged, the police used 'excessive power' against them and did not allow them to 'enter the Bapu market area on the scheduled day of the protest'. The petitioners accused 'an unknown person, not part of their group' of 'intentionally raising slogans like '*Hindustan mein rehna hai toh Jai Shri Ram kehna hoga*' (If you wish to stay in India, you need to say Jai Shri Ram) during the march, after which the police got a legitimate reason to crack down on the protesters'.[19]

Democratic Iterations

The robust opposition to the CAA in the Rajya Sabha, where the pro-CAA numbers eventually prevailed with a narrow margin, reverberated in the state assemblies. In an iteration of the federal process, the legislatures of states ruled by parties that had opposed the CAA in the Parliament resolved not to implement it in their states. On 31 December, the Left Democratic Front government (LDF) in Kerala led by Pinarayi Vijayan passed a resolution against the CAA in the state assembly and put a stay on the NPR process in the state. In a significant move, the state of Kerala filed a suit in the Supreme Court of India challenging the constitutional validity of the CAA under the provisions of Article 131 of the Constitution. Under this Article the Supreme Court has original jurisdiction in a dispute

---

[19] 'Rajasthan HC Pulls Up Police for Coercive Action against Anti-CAA Protesters', *The Wire*, 15 February 2020.

between the Centre and a state government, if the dispute involved 'any question (whether of law or fact) on which the existence or extent of a legal right depended'. In its plea before the Supreme Court, filed on 13 January 2020, the government of Kerala argued that the compulsion to implement the CAA and the Passport (Entry into India) Rules and Foreigners Order, which the state government considered 'manifestly arbitrary and unconstitutional', had resulted in a 'legal dispute' between the state and the Centre in which questions of legal rights were involved:

> In accordance with the mandate of Article 256 of the Constitution, the Plaintiff State will be compelled to ensure compliance of the provisions of the Impugned Amendment Act, the Impugned Passport Rules Amendments and the Impugned Foreign Order Amendments, which are manifestly arbitrary, unreasonable, irrational and violative of fundamental rights under Articles 14, 21 and 25. Thus, there exists a dispute, involving questions of law and fact, between the Plaintiff State of Kerala and the defendant Union of India, regarding the enforcement of legal rights as a State and as well for the enforcement of the fundamental, statutory, constitutional and other legal rights of the inhabitants of the State of Kerala. Hence, this Original Suit under Article 131 of the Constitution is being led.[20]

Saskia Sassen (2011) and Aihwa Ong (2006) see the urban street and the cyberworld as spaces of citizenship formation and performance, where diverse groups may come together as epistemic communities to protest against the state and demand an end to corruption, nepotism, and autocratic rule. Seyla Benhabib (2007) stresses the need for a different kind of resistance, which she calls a politics of democratic iterations, referring to complex processes of public deliberations which take place in institutions of the state and civil society. The sites at which democratic iterations can take place are the entrenched and structured political and representative public institutions like the legislatures, decision-making bodies like the executive and the judiciary, as well as in what Benhabib calls the 'informal' and 'weak' publics of civil society associations and the media.

---

[20] 'State of Kerala Files Suit in SC Against Union Govt Challenging Citizenship Amendment Act', *Live Law.in*, 14 January 2020.

With the iterative processes set in motion by the Kerala government, which may be seen as a continuum of the 'political' created in the streets, several states followed suit. The Congress-ruled Punjab Assembly passed a resolution on 17 January 2020 seeking repeal of the CAA by the Central government, arguing that it was an attack on the secular fabric of the country. Stating that the contexts surrounding its passage were reminiscent of Germany under Hitler in the 1930s, the Chief Minister sent a copy of the *Mein Kamph* to Sukhvinder Singh Badal of the Shiromani Akali Dal (SAD), the main opposition party in the state and an NDA ally, to stress his point.[21] In addition, the state assembly asked the Central government to put the NPR process on hold till the time apprehensions among people that the NPR was a prelude to the NRC and would facilitate the implementation of CAA was allayed. Passing the resolution after a three-hour discussion, the Parliamentary Affairs Minister in the Punjab government, in an indication of the ties between the people's demands and their iteration in institutionalized spaces, referred to the 'countrywide anguish' caused by the CAA and the peaceful protests in Punjab which 'involved all segments of society'. Asking that the NPR forms be changed, Chief Minister Amarinder Singh confirmed that the census in Punjab would be prepared based on past practices.[22] The Rajasthan Assembly became the third state legislature to pass a resolution against the CAA, NPR, and NRC urging the Central government to repeal the CAA, after a five-hour debate in the Assembly. The Congress-ruled state under Ashok Gehlot, like Punjab, asked the Central government to withdraw the 'new fields of information' that were being sought in the NPR process, since 'a substantial section of the population believed that the NPR and the NRC had the same base as the CAA'. In an important intervention, the resolution drew attention to the fact that the rules under the CAA had not yet been framed, which he attributed to the Centre's concern that they too would face challenge in the Supreme Court.[23] On 27 January 2020, the West Bengal Assembly passed a resolution against the CAA, brought by

---

[21] 'Amarinder Sends Sukhbir Copy of Mein Kamph', *The Hindu*, 23 January 2020.
[22] 'After Kerala, Punjab Assembly Passes Resolution against the CAA,' *Newsclick*, 17 January 2020; 'Punjab Assembly Passes Resolution against CAA by Voice Vote,' *The Times of India*, 17 January 2020.
[23] Mohammed Iqbal, 'Rajasthan Assembly Passes Resolution against CAA', *The Hindu*, 25 January 2020.

the TMC, supported by the Congress, and left parties. Mamata Banerjee's government had passed resolutions against the NRC in the state assembly in July 2018, demanding its withdrawal in Assam and in September 2019, opposing its possible application in West Bengal.[24] Banerjee had on several occasions challenged the Central government over the NRC saying that it could be implemented in West Bengal only 'over her dead body'.[25] On 30 January 2020, the Congress-ruled Chhattisgarh Cabinet under Chief Minister Bhupesh Baghel, passed a resolution against the CAA.[26] The Madhya Pradesh Assembly, then under Congress rule under Chief Minister Kamal Nath, passed a resolution against the CAA on 5 February 2020 for being against the spirit of the Constitution and asked the Central government to scrap it. In line with the other state governments which voiced apprehensions against the NPR, the MP government too asked the Central government to continue with the NPR exercise only after withdrawing the requirement of new information which had caused apprehension among the people.[27] On 12 February 2020 Congress-ruled Puducherry Assembly became the first Union Territory to pass a resolution against the CAA and lodge a protest against the NRC and NPR, amidst boycott and walkout by opposition members including the AIADMK, AINRC, and BJP.[28]

The JD(U) had voted in favour of the CAA in the Parliament, where its representatives had made it clear that Muslims in Bihar felt secure due to a number of measures that the government of the state had undertaken. On 25 February 2020, Bihar became the first NDA ruled state to move a resolution against the NRC. Nitish Kumar, Chief Minister of Bihar, veered to what may be perceived as a neutral position on the CAA saying that it was a central law whose constitutionality was being evaluated by the Supreme Court, but manoeuvred to support a resolution against the NRC which was brought by the opposition party—Rashtriya Janata Dal.

---

[24] Shiv Sahay Singh, 'West Bengal Assembly Passes Resolution against CAA', *The Hindu*, 27 January 2020.
[25] 'NRC, New Citizenship Law over my Dead Body, Mamata Banerjee', *The Indian Express*, 17 December 2020.
[26] 'Chhattisgarh Cabinet Passes Resolution against the CAA, Urges PM to Withdraw It', *The New Indian Express*, 30 January 2020.
[27] 'Madhya Pradesh Cabinet Passes Resolution against the CAA', *Business Standard*, 5 February 2020.
[28] 'Now Puducherry Assembly Also Passes Anti-CAA Resolution', *India Today*, 12 February 2020.

As a result, the Bihar Assembly passed the resolution unanimously. The Chief Minister also sought to assure the people of Bihar that the contentious questions pertaining to the place and date of birth of parents in the preparation of the NPR will no longer be asked.[29] Two other states with newly elected legislative Assemblies—Delhi and Jharkhand—led by the Aam Aadmi Party (AAP) of Arvind Kejriwal and Jharkhand Mukti Morcha (JMM) of Hemant Soren, respectively, passed resolutions against the NRC and the NPR in its new format, soon after the new governments assumed office. It is significant that by this time Home Minister Amit Shah had begun clarifying the BJP government's position saying that no decision had been taken on a nationwide NRC and no documents would be required in the preparation of the NPR, supplying information would be optional, and no one would be marked doubtful.[30] On 16 March 2020, the Telangana Assembly passed a resolution against CAA, NRC, and NPR for being 'divisive' and 'endangering the unity and integrity of the census'. The resolution also asked the Central government to amend the CAA to remove references to religion and foreign countries. The resolution was moved by the Chief Minister K. Chandrashekhar Rao who challenged those who saw opposition to the CAA as anti-national, to label the Telangana Assembly 'traitor' for passing the resolution. The ruling party in Telangana, the Telangana Rashtra Samiti (TRS) had opposed the CAB in the Parliament.[31] On 17 June, in the middle of a Covid-19 lockdown the Jagan Reddy government in Andhra Pradesh passed a resolution against the NPR and NRC. The YSR Congress Party had supported the CAB in Parliament and had been under pressure from opposition parties in the state to pass a resolution against the CAA, NPR, and NRC. The CPI gave a 'Chalo Assembly' call to put pressure on the state government to join other states which had already done so.[32] In a massive anti-CAA rally led by AIMIM, Asaduddin Owaisi had appealed to the Chief Minister to

---

[29] Anirban Guha Roy, 'Bihar Assembly Rejects NRC, Says NPR to Be Rolled Out with No New Questions', *Hindustan Times*, 25 February 2020; Nalin Verma, 'How Nitish Kumar Made the BJP Vote for an Anti-NRC Resolution in Bihar', *The Wire*, 27 February 2020.

[30] 'Jharkhand House Passes Resolution against NRC, Seeks NPR in the 2010 format', *The Outlook*, 23 March 2020; 'Delhi Legislative Assembly Passes Resolution against NRC & NPR', *Live Law.in*, 13 March 2020.

[31] 'Telangana House Adopts Resolution against CAA, NPR and NRC', *The Economic Times*, 17 March 2020.

[32] 'Opposition Parties Urge YRSCP, TDP to Oppose CAA, NRC in Assembly', *The Hindu*, 13 January 2020.

reconsider his decision of supporting the BJP on CAA.[33] Thus, Andhra Pradesh, Bihar, Delhi, Tamil Nadu, Kerala, West Bengal, and Madhya Pradesh opposed the NPR in its current format—demanding the restoration of the 2010 version. States like Rajasthan, Punjab, Kerala, West Bengal, Telangana, and Chhattisgarh have, in addition, passed anti-CAA resolutions too. On 8 September 2021, the DMK which formed the government in Tamil Nadu after the state Assembly election in April 2021, passed a resolution in the Assembly against the CAA for 'betraying' and 'usurping' the rights of Sri Lankan Tamil refugees in India.[34]

While the CAA was being opposed in the city streets and chowks, on 22 January 2020, a Supreme Court bench consisting of the then Chief Justice of India, Justice S. A. Bobde, Justice S Abdul Nazeer, and Justice Sanjeev Khanna, heard 144 petitions against the CAA 2019.[35] The Bench refused to pass an interim order to put a stay on the implementation of CAA until the Central government had been given a chance to be heard and segregated the petitions pertaining to Assam from the rest owing to what the bench considered to be special conditions prevailing in the state.[36] Among the latter was the petition filed by the Indian Union Muslim League (IUML) on 12 December 2019 after the CAA was passed in the Rajya Sabha and before it received the President's assent. The petition filed under Article 32 of the Constitution, joined by the IUML Members of Parliament, was the first petition filed in the Supreme Court challenging the CAA. The petitioners pleaded that they did not oppose the grant of citizenship to 'migrants', but in its present form the CAA was based on an 'illegal classification based on religion', which resulted in the exclusion of Muslims and amounted to 'religion based discrimination'. The IUML's petition was premised on the argument that illegal migrants

---

[33] 'No NRC in Andhra Pradesh, Says Jagan Mohan Reddy Amid Nationwide Anti-CAA Protests', https://www.news18.com/news/politics/no-nrc-in-andhra-pradesh-says-jagan-mohan-reddy-amid-nationwide-anti-caa-protests-2433947.html, https://www.news18.com/news/politics/no-nrc-in-andhra-pradesh-says-jagan-mohan-reddy-amid-nationwide-anti-caa-protests-2433947.htmly (accessed on 4 July 2020).

[34] 'Tamil Nadu Assembly Passes Resolution Urging Centre to Repeal CAA', *The Hindu*, 8 September 2021.

[35] Several petitions—about 16—were also made to urge the Supreme Court to declare the amendments constitutional.

[36] Murali Krishnan, 'In 10 Points, Supreme Court Hearings on Citizenship Act Petitions Explained', *The Hindustan Times*, 22 January 2020.

constituted a 'class by itself' and the application of any law to them should not differentiate on the basis of religion, caste, or nationality.[37] The 'religious segregation' in the Bill was not based on 'reasonable differentiation' in violation of Article 14 of the Constitution and went against the idea of India as a country 'which treats people of all faiths equally'. This petition was followed up by two applications filed on 16 January 2020 seeking interim directions from the Supreme Court till its petition challenging the constitutionality of CAA was heard. In these applications, the IUML sought a stay on the CAA and a declaration from the Central government that the CAA, NPR, and NRC were not related. The first application referred to the contradictory statements made by Union Home Minister Amit Shah and earlier Minister of State Kiren Rijiju that NPR is the first step towards NRC, and subsequent statements by the Prime Minister, Home Minister, and the Union Law Minister denying plans for a nationwide NRC and any link between NPR and NRC. These statements were made in the wake of countrywide protests against CAA and NRC. Such 'contradictory statements', the application stated, were creating 'widespread confusion and panic among people at large'.[38] The second application filed the same day sought a stay on the 10 January notification which brought the CAA 2019 into force.

While most petitions filed in the CAA were based on more or less similar premises referring to the jurisprudence around Articles 14 and 21, secularism as part of the basic structure of the Constitution, the citizenship provisions in the original constitutional text, international conventions and human rights obligations, and the ramifications the CAA would have on the ongoing NRC process in Assam—there were variations in *what* was given salience in the petition, making each petition also distinctive.[39] A perusal of two petitions among those associated with Assam—by AASU (through its President Dipanka Kumar Nath and

---

[37] 'Breaking: Indian Union Muslim League Moves SC Challenging Citizenship Amendment Bill', 12 December 2019, *Live Law.in*.

[38] 'Centre Must Clarify If Nationwide NRC Will Be Prepared': Indian Union Muslim League Files Application in SC', 16 January 2020; https://www.livelaw.in/top-stories/centre-must-clarify-if-nationwide-nrc-will-be-prepared-indian-union-muslim-league-files-application-in-sc-151684 (accessed on 8 July 2020).

[39] These petitions may be accessed on *Live Law.in*; for example, https://www.livelaw.in/top-stories/four-new-petitions-against-caa-in-sc-say-it-privileges-specified-religious-persecution-read-petitions-150903 (accessed on 7 July 2020).

General Secretary Lurinjyoti Gogoi) and by Debabrata Saikia the leader of the opposition in the Assam Legislative Assembly (along with Abdul Khaleque, Congress MP from Barpeta and Rupjyoti Kurmi, a Congress MLA from Mariani legislative Assembly constituency)—shows the centrality given to the *Assam perspective*, even as the general points of challenge to the CAA, consistent with other petitions, persist.[40] It is also significant that even when the Assam perspective is given primacy in these petitions, the petitioners do not seek an exemption from the CAA exclusively for Assam. The AASU petition, for example, appealed to the Supreme Court to direct the Central government to 'take effective steps for implementation of Assam Accord in general and for conservation and preservation of the distinct culture, heritage, and traditions of the indigenous people of Assam in furtherance to Clause 6 of the Assam Accord, in particular'. At the same time, its first prayer to the court was to declare the CAA as a whole or its specific sections 'discriminatory, arbitrary and illegal' and set it aside as *ultra vires*—going beyond the authority given by the Constitution of India. The petition by Debabrata Saikia asked the Supreme Court 'in the interest of justice' to quash the CAA, declaring it unconstitutional and *ultra vires* Articles 14, 21, the Assam Accord, the law laid down by the Supreme Court in *S. R. Bommai vs. Union of India* (1994) and in violation of the basic structure of the constitution of India'. The trajectory of the background events they draw to place their prayers and make their appeal effective is a historical timeline of Indian citizenship's exceptional relationship with Assam. In its petition the AASU describes itself as a 'non-political' student organization whose aims and objectives, among others listed, are to protect the independence and sovereignty of India, the interests of the indigenous Assamese, raising social, political, and cultural consciousness amongst students, and strengthening national integration. The AASU claimed 'representative capacity' in making the petition by flagging the leadership it gave to the Assam Movement (1979–1985) against illegal migration and 'in formalizing a solution' through the Assam Accord to ensure the 'academic, cultural and developmental requirements of the State of Assam'. It challenged the CAA citing the long suffering of the people of Assam from the 'consequences of illegal immigration of Bangladeshi citizens in Assam'

---

[40] I am grateful to Abhinav Borbora for giving me access to the Congress petition.

and seeking the 'enforcement' of their fundamental rights', in particular, the 'identity of the Assamese people', and the larger question of 'national security'. Enumerating the long list of legal measures the Assamese people through their various organizations had taken to address these concerns, including the Sarbananda Sonowal case (2005) which led to the repeal of the IMDT Act, through the Assam Sanmilita Mahasangha (2005) case which resulted in the Supreme Court-monitored NRC in Assam, to the petition by Hiren Gohain led Nagarikatwa Aain Songsudhan Birodhi Mancha (Forum Against Citizenship Act Amendment Bill) which was filed when the CAB 2019 was pending in the Rajya Sabha in February 2019, the petition made a case before the Supreme Court to declare the three notifications by the Home Ministry ultra vires.[41] The petition by Debabrata Saikia too traced the ramifications of the CAA for the people of Assam in particular. Calling the CAA a 'colourable legislation', for ensuring 'by design and default' that the people excluded from the NRC, who belong to specific religions may be able to seek protection under the CAA, the petitioners raised concerns over the suspicion this would cast over the proceedings of the Foreigners Tribunals: 'CA, Act 2019 ensures that the proceeding before the Foreigner Tribunal and detention would be directly targeted against the Muslims alone. This will only make the Foreigners Tribunal more arbitrary'. The CAA, they argued, would subsequently 'render National Register of Citizens (NRC) in Assam meaningless' making large numbers of illegal migrants 'prospective beneficiaries of the Act', by proposing to 'drop all charges against Non-Muslim illegal migrants', with the result that the Foreigners Act would apply 'only on Muslims and Foreigners Tribunals will adjudicate only Muslims'. In addition, the CAA would contravene the Assam Accord, 'destroy the fragile ethnic and socio-economic fabric' of Assam and would thereby violate Clause 6 of the Assam Accord'.[42]

---

[41] These notifications were the Foreigners (Amendment) Order, 2015 and the Passport (Entry into India) Amendment Rules, 2015 which exempted six non-Muslim communities from Afghanistan, Bangladesh, and Pakistan from the application of Foreigners Act, 1946, if they had fled these countries due to religious persecution and entered the country before 31 December 2014. A third notification was made by the MHA in 2016 empowering the district administration to register as citizens of India and issue certificates of naturalization under the Citizenship Act, 1955 to the earlier mentioned non-Muslim communities, residing in specified districts in the states of Chhattisgarh, Gujarat, Madhya Pradesh, Maharashtra, Rajasthan, Uttar Pradesh, and Delhi.

[42] A copy of the petition is available with the author.

Three former civil servants—Deb Mukharji, Somsundar Burra, and Amitabh Pande—filed a petition as 'public servants' who had 'dedicated their careers to protecting the interests of the nation and upholding the principles of the Constitution'. The petitioners requested the Supreme Court to either declare CAA 2019, its specific sections, and the various executive orders to which the Act was giving effect unconstitutional or to make their provisions applicable to all persecuted persons on the territory of India. This would be commensurate with the 'moral necessity' of having a just and fair legal regime of citizenship 'consistent with India's historic place in the world as an open, plural and diverse society, which has *always* protected those who need protection, which has *always* welcomed persons of all faiths, beliefs, and ways of life, and whose civilisational character has *always* been defined by tolerance and assimilation'. The petitioners believed that the CAA was inconsistent with all these principles and violated 'every known principle of equality and equal treatment', 'damaged and destroyed' the Indian Constitution's basic feature of secularism and the 'founding principles' of the Republic of India— the idea of 'civic nationalism'—which was premised on 'allegiance to the Constitution' and informed the values which defined what it meant to be 'Indian', and the rejection of the 'two-nation theory' that triggered Partition'.[43] Moreover, by deploying nationality and religion as principles of differentiation, the CAA made a distinction between those exempted from prosecution as 'illegal migrants', who could be put on a fast track to citizenship, and others who were subjected to an 'individualized executive procedure' for the grant of Long Term Visas (LTVs) under the Standard Operating Procedure (SOP) laid down by the MHA in 2011. The petitioners emphasized also the point that had been raised in the Parliamentary debate and other petitions on the arbitrariness of classification. While agreeing that the protection of religious minorities from persecution was 'a noble' and 'worthy' goal, they argued that the CAA ignored that there existed religious persecution of minorities in other neighbouring countries, which too professed a state religion, and that religious persecution of groups other than Hindus, Sikhs, Buddhists, Jains, Parsis, and Christians took place in all the three specified countries. The

---

[43] This petition can be accessed on *Live Law.in*.

Act created therefore, 'an invidious and unjustifiable discrimination between individuals in identical circumstances'. It was, therefore, 'devoid of rationality, devoid of compassion, devoid of humanity, and devoid of constitutional validity'.[44] Moreover, the petitioners argued, by elevating religious persecution 'to the level of constituting justified claims to citizenship, while refusing to accord the same sanctity to other forms of (equally serious) non-religious persecution', the Act violated the basic feature of secularism. 'Indian secularism does not permit religion and faith to determine an individual's *civil status* in the polity (through citizenship), either directly or indirectly. And it certainly does not permit that to be done in a colourable and discriminatory fashion'. Indeed, dispelling the argument that the basic structure doctrine could be applied *only* to a constitutional amendment, the petitioners cited the Supreme Court judgement in *Madras Bar Association v. Union of India* (2014), which lay down that an ordinary legislation too could be held unconstitutional if it violated the basic structure of the constitution. Asserting that laws that dealt with legal status of non-nationals and conferred or withdrew citizenship 'must be subjected to a rigorous standard of judicial review', since citizenship has been affirmed in judgements by the Supreme Court, as 'a most precious right' (*State of Arunachal Pradesh v Khudiram Chakma* 1993), which constitutes the foundation from which 'critical human rights' flow. Citing the Supreme Court's caution in the case *Navtej Johar v. Union of India* (2018), the petitioners pointed towards the powerlessness of 'discrete or insular minorities' to 'protect themselves through the normal channels of the political process'—who must be protected by the constitutional courts. Refugees and asylum seekers according to the petitioners were 'discrete and insular minorities', who were 'fleeing from persecution', and lacked the 'basic rights that enabled participation in the political process'—the right to vote, freedom of speech, assembly, and association—among them required 'searching and anxious' scrutiny of the Supreme Court. In making this scrutiny, it was desirable that the court 'should impose a high burden upon the State to justify laws that are facially discriminatory'.

The petitioners argued that the CAA violated Article 14 of the constitution by 'entrenching and perpetuating existing disadvantage, without any

[44] Ibid.

reasonable justification'. Asserting that Article 14 jurisprudence has been 'continuously enhanced' by the Supreme Court, and is no longer confined to the 'traditional' *classification* and *arbitrariness* tests, the CAA would have to satisfy the 'vision of equality and equal treatment' articulated by the Supreme Court which focuses on *social context* and 'prohibits the entrenchment or perpetuation of *disadvantage*'. Referring to *Navtej Johar* (2018), the petitioners contended that the CAA was perpetuating disadvantage by focusing on 'personal or immutable characteristics, which are either beyond the control of individuals to alter (countries of origin), or at the heart of individual autonomy and personal self-determination (religion)'. The CAA similarly violated Article 21, because it violated the right to dignity as established in *Justice K. S. Puttaswamy v Union of India* (2017).

On 17 March 2020, the Ministry of Home Affairs (MHA) filed a *preliminary* counter-affidavit (henceforth, counter-affidavit) on behalf of the Union Government, in response to the petition filed by the IUML on 12 December 2019 (IUML vs. Union of India, WP (C) NO. 1470 OF 2019). The 'preliminary' counter-affidavit was filed by the government to oppose the grant of any interim order by the Supreme Court and to seek time to peruse other petitions in detail. In its 129-page counter-affidavit, the government gave a systematic defence of the CAA on 'legal, factual, and political' grounds and claimed the right to respond to all other petitions on a later date. Like all petitions pleading for the evaluation of the CAA against the standards of validation inscribed in the Constitution, the government's affidavit too began with a 'brief list of dates' to lay down the 'bare facts' pertaining to the case. Like most petitions, the affidavit traced the historical trajectory of CAA 2019 to the Passports Act 1920 and the Foreigners Act 1946 followed by the Partition of India as the anchor from which other dates that are subsequently identified, followed. The counter-affidavit, however, went beyond listing the dates as 'bare facts' and turned them into a chronology of 'events' through an 'evaluation' of their ramifications for the 'turns' in history that the dates represented.

Concerning itself in a large measure with establishing that the Parliament had the 'competence' to legislate on matters concerning citizenship, the affidavit drew upon Part II of the Constitution which carries the citizenship provisions and Schedule Seven under Article 246 which maps the legislative relations between the Centre and the states and the subjects over which they had exclusive jurisdiction. Through the former, it sought to establish both the *indisputability* of the power of the Parliament to legislate on all matters concerning the acquisition and termination of citizenship and also the authority to deviate from the citizenship provisions laid down from Article 5 to Article 10 (Page 3, Para 5). In the distribution of legislative powers between the Centre and the states in the Seventh Schedule, citizenship is placed in the list of subjects assigned to the Central government.

Yet, there can also be identified a line of argument in the counter-affidavit which seeks to demonstrate that the CAA had not really changed anything and merely inscribed in law what had always existed in practice. The list of dates gave prominence, through detailed enumeration and description, to the emergence and development of the policy of giving LTVs to persons who entered India from the three specified countries because of religious persecution and intended to make India their home. The counter-affidavit emphasized that the need for such a policy emerged from the failure of the Liaquat–Nehru Pact, which was signed on 8 April 1950, to commit both countries to the protection of religious minorities residing in their territories. It was in 1964 that the implications of this failure, because of Pakistan's non-adherence to its part of the commitment, became evident. This argument corresponds closely with the position taken by the Home Minister in the debates on the CAB in the Parliament. In the narrative of events, the criticality of 1964 lay in the communal violence unleashed in East Pakistan following the theft of the holy relic in the Hazratbal shrine in Srinagar in December 1963, resulting in large numbers of 'refugees' fleeing into Assam, Tripura, and West Bengal. The debates that ensued in the Lok Sabha at that time led to the decision that India could not take 'a purely legal and constitutional view' on the matter. The fleeing people 'were part of ourselves, with whom we have ties of blood … if they find it impossible to breathe the air of security in their country and they feel that they must leave it, then we cannot bar their way. We have no heart to tell them "You go on staying there and be butchered".' It was the 'historical' and 'special' circumstances of the 'specified communities' in Pakistan, Bangladesh, and Afghanistan that necessitated a 'liberal and accommodative visa regime' for minority communities from these countries. In the 1980s, successive announcements of change in 'the policy regarding illegal entrance and settlement in India of minority communities' installed a 'relaxed/preferential LTV regime', initially for Hindus and Sikhs and since 2011 for Christians and Buddhists as well. These were 'executive instructions' that flowed from the powers given to the Central government under the Foreigners Act 1946 and the Passport Act 1920. Much of the burden of the history of the LTV regime traced in the counter-affidavit was to argue that 'a classification based on special circumstances of specified minorities migrating into India from Pakistan and Bangladesh for long term stay has been in existence since last many decades'. Indeed, the affidavit lists a series of instances to show how a border state like Rajasthan, which like Gujarat, received refugees from Pakistan over a long period of time, requested for rules which would enable the government to give citizenship to Hindu migrants. The requests made by CM Ashok Gehlot of the Congress Party over a period of time were cited as having paved the way for rules allowing designated District Collectors in Rajasthan and Gujarat to grant citizenship to 'Pakistan nationals of minority Hindu community'. The CAA 2019 could then be seen simply as legal affirmation of a long-standing policy addressing the special conditions of refugees from neighbouring countries—'a benign piece of legislation'—all it sought to do was to 'provide a relaxation, in the nature of an amnesty to specific communities from the specified communities with a clear cut-off date'.

Deflecting the allegations that it ignored other forms of persecution by isolating *religious* persecution for consideration of citizenship protection, the affidavit admitted that the CAA 2019 was a 'narrowly tailored legislation'—a 'limited legislative measure circumscribed in its application'—not designed to 'provide answers to all kinds of purported persecutions'. It did not, moreover, change the already existing legal regime for foreigners who wished to acquire Indian citizenship. The assertions that it violated Article 14 of the Constitution did not, therefore, hold.

In buttressing the CAA against the charge that it violated the basic structure of the Constitution and constitutional protections to equality and life, the counter-affidavit sought a foreclosure in the argument that the CAA was protected from judicial scrutiny on any of these grounds. The protection was drawn from what the counter-affidavit referred to as the averments by the Supreme Court, which it asserted had 'repeatedly held that in matters concerning foreign policy, citizenship, economic policy, etc., a wider latitude for classification is available to the Parliament/

Legislature considering the subject matters of the challenge and the nature of the field which the Legislature seeks to deal with'. Claiming that the question of 'entitlement and conferment of citizenship' fell 'within the plenary domain of the competent legislature', the legislature had the power to 'devise its own legislative *policy*' on citizenship, which 'may not be within judicial review and may not be justiciable'. Decisions which are an outcome of 'Parliamentary legislative policy' emerging from 'executive foreign policy decision making', it argued are not only outside the purview of the constitutional court, the courts may not have the 'requisite expertise to examine the parameters based upon which such legislative policy is enacted'. The 'wider width of legislative policy and legislative wisdom' was available only with the 'competent legislature'. Indeed, the affidavit takes this argument further to emphasize that decisions in citizenship matters which are concerned with immigration policy are generally governed by 'executive policy of the sovereign manifested by competent legislation'. As a matter of foreign policy and security integral to the exercise of sovereign power of a nation-state, they were exclusively within the domain of the state and could not come under the scrutiny of the court in the form of a Public Interest Litigation:

> ... matters concerning the sovereign plenary power of the Parliament, especially in regard to citizenship and the contours thereof, cannot be questioned before this Hon'ble Court by way of a public interest petition. It is submitted that the cardinal principle of *locus standi* has been diluted by this jurisprudence evolved by this Hon'ble Court only in limited fact situations which cannot be extrapolated to include the present constitutional challenge to the legislative measure of the Indian Parliament in the domain of issues concerning citizenship/immigration. It is therefore submitted that the scope of public interest petitions, and the maintainability thereof, especially in matters concerning immigration policy must be decided as question of law by this Hon'ble Court.[45]

---

[45] Preliminary Counter-Affidavit, available on *Live Law.in*.

The Pandemic Effect

On 12 March 2020, the Director-General of WHO announced that Covid-19 was a pandemic, a conclusion drawn from the rapid spread of Cornona virus cases outside China—the epicenter—where it had all started in November 2019. The declaration by WHO called for a 'containment strategy' which required that countries escalated their efforts towards taking preemptive action to delay the spread to ensure that the health care system reached an appropriate state of preparedness to curb the impact and eventually eradicate the virus. It was expected that these preemptive actions would balance the overwhelming necessity to protect people's health with the need to alleviate the social and economic disruptions and human rights violations these measures were likely to cause. These, the WHO admitted, were likely to present dilemmas before governments in all countries.

On 22 March 2020, the Prime Minister of India exhorted citizens to observe a voluntary *janata* (people's) curfew. From 24 March, India went into complete lockdown. 'Social distancing'—the expression used for what was supposed to be physical distancing considered integral to the so called 'war' against the Coronavirus—captured the impact the lockdown had on the hitherto teeming public space. The streets in Delhi and other parts of the country had seen continuous sit-ins and demonstrations against the CAA-NRC since the CAA was passed by the Parliament in December 2019. In January 2020 a massive nation-wide strike was called by the trade unions to protest the government's 'anti-people' economic policies and its plans for disinvestment and privatization of public sector undertakings including those in the banking sector. The pandemic had the effect of making the 'public' a potentially dangerous space—a source of contagion—where 'the public' as a cluster of infected bodies became a risk. The public was folded up and in, as bodies were isolated and quarantined.

As an immediate effect, the streets were emptied out of people—protests were lifted or deferred—announcing a period of hiatus till they reconvened. The almost five thousand women of Mumbai Bagh in Mumbai went home in deference to the health emergency and the women of Hauz Rani in Delhi lifted their sit-in with the resolve to continue it online.[46] On

---

[46] 'Jamia, Hauz Rani, Mumbai Bagh: Coronavirus Forces Anti-CAA Organisers to Suspend Protests', *The Print*, 23 March 2020.

24 March, after a hundred days of incessant sit-in, the women of Shaheen Bagh, who had become the face of the anti-CAA protest in the country, also dispersed. On 7 October 2020, several months after the Shaheen Bagh sit-in folded up, the Supreme Court of India delivered an order giving closure to an appeal to issue directions to the Commissioner of Delhi police to clear the road occupied by 'persons opposing' the CAA and the NRC. The appeal was in the form of a Special Leave Petition (SLP) against the order of the Delhi High Court, which had disposed off the petition on 14 January 2020, the day that it was first heard, with directions to the Delhi police to discharge their powers 'to control traffic' wherever protests were taking place, in 'the larger public interest'. The petitioner turned to the Supreme Court when the order had no impact on the protests. On 17 February, the Supreme Court appointed two interlocutors 'to meet the protestors at the site'. While giving the order, the judges confirmed that those who felt aggrieved by the law had the right to protest, but the 'question was where and how the protest can be carried on, without the public being affected'. By March 2020, after receiving what it called 'the second report' from the two interlocutors—senior counsel Sanjay R. Hegde and mediator trainer Sadhana Ramachandran—the Supreme Court came to the conclusion that despite their best efforts, the mediation process 'could not fructify into success'. The judgement goes on to refer to the Coronavirus pandemic as 'the hand of God' that 'subsequently intervened and overtook the situation'. The protestors, the judges wrote, showed 'wisdom' and returned to their homes, although some 'police action' was deployed to clear the 'infrastructure' that had been created at the site of protest. Against this background, the three-judge bench of Justice S. K. Kaul, Justice Aniruddha Bose, and Justice Krishna Murari turned their attention to the question of the relationship between dissent and democracy. While starting from the premise that 'democracy and dissent go hand in hand', the judges made it clear that dissent must take form that 'yields to social interest':

> ... [W]e have to make it unequivocally clear that public ways and public spaces cannot be occupied in such a manner and that too indefinitely. Democracy and dissent go hand in hand, but then the demonstrations expressing dissent have to be in designated places alone. The present case was not even one of protests taking place in an undesignated area

but was a blockage of a public way which caused grave inconvenience to commuters. We cannot accept the plea of the applicants that an indeterminable number of people can assemble whenever they choose to protest. (Judgement, Amit Sahni vs. Commissioner of Police 2020, para. 17)

Indeed, while stating that the Shaheen Bagh protests were 'blockage of a public way' and not even a case of protest in an undesignated space, the judges drew attention to the dangers of social media which had the potential of scaling up 'leaderless protests' and create 'highly polarized environments'.[47]

The interruption of Shaheen Bagh and other 'mini-Shaheen Baghs' that had proliferated in Delhi and in other cities set in a period of deferral and interregnum in citizen democracy. It may be worthwhile to see the pandemic as producing conditions with specific attributes which gave coherence to a new set of constraints, challenges, and even possibilities of citizenship. In a sustained environment of fear of getting sick and dying, the fear of the contagion ushered in the isolated monad as the best defence in the 'war on corona', which worked on the logic of changing people's behaviour. At the crux of this logic was the belief that the fear of an unbridled and lethal contagion would make people participate in legal/punitive and medical regimes if they believed that it is for their and society's defence. Ordinary penal laws that facilitated policing of the public were buttressed by special laws that allowed the government to use emergency powers to protect the people against disasters and epidemics.

Among the changes that the pandemic regime brought was the re-privatization of home and privatization of work as the home became the world of work. Through much of the 1970s and 1980s, the women's movement had striven to make the 'home' visible by rolling back the devaluation of housework, the recognition of housework as unpaid work, and contesting the idea of the domestic as a private space of intimacy and un-coerced consent. The women's movement had sought to make the boundaries between the public and private permeable, to make their relationship non-hierarchical, and open it up to scrutiny against

---

[47] Supreme Court Judgement in *Amit Shani vs. Commissioner of Police* (Civil Appeal no. 3282 of 2020) delivered on 7 October 2020.

constitutional norms so that it became possible to see that the domestic was a space of contestation, power relations, and gendered violence. The pandemic saw rapid reversal of these gains. The sudden conflation of the spaces of work—amidst the uncertainty of the times—reinforced gendering of work—care work and housework—while cloistering questions of reproductive health, bodily integrity and dignity, and intimate relationships. The phenomenon of privatization of violence occurred alongside the participation of people in cultures of violence because of rampant fear that has been part of the force of the pandemic.[48]

Domestication of the public occurred alongside cloistering of the private space. The decline of the idea of the public as a space of trust, empathy, and reciprocity made way for distance and suspicion—quarantine, isolation, containment zones, contact tracing—became governmental practices and strategies facilitated by tools/apps for tracing and isolating, sifting, and sorting, and policing the public. Ideas of the public based on equality, fraternity, and public conscience were not part of the discursive framework of 'prevention through policing'. The images of millions of migrant workers making their way home back from the city, which was never home but was mostly hospitable, to return home, where they would still face rejection, became the most emphatic statement of estrangement from citizenship. The estranged bodies—walking carcasses (Guru 2016)—of the migrant workers/pandemic refugees, the untouchable, isolated, and stigmatized body of the infected, represented the ways in which they were pushed into the penumbra of citizenship—their bodies were made visible in an absent public. The stigmatized body of the 'covid-infectee' became untouchable even as untouchable bodies became frontline warriors, producing a blurred spectrum of precarious lives.

For quite some time now, T. H. Marshal's post-War trajectory of social citizenship model has stood eroded. The solidarity of citizenship for Marshall was established in a growing national consciousness and 'awakening' public opinion which produced the 'first stirrings' of community membership. The social inequalities and class structure, however, remained till the working class learnt to wield 'effective political power'. Both—the welfare models of the post-war contexts and the workfare

---

[48] 'Domestic Violence during Covid-19 Lockdown Emerges as Serious Concern', *Hindustan Times*, 26 April 2020.

model—were associated with citizens' participation in the workforce and strengthening of labour in employment through negotiation and collective bargaining. The acceleration of processes of disarticulation that had set in with neo-liberal citizenship—proletarianization as a condition of political citizenship accruing from the political power of collective bargaining—to neoliberal citizenship, where proletarianization meant loss of power and disenfranchisement, was starkly evident when the cities locked down. Rather than encouraging workers to stay or to return by securing wages and improving working conditions, amendments in labour laws were suggested to remove protections. Several states contemplated either suspending them altogether or increasing working hours, despite the protection extended by the Supreme Court in its judgment in *PUDR vs Union of India* (1982). In this judgement, the Supreme Court noted that no one would willingly work for less than the minimum wage without some force or compunction—and that compunction could include hunger or poverty.

The abandonment of the citizen by the state corresponded with the accentuation of vertical relationship between the citizen and the state. In a context where the deliberative spaces within the political apparatus of the state—government and opposition, government and political party, Centre and the states—waned, the policing functions of the state enhanced exponentially. From public order to public health, the Ministry of Home Affairs has become more pronounced as it has seeped into all spaces vacated by public power. The augmentation of emergency powers of the state through the Epidemic Act 1892 and the protective role of the state through the National Disaster Management Act 2005 have devolved enormous responsibility and simultaneously powers onto 'Home' in the governmental apparatus. The overdevelopment of Home in the state apparatus has also been evident in the context of anti-CAA protests and sit-in against the CAA/NRC in parts of North-Delhi where communal riots broke out in February 2020. In these contexts the precariousness of citizenship was made manifest as the functions of *Home* became more pronounced in its coercive role of securing public order and the Parliament remained deferred. The use of draconian sedition provisions and the Unlawful Activities Prevention Act (UAPA), which since 2004 after the repeal of Prevention of Terrorism Act 2002 has become the foremost central law to deal with terrorism, against students and activists reflect the way in which the CAA has been sutured to the national security architecture. It is also a testimony to both the limits and possibilities of citizenship and the need for a reflexive citizenship practice founded in shared life and a state that has the capacity to empathize and not merely to enforce consent.

Conclusion

This work traces the antecedents of citizenship in contemporary India to the regimes of citizenship that were installed through successive amendments in the Citizenship Act 1955. A *citizenship regime*, it is argued, is not simply the Bare Act or the provisions of a law and the rules made under it, but the way in which law is structured to produce specific power effects. Through successive regimes of law, citizenship in India has gravitated towards the principle of *jus sanguinis* which is founded in an ideology of majoritarian communitarianism. The Citizenship Amendment Act (CAA) 2019 and the National Register of Citizens (NRC) which constitute the core components of the contemporary regime of citizenship are an emphatic statement of this ideology. The procedure for the 'updating' of NRC in Assam with the requirement of establishing a link through appropriate 'public documents' proving an Assamese 'legacy' has generated a form of 'hyphenated citizenship' within Indian citizenship. The NRC, as it unfolded in Assam established the relationship between legal status and blood ties. Extended to the entire country, it envisions a 'national order of citizenship' (Baruah 2009) based on the principle of parentage. The 2015 Land Border Agreement Treaty between India and Bangladesh is an example of the possibility of legibility for those with ambivalent citizenship, with the resolution of the question of legal-juridical sovereignty of states over their territories.

Although citizenship is understood as a condition of equality, it is dependent on a prior status of membership and the distinction, therefore, between citizens and non-citizens. The association of citizenship with 'legal status' is a continuing legacy of passive citizenship of the absolutist states which were concerned with imposing their authority over heterogeneous populations. Yet, citizenship is also about identity and belonging which are both constrained *and* enabled by the understanding of citizenship as legal status, determined by the modes through which people acquire citizenship and the conditions in which they can retain, relinquish, or lose it. The idea that citizenship can be passed on as a legacy of ancestry and descent has become part of the contemporary legal landscape of citizenship in India. It transmits the idea of blood as an organizing principle of a bounded political community and citizenship as inheritance. These can be traced across generations and establish ties with a homeland that holds out the promise of return, generating ideas of belonging which construe citizenship as a natural and constitutive identity.

The contemporary regime of citizenship, this work argues, has its origin in CAA 2003, which constituted a hinge point, from which the NRC and CAA 2019 emerged as two discrete *tendencies*. The CAA 2003 constrained citizenship by birth, by limiting it to only those whose parents were Indian citizens or one of the parents was an Indian citizen and the other was not an illegal migrant. The amendment also put in place the requirement of identification of citizens and the compilation of a National Register of Indian Citizens (NRIC). This requirement activated documentary practices associated with the structuration and standardization of state power, state-formative practices and the intensification and accentuation of state authority, internally and externally. The CAA 2019 gives exemption to a 'class of persons' from the category of 'illegal migrants' prescribed by CAA 2003, in citizenship by birth and naturalization provisions. In the process, CAA 2019 has put in place a citizenship regime that extends the protection of Indian citizenship to those persecuted on grounds of religion, making way for a form of de-territorialized citizenship. Yet, the de-territorialization is deceptive since the protection of CAA 2019 is available only to persons belonging to specific religions, namely those Hindus, Sikhs, Buddhists, Jains, Parsis, and Christians, who are citizens of Pakistan, Bangladesh, and Afghanistan, and had entered India before 31 December 2014. The CAA 2019, therefore, puts in place a regime of citizenship 'bounded' by religious preference, concealed behind the veneer of liberal citizenship. In binding citizenship to a preferential regime based on religion, the CAA 2019 has 'entrenched' a religious-majoritarian order of citizenship. The legal ordering of citizenship is a manifestation of the standardization and intensification of state practices of ruling that takes recourse to bureaucratic practices of enumeration and identification to make citizens legible. At the same time, by making the identification regime dependent on the 'distinguishability assumption' (Sadiq 2009)—based on 'legacy' in the case of the NRC and religion in CAA 2019—it has projected citizenship, tied to blood and inheritance, onto a national scale.

The Joint Parliamentary Committee (JPC) which recommended that the CAB 2016 be considered in Parliament, argued against what it called 'misconceived and mistaken notions of secularism' coming in the way of stopping the influx of illegal migrants into Assam and India (JPC Report 2019, p. 12). Earlier, on 17 December 2014, Justice Ranjan Gogoi and R. F. Nariman of the Supreme Court of India, had delivered a judgement in the case *Assam Sanmilita Mahasangha and Others v. Union of India and others* [Writ Petition (Civil) No. 562 of 2012] laying down the modalities and the schedule for updating the NRC in Assam. In its administrative guidelines, the Supreme Court followed its decision in *Sarbananda Sonowal v. Union of India and Others* (2005) in construing the 'influx of illegal migrants into the state of India as external aggression'. As a register of Indian citizens, the NRC is simultaneously an exercise of identification of illegal migrants/foreigners—termed 'infiltrators' (*ghuspaithiya*) by the state. It is in this endorsement of closure that the NRC converges with the CAA, even though the NRC and the CAA are based on different logics of determining citizenship—the NRC as a modality of identification of citizens through the logic of documentary citizenship (Sadiq 2009) to eliminate illegal migrants—and the CAA as the extension of Indian citizenship to specified religious minorities to affirm their right to return to their homeland. The alignment of the NRC with an Assamese legacy embedded the NRC, like the CAA, in an idea of citizenship, which was ultimately based on identity drawing upon ethno-cultural belonging. The NRC initially found legitimacy in the ideological and political consensus on the citizenship question in the Assam Accord, even though the Accord itself does not mention an NRC. With the announcement of the CAA, and the imbrication of the NRC and CAA in the electoral politics of Assam, the NRC was woven into the agenda of Hindutva. The reluctance of the ruling regime to take the NRC forward after the declaration of the final list, which, contrary to expectations, excluded large numbers of Hindus, manifests this alignment.

The coincidence of citizenship regimes based on different logics exacerbated the contradictions that had emerged during the preparation of the NRC in Assam. These precipitated ferment in specific sites of assemblage of citizenship. James Holston describes *assemblage* as a space of 'entrenched and insurgent forms' which exist 'in tense and often dangerous' relationship with each other (2008, p. 33). The tension in the space of assemblage occurs owing to the insurgent 'irrupting' in and unsettling the site inhabited by the entrenched. In a different formulation, the CAA and the NRC are seen as manifestations of contradictions in the state formative practices following Partition, and the 'nationalizing' tendencies inherent in citizenship regimes. The 'reality of a post-Partition space', argues Sanjib Baruah is not in conformity with the 'idealized notion of a bounded national territory with a clearly defined community of citizens' (2009, p. 593). The contemporary landscape of citizenship in India presents a space of assemblage where the CAA 2019 and the NRC exist in a tense relationship, but also converge in their articulation of bounded citizenship, producing disturbed zones of citizenship.

An identification practice based on specified documents recognized as 'public' is a significant aspect of entrenchment of the contemporary regime of citizenship. As seen in the process of updating the NRC in Assam, documents became embodiments of citizenship identity. The nature of the documents and the problems of accessibility and ownership associated with each made some documents more *worthy* than others in proving identity through legacy. This created a hierarchy among documents and among people, since some were more likely to possess those documents than others. The hierarchy among documents based on their effectiveness in providing evidence of citizenship was also reflected in the articulation of preferred identities, and their selective use for the purpose of identification and expulsion. Proving legacy through documents required a more difficult and a higher threshold for some, including married women in rural areas who shifted residence after marriage. The invocation of legacy through the NRC also unsettled the relationship between the constitutional/legal frameworks of citizenship and the statutory frameworks determining who can vote. Indeed, the peculiarity of the electoral roll and the legal and conceptual association/dissociation of the two—voter and citizen—is evident in the contests over the electoral roll in Assam. A citizen-resident of Assam was required to trace his/her lineage to the electoral roll of 1971 in Assam, and then buttress it with the legacy data going back to the 1951 NRC of the state. Paradoxically, the association of the electoral roll with legacy has ensured that the mere presence of a person's name on the electoral roll did not prove citizenship, unless a link with a legacy person was also established.

The requirement of 'legacy' made citizenship a condition of constitutive belonging. Ranabir Samaddar (2019) has argued that the constitutive power of citizenship unfolds in two ways: as a procedure to arrest the power of the family through the construction of a legal myth called legacy, and as a process that results in the pruning of the power of an individual to claim citizenship as a *person*. Samaddar calls this 'technical power' that drives a wedge in the 'broad continuum of the family reaching up to the state'. Samaddar's framework helps us understand how both these practices work through contradictory logics—the substitution of the power of the family to absorb the 'awkward' citizen to make her inaccessible to the state, and on the other hand, reinstalling the order of the state through the power of legacy—traced through the family tree and verifiable by public evidence. The expulsion of the individual in the new identification regime reinforced the power of the state through its capacity to unsettle the family by summoning individual members—who consequently became the nodes through which the entire family could be rendered suspect.

The citizenship regime put in place at the founding moment of the Republic was structured by legal provisions that were premised on principles of inclusion to ameliorate the effects of Partition. By giving legibility to different kinds of movements across the newly created borders, the 'crisis' precipitated by the cartographic sundering of people's relationship with land was resolved through inclusive citizenship. The contemporary narrative of 'crisis' in citizenship is sutured around the spectre of 'indiscriminate' immigration and the risks presented by 'strangers' among *us* (Miller 2016). Such narratives of crisis have spelt out the conditions of 'extreme necessity' which have given impetus to legal regimes of citizenship across the world that have been averse to immigrants. These regimes have recalled the sovereign's power to command by controlling the borders in the interest of a national community based on social cohesion, trust, and shared interests. A corresponding tendency has been to consolidate the 'stock', manifested in different modalities for providing legal affirmation of affective belonging. One of these was the extension of 'overseas' citizenship to those who left 'home' to become citizens of another country, made possible through CAA 2003. In 2019, the promise of return and absorption in the 'home' country from adopted countries, which are inhospitable or hostile, has been invoked as a statement of citizenship identity based on descent. Shachar (2012) suggests that the principle of descent underlying *just sanguinis* enables the sustenance of ties with citizens and their descendants living abroad, often up to several generations. Citizenship regimes of Poland, Hungary and other Central and East European countries have displayed this approach. The Irish Constitution makes it explicit that those of 'Irish ancestry' living abroad share a 'special affinity' with the Irish nation owing to their common cultural identity and heritage. A strong statement of cultural bonds and its association with a right to return is found in Israel. The Law of Return 'establishes an entitlement to citizenship' for those with a Jewish ancestry 'treating them as *inpotentia* members of the state, thus creating a legal and symbolic link between existing members of the polity and a large diaspora community. This "right to return" is extended to family members, up to a third generation, regardless of their own religious affiliation or place of birth, as long as they can claim a lineage to a person who would have been entitled to make *aliyah* (Hebrew: "to ascend") to Israel, even if that person is already deceased or never actually settled there' (Shachar 2012, p. 1010). Apart from the ethno-national and cultural turn in citizenship, tendencies of 'solidification' of citizenship in relationship with the 'outsider' are seen in citizenship regimes that had hitherto professed republican or multicultural models of inclusion.

In November 2018, President Trump used 'invasion' as a metaphor to refer to the caravan of thousands of asylum seekers approaching the American borders along Mexico: 'It's like an invasion. They have violently overrun the Mexican border … These are tough people, in many cases. A lot of young men, strong men. And a lot of men that maybe we don't want in our country' (Flynn 2018). The invocation of a crisis ridden border, the need to deploy troops and install a wall at the border, along with the attack on birthright citizenship was a common refrain by President Trump in his election campaigns. In her novel *Home Fire*, Kamila Shamsie (2017) writes about the estrangement of young Muslim men and women born and brought up in England in the post 9/11 and the rise of the ISIS contexts. Their religious and cultural othering was, however, only part of the narrative of estrangement. Deeper and more consequential was the complete withdrawal of state protection and the refusal of a right to return to a young man, who joined the ISIS and subsequently wanted to exit. Shamsie's fictional rendition of the conditions in which citizenship can be reduced to a privilege is evident in most countries. It is, however, especially significant for understanding the turn towards strengthening those provisions that facilitate the deprivation of citizenship for public good and in the national interest. The loss of citizenship in such contexts, relegates the *political* relationship between citizens and the state, to revert to a stage where citizenship becomes a privilege that can be withdrawn. The distinction between those who deserve protection and those who do not depends on what is construed as the capability of a person to show sufficient and effective allegiance to the state. It also demands conformity to an idea of citizenship, which is aligned with constitutive conditions of belonging, such as ancestry and culture. By forming a community of descent, the state no longer establishes its authority as the primary source of universal membership, by standing above and independent of other local communities of belonging. Indeed, the state itself becomes the community to which citizens are tied constitutively.

The narrative structuring of a 'crisis' that makes an 'appropriate' citizenship law imperative mystifies the ways in which law serves as a 'cultural and institutional artefact' that masks the claims of ruling regimes to organize the different aspects of social relations. Those who see laws as part of the 'superstructure' would see them as instrumental in mediating, reinforcing and consolidating existing class relations and power, which is reflected also in the implementation of law through 'rules and sanctions' and 'class bound' institutions, including the courts. Law may, however, also be seen as an ideology which legitimates these practices, but stands in an 'active relationship' with society, often in a field of conflict (Thompson [1975] 1990). The space of citizenship assemblage precipitated by CAA and NRC has been replete with 'irruptions' which took 'insurgent' (Holston 2007) and 'iterative' (Benhabib 2007) forms. The debates in the Parliament represented a strong opposition to the ideology of citizenship embodied in the CAA and recalled the constitutional secularism of the founding moment of the Republic. The Constitution was recalled and reclaimed in the city streets and became emblematic of the transformative moment of constitutional founding, which was resurrected by the people in their search for democracy as a 'permanent ideal' (Langa 2006). Pius Langa's use of the 'metaphor' of the bridge (Langa 2006) as an embodiment of the constituent moment suggests a continuous quest for the 'magnificent goal of democracy'. It is also a reminder that the search for democratic citizenship does not have a terminal point. It demands a continual flow of people 'on the bridge', and its constant replenishment to make it a zone of sustained inhabitation to guard against the breach of democracy.

Bibliography

Ackerman, B. (1988). Neo-federalism. In J. Elster, and R. Slagstad (eds.), *Constitutionalism and Democracy: Studies in Rationality and Social Change* (153–193). Cambridge: Cambridge University Press.
Ackerman, Bruce. (1991). *We the People: Foundations*. Cambridge, MA: The Belknap Press of Harvard University Press.
Ahuja, Naman. (25 January 2020). 'Can the Historic Art of our Constitution Look to the Future?', *The Mint*, available on https://www.livemint.com/mint-lounge/features/can-the-historic-art-of-our-constitution-look-to-the-future-11579885322689.html (accessed 30 January 2020).
Akerman, James R. (1984). 'Cartography and the Emergence of Territorial States in Western Europe'. *Proceedings of the Tenth Annual Meeting of the Western Society for French History* (84–93). Lawrence: Western Society of French History.
Ambedkar, B. R. (2013). 'English Address at Poona District Law Library, Pune 22 December 1952'. In Narendra Jadhav (ed.), *Ambedkar Speaks* (Vol. 1, 287–294). Delhi: Konark Publishers.
Amin, Shahid. (1995). *Event, Metaphor, Memory: Chauri Chaura 1922–1992*. New Delhi: Oxford University Press.
Austin, Granville. ([1966] 2010). *The Indian Constitution: Cornerstone of a Nation*. New Delhi: Oxford University Press.
Austin, Granville. (2002). 'The Expected and the Unintended in the Working of a Democratic Constitution'. In Zoya Hasan, Eswaran Sridharan, and R. Sudarshan (eds.), *India's Living Constitution: Ideas, Practices, Controversies* (319–343). New Delhi: Permanent Black.
Austin, John. ([1832] 1995). *The Province of Jurisprudence Determined* (ed. W. Rumble). Cambridge: Cambridge University Press, 1995.
Bandes, Susan A. (ed.) (1999). *The Passions of Law*. New York: New York University Press.
Banerjee, Paula. (2010). *Borders, Histories, Existences: Gender and Beyond*. New Delhi: SAGE, 2010.
Banerjee, Sreeparna, Ambalika Guha, and Anasua Basy Ray Chaudhury. (July 2017). 'The 2015 India-Bangladesh Land Boundary Agreement: Identifying Constraints and Exploring Possibilities in Cooch Behar'. ORF Occasional Paper # 117, available on https://www.orfonline.org/wp-content/uploads/2017/07/ORF_OccasionalPaper_117_LandBoundary.pdf (accessed on 14 June 2019).
Barkley-Brown, Elsa. (1991). 'Polyrhythms and Improvisations: Lessons for Women's History'. *History Workshop Journal*, (Spring), 85–90.
Barpujari, Indrani. (2006). *Illegal Migrants (Determination by Tribunals) Act 1983, Promulgation and Repeal: A Contextual Analysis*. Guwahati, Assam: Omeo Kumar Das Institute of Social Change and Development.

Baruah, Sanjib. (1986). 'Immigration, Ethnic Conflict, and Political Turmoil—Assam 1979-1985'. *Asian Survey*, 26 (11), 1184-1206.
Baruah, Sanjib. (1999). *India Against Itself: Assam and the Politics of Nationality*. New Delhi: Oxford University Press.
Baruah, Sanjib. (2005). *Durable Disorder: Understanding the Politics of Northeast India*. New Delhi: Oxford University Press.
Baruah, Sanjib. (2009). 'The Partition's Long Shadow: The Ambiguities of Citizenship in Assam, India'. *Citizenship Studies*, 13 (6), 593-606.
Baruah, Sanjib. (19 January 2018). 'Stateless in Assam'. *Indian Express*, available on https://indianexpress.com/article/opinion/national-register-of-citizens-5030603/.
Baxi, Upendra. (2008). 'Outline of a "Theory of Practice" of Indian Constitutionalism'. In Rajeev Bhargava (ed.), *Politics and Ethics of the Indian Constitution* (93-118). New Delhi: Oxford University Press.
Baxi, Upendra. (2011). 'Dignity in and with Naz'. In Arvind Narrain, and Alok Gupta (eds.), *Law Like Love: Queer Perspectives on Law* (210-252). New Delhi: Yoda Press.
Baxi, Upendra. (2013). 'Preliminary Notes on Transformative Constitutionalism'. In Oscar Vilhena, Upendra Baxi, and Frans Viljoen (eds.), *Transformative Constitutionalism: Comparing the Apex Courts of Brazil, India and South Africa* (19-47). Johannesburg: Pretoria University Law Press.
Becker, Michael. (2020). 'Constitutionalism and Nationalism – Revisited'. In Anupama Roy and Michael Becker (eds.), *Dimensions of Constitutional Democracy: India and Germany* (31-50). Singapore: Springer.
Benhabib, Seyla. (2007). 'Twilight of Sovereignty or the Emergence of Cosmopolitan Norms? Rethinking Citizenship in Volatile Times'. *Citizenship Studies*, 11, 19-36.
Bhatia, Gautam. (2019). *The Transformative Constitution: A Radical Biography in Nine Acts*. Noida: Harper Collins.
Bhatia, Udit. (ed.) (2018). *The Indian Constituent Assembly: Deliberations on Democracy*. London and New York: Routledge.
Bockenforde, Ernst-Wolfgang. (2016). 'Citizenship and the Concept of Nationality'. In Mirjam Kuenkler, and Tine Stein (eds.), *Constitutional and Political Theory: Selected Writings of Ernst-Wolfgang Bockenforde* (Vol. I, 318-324). Oxford: Oxford University Press.
Boehme-Neßler, Volker. (2011). *Pictorial Law: Modern Law and the Power of Pictures*. Heidelberg: Springer.
Borbora, Sanjay. (23 December 2019). 'Essential Guide to the Crisis of Citizenship in Assam'. *RAIOT*, available on https://www.raiot.in/essential-guide-to-the-crisis-of-citizenship-in-assam/ (accessed 21 January 2020).
Brouard, Sylvain, Emiliano Grossman, Isabelle Guinaudeau, Simon Persico, and Caterina Froio. (2018). 'Do Party Manifestos Matter in Policy-Making? Capacities, Incentives and Outcomes of Electoral Programmes in France'. *Political Studies*, 66 (4), 1-19.
Brubaker, Rogers. (1992). *Citizenship and Nationhood in France and Germany*. Cambridge, MA: Harvard University Press.
Buragohain, Romesh. (2004). 'The All Assam Ahom Association and Ahom Politics of Surendranath Buragohain'. In Manorama Sharma (ed.), *Proceedings of North East India History Association, Twenty Sixth Session*. Shillong: North-Eastern Hill University.

Chatterjee, Himadri. (31 December 2019). 'Why Scheduled Caste Refugees of Bengal are Resisting CAA and NRC', *The Wire*, available on https://thewire.in/rights/scheduled-caste-refugees-bengal-caa-protest (accessed on 4 January 2020).

Chowdhory, Nasreen. (2018). *Refugees, Citizenship and Belonging in South Asia: Contested Terrains*. Singapore: Springer.

Collier, Stephen, and Aihwa Ong. (2005). 'Global Assemblages, Anthropological Problems'. In Aihwa Ong, and Stephen Collier (eds.), *Global Assemblages: Technology, Politics, and Ethics as Anthropological Problems* (3–21). Malden MA: Blackwell Publications.

Das, Veena. (1995). *Critical Events: An Anthropological Perspective on Contemporary India*. New Delhi: Oxford University Press.

Derrida, Jacques. (1992). 'Force of Law: The "Mystical Foundation of Authority"'. In Drucilla Cornell, Michel Rosenfeld, and David Gray Carlson (eds.), *Deconstruction and the Possibility of Justice*. New York: Routledge.

De, Rohit. (2016). 'Constitutional Antecedents'. In Sujit Choudhry, Madhav Khosla, and Pratap Bhanu Mehta (eds.), *The Oxford Handbook of the Indian Constitution* (17–37). Oxford: Oxford University Press.

De, Rohit. (2018). *A People's Constitution: The Everyday Life of Law in Indian Republic*. Princeton: Princeton University Press.

Desai, Rajvi. (6 January 2020). 'In Shaheen Bagh, Muslim Women Redefine Carework as Resistance'. *The Swaddle*, available on https://theswaddle.com/in-shaheen-bagh-muslim-women-redefine-carework-as-resistance/ (accessed on 14 March 2020).

Deshpande, Satish. (2003). *Contemporary India: A Sociological View*. New Delhi: Viking.

D'Entreves, Maurizio Passerin. (1994). *The Political Philosophy of Hannah Arendt*. London: Routledge.

Dhabahi, Garima. (2020). 'Paramount State and the "Princely Subject": Privy Purses Abolition and Its Aftermath'. In Anupama Roy, and Michael Becker (eds.), *Dimensions of Constitutional Democracy: India and Germany* (169–182). Singapore: Springer.

Đokić, Vladimir. (1998). 'Reading Derrida's "Force of Law: The Mystical Foundation of Authority"'. *Philosophy and Sociology*, 1 (5), 449–454.

Dutt, Bishnupriya. (2015). 'Performing Resistance with Maya Rao: Trauma and Protest in India'. *Contemporary Theatre Review*, 25 (3), 371–385.

Dutta, Akhil Ranjan. (24 February 2018). 'National Register of Citizens: Political Destiny of Immigrants in Assam'. *Economic and Political Weekly*, 53 (8), 18–21.

Dutta, Akhil Ranjan. (2021). *Hindutva Regime in Assam: Saffron in the Rainbow*. New Delhi: SAGE.

Dworkin, Ronald M. (1967). 'The Model of Rules'. Faculty Scholarship Series Paper 3609, Yale Law School Legal Scholarship Repository, 14–46, available on http://digitalcommons.law.yale.edu/fss_papers/3609

Elangovan, A. (2018). '"We the People?": Politics and the Conundrum of Framing a Constitution on the Eve of Decolonization'. In Udit Bhatia (ed.), *The Indian Constituent Assembly: Deliberations on Democracy* (10–37). London and New York: Routledge.

Faulks, Keith. (2000). *Citizenship*. London and New York: Routledge.

Flynn, Meagan. (2 November 2018). '"An Invasion of Illegal Aliens": The Oldest Immigration Fear-Mongering Metaphor in America'. *The Washington Post.*

Ghosh, Sahana. (December 2019). '"Everything Must Match": Detection, Deception and Migrant Illegality in India-Bangladesh Borderlands'. *American Anthropologist,* 121 (4), 870–883.

Gilmartin, D. (2009). 'One Day's Sultan: T.N. Seshan and Indian Democracy'. *Contributions to Indian Sociology,* 43 (2), 247–284.

Gohain, Hiren. (2019). *Struggling in a Time Warp.* Guwahati: Bhabani Books.

Guha, Ranajit. (ed.) (1982). *Subaltern Studies* (Vol. I). New Delhi: Oxford University Press.

Hart, H. L. A. ([1961] 2011). *The Concept of Law, Oxford Indian Paperbacks* (Second Edition). New Delhi: Oxford University Press.

Hart, H. L. A. (1982). *Essays on Bentham: Jurisprudence and Political Theory.* Oxford: Clarendon Press.

Heater, Derek. (1999). *What Is Citizenship?* Cambridge: Polity.

Holston, James. (2007). *Insurgent Citizenship: Disjunctions of Democracy and Modernity in Brazil.* Princeton: Princeton University Press.

Hull, Matthew. (2012). *Government of Paper: Materiality of Bureaucracy in Urban Pakistan.* Berkeley and Los Angeles: University of California Press.

Hussain, Monirul. (1993). *The Assam Movement: Class, Ideology and Identity.* New Delhi: Manak Publications in Association with Har-anand Publications.

Ignatieff, Michael. (1993). *Blood and Belonging: Journeys Into the New Nationalism.* London: BBC Books.

Jacobsohn, G. J. (2010). *Constitutional Identity.* Cambridge: Harvard University Press.

Jayal, Niraja Gopal. (2013). *Citizenship and Its Discontents: An Indian History.* Cambridge: Harvard University Press.

Jones, Reece. (2009). 'Sovereignty and Statelessness in the Border Enclaves of India and Bangladesh.' *Political Geography,* 28, 373–381.

Khosla, Madhav. (2020). *India's Founding Moment: The Constitution of a Most Surprising Democracy.* Cambridge: Harvard University Press.

Knops, Andrew. (2007). 'Agonism as Deliberation—On Mouffe's Theory of Democracy'. *Journal of Political Philosophy,* 15 (1), 115–126.

Kraidy, Marwan M. (2017). *The Naked Blogger of Cairo: Creative Insurgency in the Arab World.* Cambridge: Harvard University Press.

Langa, Pius. (2006). 'Transformative Constitutionalism'. *Stellenbosch L R,* 17 (3), 351–360.

Lerner, Hanna. (2016). 'The Indian Founding: A Comparative Perspective'. In Sujit Choudhary, Madhav Khosla, and Pratap Bhanu Mehta (eds.), *The Oxford Handbook of the Indian Constitution* (55–70). New Delhi: Oxford University Press.

Lohia, Prachi. (2019). *Erstwhile Enclaves in India: A Post LBA Analysis.* Kathmandu: Forum Asia.

Marshall, Thomas Humphrey. (1950). *Citizenship and Social Class and Other Essays.* Cambridge: Cambridge University Press.

Mbembe, Achille. (2001). *On the Postcolony.* Berkeley: University of California Press.

Mehta, Pratap Bhanu. (2002). 'The Inner Conflict of Constitutionalism: Judicial Review and the Basic Structure'. In Zoya Hasan, E. Sridharan, and R. Sudarshan

(eds.), *India's Living Constitution: Ideas, Practices, Controversies* (179–206). New Delhi: Permanent Black.
Mehta, Uday. (2010). 'Constitutionalism'. In N. G. Jayal, and P. B. Mehta (eds.), *The Companion Volume to Politics in India* (15–27). New Delhi: Oxford University Press.
Miller, Patrick R. (May 2011). 'The Emotional Citizen: Emotion as a Function of Political Sophistication'. *Political Psychology*, 32 (4), 575–600.
Miller, David. (2016). *Strangers in Our Midst*. Cambridge/Mass and London: Harvard University Press.
Misra, Udayon. (2000). *The Periphery Strikes Back: Challenges to the Nation-State Assam and Nagaland*. Simla: IIAS, 2000.
Misra, Udayon. (2014). *India's North-East: Identity Movements, State and Civil Society*. New Delhi: Oxford University Press.
Misra, Udayon. (2017). *Burden of History: Assam and the Partition—Unresolved Issues*. New Delhi: Oxford University Press.
Mitchell, Timothy. (March 1991). 'The Limits of the State: Beyond Statist Approaches and Their Critics'. *The American Political Science Review*, 85 (1), 77–96.
Nader, Laura. (2002). *The Life of the Law: Anthropological Projects*. Berkeley: University of California Press.
Narayan, R. K. (3 February 1952). 'The Election Game'. *The Hindu*.
Naresh, Vatsal. (2018). 'Pride and Prejudice in Austin's Cornerstone: Passions in the Constituent Assembly'. In Udit Bhatia (ed.), *The Indian Constituent Assembly: Deliberations on Democracy* (58–82). London and New York: Routledge.
Nariman, Fali. (2006). *India's Legal System: Can It Be Saved*. New Delhi: Penguin.
Nehru, Jawaharlal. (1947). Tryst with Destiny, Speech available at https://www.cam.ac.uk/files/a-tryst-with-destiny/index.html (accessed on 15 August 2020).
Neveu, Catherine, John Clarke, Kathleen Coll, and Evelina Dagnino. (2011). 'Introduction: Questioning Citizenships/Questions de citoyennetés'. *Citizenship Studies*, 15 (8), 945–964.
Niloy, Suliman. (15 May 2015). 'Indian Enclave Dweller's Son Prefers Living as a Bangladesh Citizen'. bdnews24.com.
Olson, Greta. (2016). 'The Turn to Passion: Has Law and Literature become Law and Affect?' *Law & Literature*, 28 (3), 335–353, http://dx.doi.org/10.1080/1535685X.2016.1232925
Ong, Aihwa. (2006). 'Mutations in Citizenship'. *Theory, Culture & Society*, 23, 499–531.
Ong, Aihwa, and S. J. Collier (eds.). (2005). *Global Assemblages: Technology, Politics, and Ethics as Anthropological Problems*. Malden MA: Blackwell.
Parker, Geoffrey. (1988). *The Geopolitics of Domination*. London: Routledge and Kegan Paul.
Philipose, Pamela. (2009). 'Borders in the Mind: Bangladeshis, a Nowhere Policy for a Nowhere People'. In Ujjwal Kumar Singh (ed.), *Human Rights and Peace: Ideas, Laws, Institutions and Movements* (192–196). New Delhi: Sage.
Pisharoty, Sangeeta Barooah. (2019). *Assam: The Accord, The Discord*. Gurgaon: Penguin Random House Press.
Pitkin, Hanna. (1987). 'The Idea of a Constitution'. *Journal of Legal Education*, 37 (2), 167–169.

Quinn, Thomas. (2014). *Mandates, Manifestos and Coalitions: UK Party Politics after 2010*. London: The Constitution Society.

Ramnath, Kalyani. (2011). 'The Runaway Judgement: Law as Literature, Courtcraft and Constitutional Vision'. *Journal of Indian Law and Society*, 3 (Winter), 1–28.

Rathore, Akash Singh. (2020). *Ambedkar's Preamble: A Secret History of the Constitution of India*. Delhi: Penguin Books India.

Rawls, John. (1993). *Political Liberalism*. New York: Columbia University Press.

Report of the Joint Parliamentary Committee on the Citizenship (Amendment Bill). (2016). Lok Sabha Secretariat. New Delhi, January 2019/Pausha 1940 (Saka).

Rodrigues, Valerian. (2008). 'Citizenship and the Indian Constitution'. In Rajeev Bhargava (ed.), *Politics and Ethics of the Indian Constitution* (164–188). New Delhi: Oxford University Press.

Rosenfeld, M. (2009). *The Identity of the Constitutional Subject: Selfhood, Citizenship, Culture, and Community*. London: Routledge.

Roy Anupama. (2010). *Mapping Citizenship in India*. New Delhi: Oxford University Press (Reprint, October 2014).

Roy, Anupama. (2014). 'Critical Events, Incremental Memories and Gendered Violence'. *Australian Feminist Studies*, 29 (81), 238–254.

Roy, Anupama. (2016). 'Liminal and Legible: Gendered Citizenship and State-Formative Practices in the 1950s'. In Anne R. Epstein, and Rachel G. Fuchs (eds.), *Gender and Citizenship in Historical and Transnational Perspective: Agency, Space, Borders* (120–142). New York: Palgrave Macmillan.

Sack, D. R. (1980). *Human Territoriality: Its Theory and History*. Cambridge: Cambridge University Press.

Saco, Giuseppe. (1991). 'A Place in the Shade'. *The European Journal of International Affairs*, 12 (2), 5–23.

Sadiq, Kamal. (2009). *Paper Citizens*. New York: Oxford University Press.

Sahai, Shrinkhla. (9 January 2020). 'Maya Rao Leads the Way in Art Uprising'. *The Hindu*, available on https://www.thehindu.com/entertainment/art/maya-rao-leads-the-way-in-art-uprising/article30521874.ece (accessed on 14 January 2020).

Sajo, A. (2011). *Constitutional Sentiments*. New Haven: Yale University Press.

Samaddar, Ranabir. (12 April 2019). 'Migrants, NRC, and the Paradox of Protection and Power'. *The Wire*.

Sassen, Saskia. (2011). 'The Global Street: Making the Political'. *Globalizations*, 8, 573–579.

Scott, David. (1995). 'Colonial Governmentality'. *Social Text*, (43) (Autumn), 191–220.

Sethi, Rajat, and Subhrashtha. (2017). *The Last Battle of Saraighat: The Story of the BJP's Rise in the North-East*. New Delhi: Penguin.

Shachar, Ayelet. (2012). 'Citizenship'. In Michel Rosenfeld, and András Sajó (eds.), *The Oxford Handbook of Comparative Constitutional Law*. Oxford: Oxford University Press.

Shamsie, Kamila. (2017). *Home Fires*. New York: Riverhead Books.

Shani, Ornit. (2018). *How India Became Democratic: Citizenship and Making of the Universal Franchise*. Gurgaon: Penguin/Viking.

Singh, Anushka. (2020). 'Law and Constitutional Democracy: Meanings, Iterations and Consequences'. In Anupama Roy, and Michael Becker (eds.), *Dimensions of Constitutional Democracy: India and Germany* (147–168). Singapore: Springer.
Singh, K. P. (1990). 'Role of the Congress in the Framing of India's Constitution'. *Indian Journal of Political Science*, 51 (2).
Singh, Ujjwal Kumar. (1999). *Political Prisoners in India*. New Delhi: Oxford University Press.
Singh, Ujjwal Kumar. (2014). 'Surveillance Regimes in India'. In Fergal Davis, Nicola McGarrity, and George Williams (eds.), *States of Surveillance: Counter-Terrorism and Comparative Constitutionalism*. London: Routledge.
Smith, Anthony D. (1983). *Theories of Nationalism*. London: Duckworth.
Spark, Holloway. (1997). 'Dissident Citizenship'. *Hypatia*, 12 (4) (Fall), 74–110.
Staatsbürgerschaft und Nationalitätskonzept. (1995). In Staat, Nation, Europa. Studien zur Staatslehre, Verfassungstheorie und Rechtsphilosophie (59–67). Frankfurt am Main: Suhrkamp, 2000.
Supiot, Alain. (2007). *Homo Juridicus: On the Anthropological Function of the Law* (translated by Saskia Brown). London: Verso.
Swaminathan, Shivprasad. (26 January 2013). 'India's benign constitutional revolution'. *The Hindu*, available on http://www.thehindu.com/opinion/lead/indias-benign-constitutional-revolution/article4345212.ece (accessed on 26 January 2013).
Thompson, E. P. ([1975] 1990). *Whigs and Hunters: The Origin of the Black Act*. London: Penguin Books.
Torpey, John. (2000). *The Invention of the Passport: Surveillance, Citizenship and the State*. Cambridge: Cambridge University Press.
Tribe, L. H. (1987). 'The Idea of the Constitution: A Metaphor-Morphis'. *Journal of Legal Education*, 37 (2), 170–173.
Tushnet, Mark. (2010). 'How do Constitutions Constitute Constitutional Identity?' *International Journal of Constitutional Law*, 8 (3), 671–676.
Urbinati, Nadia. (December 2000). 'Representation as Advocacy: A Study of Democratic Deliberation'. *Political Theory*, 28 (6), 758–786.
Van der Veer, Peter. (1996). *Religious Nationalisms: Hindus and Muslims in India*. Delhi: Oxford University Press.
Vilhena, Oscar, Upendra Baxi, and Frans Viljoen. (eds.) (2013). *Transformative Constitutionalism: Comparing the Apex Courts of Brazil, India and South Africa*. Johannesburg: Pretoria University Law Press.
Walzer, Michael. (1983). *Spheres of Justice*. New York: Basic Books.
Wankhede, Harish. (19 March 2010). 'Dalit Symbolism and the Democratisation of Secular Spaces'. *Mainstream*XLVIII (12).
Weiner, Myron. (1965). 'India: Two Political Cultures'. In Lucian W. Pye, and Sydney Verba (eds.), *Political Culture and Political Development* (199–244). Princeton: Princeton University Press.
Weiner, Myron. (1983). 'The Political Demography of Assam's Anti-Immigrant Movement'. *Population and Development Review*, 9 (2), 279–292.
Wood, Bronwyn Elisabeth. (November 2013). 'Young People's Emotional Geographies of Citizenship Participation: Spatial and Relational Insights'. *Emotion, Space and Society*, 9, 50–58.

Young, Iris Marion. (1989). 'Polity and Group Difference: A Critique of the Ideal of Universal Citizenship'. *Ethics*, 99 (2), 250–274.

List of Cases Cited

Ajay Hasia vs. Khalid Mujib Sehravardi, 1 SCC 722 1981 AIR 487, 1981 SCR (2) 79, available on https://indiankanoon.org/doc/1186368/

Amit Sahni vs. Commissioner of Police, 2020 [WP (Civil) No. 3282 of 2020], available on https://indiankanoon.org/doc/145656971/

Assam Sanmilita Mahasangha and Others vs. Union of India and others [WP (Civil) No. 562 of 2012], available on https://indiankanoon.org/doc/50798357/

Budhan Choudhry vs. State of Bihar, AIR 1955 SC 191, available on https://indiankanoon.org/doc/1905739/

Deepak Kumar Nath vs. Union of India [WP (Civil) No. 311 of 2015], available on https://indiankanoon.org/doc/1514020/

Deepak Sibal vs. Punjab University, 1989 2 SCC 145, available on https://indiankanoon.org/doc/1461661/

E. P. Royappa vs. State of Tamil Nadu, 1974 AIR 555, 1974 SCR (2) 348, available on https://indiankanoon.org/doc/1327287/

Jabeda Begum @ Jabeda Khatun vs. The Union of India and Others [WP (Civil) No. 7451 of 2019], available on https://indiankanoon.org/doc/161150352/

Justice K. S. Puttaswamy (Retd) vs. Union of India [WP (Civil) No. 494 of 2012], available on https://indiankanoon.org/doc/91938676/

Kamalakhya Dey Purkayastha and Others vs. Union of India and others [WP (Civil) No. 1020 of 2017], available on https://indiankanoon.org/doc/132044439/

Madras Bar Association vs. Union Of India & Anr [Transferred Case (C) No. 150 OF 2006], available on https://indiankanoon.org/doc/181443842/

Maneka Gandhi vs. Union of India, 1978 AIR 597, 1978 SCR (2) 621, available on https://indiankanoon.org/doc/1766147/

Manowara Bewa @ Manora Bewa vs. Union of India and the State of Assam [WP (Civil) No. 2364 of 2016], available on https://indiankanoon.org/doc/105245883/

Md. Babul Islam vs. State of Assam [WP(Civil) No. 3547 of 2016].

Navtej Johar vs. Union of India [WP (Criminal), No. 76 of 2016], available on https://indiankanoon.org/doc/168671544/

Naz Foundation vs. Government of NCT of Delhi [WP (Civil) No. 7455 of 2001], available on https://indiankanoon.org/doc/100472805/

PUDR vs. Union of India, 1982 AIR 1473, 1983 SCR (1) 456, available on https://indiankanoon.org/doc/496663/

Rupajan Begum vs. Union of India and Others [WP (Civil) No. 20858 of 2017], arising out of Special Leave Petition (Civil) No. 13256 of 2017], available on https://indiankanoon.org/doc/7961750/

S. R. Bommai vs. Union of India 1994 AIR 1918, 1994 SCC (3) 1, available on https://indiankanoon.org/doc/60799/

Sarbananda Sonowal vs. Union Of India & Anr [WP (Civil) 131 of 2000], available on https://indiankanoon.org/doc/907725/

The State of West Bengal vs. Anwar All Sarkar Habib, 1952 AIR 75, 1952 SCR 284, available on https://indiankanoon.org/doc/1270239/
State of Arunachal Pradesh vs. Khudiram Chakma, 1994 AIR 1461, 1993 SCR (3) 401, available on https://indiankanoon.org/doc/473806/

Debates in the Constituent Assembly and Parliament

Constituent Assembly Debates, Official Report, Book no. 4, Vol. IX, Lok Sabha Secretariat, New Delhi, 2003 (fourth reprint), available on https://www.constitutionofindia.net/constitution_assembly_debates
Lok Sabha Debates, available on http://164.100.47.194/Loksabha/Debates/debatelok.aspx
Rajya Sabha Debates, available on https://rsdebate.nic.in/

Index

For the benefit of digital users, indexed terms that span two pages (e.g., 52–53) may, on occasion, appear on only one of those pages.

Tables and figures are indicated by *t* and *f* following the page number

Ackerman, Bruce
   and theory of constitutional moments, 30–31, 103
Ambedkar, B.R.
   in art installation, 207–8
   constitutional morality, 30–31, 127, 128
   debate on citizenship in the Constituent Assembly, 14–15, 97, 99–103
   invocation in anti-CAA protests, 203–4, 212–13
Article 11
   and legislative powers of Parliament, 24, 28, 46–47, 100, 102, 120–21
Assam
   'additional load', 18–19, 58–59
   Assam exception, 6, 15–22, 26–27
   CAA 1985, 6, 18–20, 35, 36, 42–43, 63–64, 76–77, 86–87, 88–89, 90*t*, 96–97
   CAA 2019 (*see* Citizenship Amendment Act 2019)
   deferred citizenship, 6, 12–13, 18–19
   Foreigners Act 1946, 4–5, 15–16, 18–19, 36, 40–41, 44–45, 71–72, 83–85, 89–97, 93*t*, 228–30, 233, 234–35
   'foreigners' question', 15–16, 35–36, 78–79, 86–87
   graded citizenship, 6, 18–19, 36, 37, 90*t*
   history of immigration, 15–16
   IMDT Act 1983, 15–19, 21–22, 36, 37–38, 40–41, 90*t*
   movement, AASU, AAGP, 35–36
   NRC (*see* National Register of Citizens)
   NRC 1951, 40
   residual citizens, 18–19, 37
Assam Accord 1985
   Clause 2, 35–36
   Clause 5, 35–37
   Clause 6, 57–58, 88, 88n.8, 160–62, 228–30
   and graded citizenship in Assam, 37
   'negotiated settlement', 18–19, 88–89
   'public contract', 18–19, 88–89
Assam Sanmilita Mahasangha, 42–43
   judgement 2014, 21–22, 34, 42–47, 49, 51–52, 53, 96–97, 245
assemblage, 6–9, 87, 246, 249–50
   aggregate of relationships, 6–8
   mobile and excluded populations, 6–8
   territorialized, 6–8
   web of contracts, 6–8
Austin, John, 22–23
   'monopoly of power', 23
   sovereign, 22–23

Baruah, Sanjib, 26–28, 35, 40, 82n.47, 85–86, 159–60, 243
Baxi, Upendra, 6, 8–9, 12, 103, 127, 149–50, 211–12
belonging, 8–10, 27–28, 215–16
   affective, 20–21, 165–66, 247–48
   ambivalence of, 29–30
   blood and, 8–9, 29–30
   commonality, 9–10
   constitutive, 247, 249–50

belonging (*cont.*)
  and identity, 9–10, 97, 101, 243–44
  inherited, 21
  and NRC, 57–58
  polyrhythmous, 8–9
  relations of *ligeance*, 9–10
  terms of, 4–5, 8–10, 30–31, 106–7
  territorial, 8–9
  zones of disturbed citizenship, 9–10, 246
Bentham, Jeremy, 23–24
demystification of law, 23–24
Bharatiya Janata Party (BJP), 3–4, 19–20, 57–58, 76–79, 87–89, 129, 134, 135–37, 138–39, 140–41, 142, 150–51, 155–56, 157–58, 225–27
borders
  anomalies, 171
  bounded geographical space, 168–69
  capacity to control, 9–10
  'cultural and political', 9–10
  decolonization and morphological models, 168–69
  Nehru-Noon Agreement and the Berubari Union, 169–70
  political and territorial sovereignty, 168–69
  Radcliffe Commission, 169–70
  and state sovereignty, 168–69
bounded citizenship, 6, 8–9, 20–21, 27–28, 85–86, 122, 129, 244–45
Brubaker, Rogers
  national citizenship in Europe, 5–6

citizenship
  acquisition and termination, 14–15, 46–47, 90*t*, 102–3, 120–21
  norms and principles, 102–3
  power to District Collectors, 83–85
  power of Parliament, 102, 233–34
  (*see entry* Article 11)
  SOP 2004 and LTV, 83–85
  by birth, 8–9, 13–15, 19–20, 36, 38, 50, 51–52, 53, 54, 86–87, 97–98
  and CAA 2003, 86–87, 91*t*
  and debates in the Constituent Assembly, 101
  and section 3 of CAA, 38–39, 89–96
  citizenship identity, 247–48
  consciousness about, 3–4, 30–31, 108, 203–4
  constitutional provisions, 13, 14–15, 46–47, 109
  impermanence of, 102–3
  creative insurgencies, 2–3
  deferred citizenship (*see entry under* Assam)
  by descent, 8–9, 13–15, 19–21, 28–29, 36, 53, 54, 68, 75, 97–98, 129, 156–57, 243–44, 248–49
  and debates in the Constituent Assembly, 105–6, 112–13, 118–19
  and NRC, 156–57
  differentiated citizenship, 35–36
  dissident citizenship, 30–31
  'documentary citizenship', 6, 27–28, 60, 245
  graded citizenship, 6, 18–19, 36, 37, 90*t*
  hyphenated citizenship, 8–9, 26–27, 34, 58, 129, 156–57, 167–68, 243
  identification regimes, 29–30, 59–60, 68–69
  as inheritance, 13–14, 97–98, 106, 111–12, 243–45
  instrument of closure, 5–8
  iterative practices, 2–3, 130–31, 223–25, 249–50
  liminality, 29–31, 163–64, 167–68
  national, 5–6, 21, 26–28, 118–19, 121–22, 129, 150–51, 156–57
  political citizenship and proletarianization, 240–41
  residual citizens (*see entry under* Assam)
  and 'strangers', 30–31, 67–68, 247–48
  terms of belonging (*see entry under* Assam)
  transformative, logic of, 6, 10–12
  uniqueness of Indian citizenship, 6, 97–98

citizenship regimes
   'aliens' and 'strangers', 30–31, 67–68, 247–48
   ancestry and the 'right to return', 247–48
   'boundary condition', 34
   conditions of 'extreme necessity', 247–48
   consecutive regimes, 6
   constitutional imaginary, 3–4
   'crisis', notion of, 9–10, 30–31, 34, 35–36, 58–59, 60, 77–78, 79, 122, 247–48, 249–50
   and indeterminate citizenship, 13, 18–19, 37, 109
   'Law of Return', 247–48
   logic of, 4–5, 6, 8–9, 11–12, 20–21, 246
      closure, 34, 58–59, 122, 245
      the security state, 56–57
   'mobility of people', 9–10, 101, 167–68
   national borders, 9–10
   solidarity models, 9–10, 34, 58–59
   sovereign's power to command, 247–48
   tendency in, 8–9, 19–20, 27–28, 85–86, 90t, 247–48
   tightening of laws, 9–10
Citizenship Act 1955, 4–5, 6, 13, 19–20, 29–30, 35, 51–52, 54–55, 56, 90t, 109, 148
Citizenship Amendment Act 1985, 6, 19–20, 35, 36, 42–43, 63–64, 86–87, 90t, 96–97
   Assam exception, 6, 15–19
   cut-off dates, 18–19, 36, 43, 45–47, 51–52, 96–97
   graded citizenship (*see entry under* Assam)
   section 6A, 18–19, 36, 51–52, 53, 90t
      constitutional validity of, 42–43, 46–47, 50, 51–52, 63–64, 76–78
Citizenship Amendment Act 1986, 19–20, 38, 51–52, 54–55, 90t
Citizenship Amendment Act 2003, 6, 19–21, 26–27, 33–34, 38–39, 45–46, 85–86, 91t, 160–62, 244–45, 247–48
   and citizenship by birth, 19–20, 53, 90t
   Citizenship Rules, 2003, 4, 4A, 38–39, 51
   the 'hinge point', 21, 86–87, 129, 156–57
   and JACBR, 50
   National Register of Citizens (NRC) (*see* NRC)
   Overseas Citizens of India (OCI), 38 , 90t
Citizenship Amendment Bill (CAB) 2016, 21–22, 34, 86–87, 88–89, 93t, 96–97, 119–20, 246
   and Joint Parliamentary Committee (JPC), 119–29
Citizenship Amendment Bill (CAB) 2019, 3–4, 101, 118–19, 129–30
   Debates in the Parliament, 131–58
      Amit Shah, 134–37
      'citizen-activist', 150–51, 153
      'communitarian majoritarianism', 150–51
      constitutional disharmony and constitutional identity, 139
      'constitutional secularism', 137–39, 150–51
      'dictatorship', 153–54
      fissures along party lines, 131–32, 141–42
      'historical necessity', 150–51
      'infiltrator', 135–36, 145–46
      and Jogendra Nath Mandal, 151–52
      law-making and judicial scrutiny, 131–33
      legislative competence or content, 134
      majoritarian politics, 140–41
      manifesto and electoral mandate, 134–35
      normal and constitutional politics, 131
      and Parliamentary democracy, 140
      partition and the Congress, 151–53
      'persecuted minorities', 137–38

Citizenship Amendment Bill (CAB) 2019 (*cont.*)
  populism as political strategy, 135–36
  regional traditions of martyrdom, 153–54
  relationship with NRC, 97–159
  violence against Hindus, 140–41
  voices from the North-East, 143–49
  Voting in Parliament, 88–89
Citizenship Amendment Act 2019, 3–4, 6, 14–15, 22–23, 27–28, 82, 83–86, 89, 94*t*, 118–19
  communitarian majoritarianism, 150–51, 243
  and executive orders, 96–97
  and illegal migrants, 96–97
  minority communities, 89–96
  national-majoritarian, 21
  protests against (*see protests against CAA*)
  veneer of liberal citizenship, 27–28, 85–86, 122, 244–45
civil disobedience in South Africa, 1–2
Constituent Assembly
  debate on citizenship, 99–118
    agonism, 101
    classes of people, 104–5
    'common citizenship', 115–16
    and constitutional disharmony, 98–99, 100
    and constitutional identity, 98–100, 114–15
    and constitutional incrementalism, 102–3
    and constitutional moments, 103
    distinguishing 'migrants' from 'returnees', 109–14
    distinguishing 'permanent home' from 'homeland', 114–15
    experience of Assam, 116–17
    evacuee property, 109–10
    as 'extraordinary provisions', 116
    fault-lines, 97–98
    non-discrimination, 115–16, 118–19
    principle of secularism, 114–15, 117–19
    and 'religious identification' of citizenship, 105–8
    tumultuous times and inclusionary citizenship, 141–42
    unbridled power of Parliament, 108
  deliberative body, 12, 14–15
  ideational disagreements, 13–14, 97
  institutional arrangements and time delays, 142
  interlocutory spaces, 103
  juridical norms, 19–20
  locating the legal sovereign, 12
  'passions' in, 12–13
  'permanent provisions' for citizenship, 97
  'principles' of citizenship, 13–15, 28–29, 99–100, 102–3, 117–18, 121, 145–46
  prior consensus, 14–15, 101, 102–3, 140
  state formative practices, 12, 59–60, 204–5
Constitution
  as best-seller, 203–4
  commencement of, 10–11, 12, 22–23
  conversations about, 30–31
  emancipatory project, 11–12
  and everyday life, 26, 206
  familiar, 26
  giving process, 99–100
  as higher-order law, 117–18
  installations and live art performance, 207–8
    cognitive and somatic experiences, 209–10
    constitutional text as image, 209
    'fear' and 'hope', 207–8
    Riyaz Komu's 'Holy Shivers', 207–8
    'The Delhi Walk' and Maya Rao, 209–11
  an insurgent text, 204–5
  dialogic space, 207–8
  intelligibility of, 213–14
  narrativized, 207
  objectives of, 14–15
  and the 'people', 26, 206–7
  people as source of authority, 3–4, 10–11

as performative text, 203–4
'popular', 26, 203–4, 206
popular sovereignty and Article
   395, 205–6
The Preamble, 203–4
Cooch Behar, 29–30, 164–65, 167–
   68, 169n.4, 171–72
Camps
   Dinhata, 29–30, 164–65, 172–73,
      180, 181, 182, 183–84, 185, 186–
      87, 188, 189, 190, 193–94, 198
   Haldibari, 29–30, 164–65, 185,
      186–87, 188, 190, 193–94
   Mekhliganj, 29–30, 164–65,
      181, 185, 186–87, 188, 191–
      92, 193–94
Chhits, 29–30, 164–65, 166–67, 197,
   198, 199–200, 201–2

democratic iteration, 8–9, 222–25
Derrida, Jacques, 'mystical foundations
   of authority of law', 25–26
discrete tendencies, NRC and CAA,
   21, 244–45
'distinguishability assumption', 6,
   60, 244–45

enclaves, 29–30, 164–65
   and ambivalent citizenship, 85–86
   'Bharat panthi', 175–76
   and border-making, 168–70
   Chhitmahal United Council
      Office, 174
   citizenship through acquisition of
      foreign territory, 87
   exchange of, 163–64, 168–73
   fragmented citizenship, 165–67
   'haphazard' borders, territoriality and
      sovereignty, 165–66
   'hoisting' the national flag, 174
   split-citizenship, 167–68
   and territorial sovereignty, 29–30
enumeration, 43
   bureaucratic practices
      of, 244–45
   and Citizenship Rules 2003, 51
   house-to house, 26–27, 38–39

legal regime of, 21
and NPR, 160–62
and NRC, 58–62
of voting population, 206–7
'event', 16–18
   critical, 16–18, 211, 234–35
   ethics of political action, 211
   modalities of political action
      of protest, 210–11
   time/space, 16–18
Executive Orders 2015, 2016
   and CAB 2016, 29–30, 231–32
   and Foreigners Act 1946, 96–
      97, 222–23
   and Passport Act 1920, 96–97,
      222–23

Gandhi, Mohandas Karamchand, 1–
   2, 114–15
   civil-disobedience, 150–51, 154–55
   Dhamma-Swaraj, 207–8, 215–16
Gauhati High Court, 26–27, 40–41, 48–
   49, 63–64, 69–73

Hindutva
   and CAA 2019, 10–11, 86–87,
      129, 245
   majoritarian order, 6
   politics of, 20–21, 212–13
homeland, 27–28, 114–15, 167–68
   and belonging, 106
   of Hindus, 86–87, 115–16
   migration and, 181–82
   promise of return, 243–44
   return to, 114
   and Sikhs, 107

identification of citizens, 36
Immigrants (Expulsion from Assam)
   Act 1950, 44–45, 50

Joint Parliamentary committee (JPC)
   and CAB 2016, 3–4, 21–22,
      28–29, 85–86, 87–88, 97,
      102, 119–29
   constitutional experts, 122–24
   constitutionality of CAB, 123–24

Joint Parliamentary committee (JPC) and CAB 2016 (*cont.*)
    Article 14 and the question of reasonableness and intelligibility, 124–26
    and authority of precedent, 128–29
    and constitutional morality, 127–29
    and critical morality, 128–29
    Naz Foundation and the 'test of reasonableness', 126–27
    in liberal democracies, 121–22
    and 'natural' citizenship, 121–22
    and opposition to CAB 2016 in the North-East, 88
    and the principle of 'legislative competence', 120–21
jus sanguinis, 6–8, 13–14, 86–87, 88–89, 97
jus soli, 6–8, 13–14, 86–87, 97

Land Border Agreement Treaty (LBAT) 2015, 8–9, 29–30, 163–65, 166–67, 171–72, 192, 200–1
    Bangladesh Vinimaya Committee, 174–76, 177
    BDO office and enclave settlements, 185, 186–87, 188
    Constitution 119th Amendment Act 2015, 170–71
    and displacement of population, 171
    exchange of population and territory, 164–65, 171
    land and homeland, 167–68
    LBAT 1974, 163–64
    'new' citizens, 164–65, 166–67, 183–84, 189, 201–182
        daily lives, 195–97, 198–99
        funds for, 197–98, 200–1
        MNREGA cards, 197
        relationship with land, 194–95, 199–200
        West Bengal Land Reforms (Amendment) Bill 2018, 200–1
        sedentary, 193
        voter ID cards, 197, 198–99
    and citizenship status, 201–2
    option taking survey, 171–72, 186–88
    possibility of legibility, 243
    Protocol of 2011, 163–64
    'returnees', 164–65, 166–67, 181–83, 185, 189, 190, 192, 194–95, 200–1
        biometric details, 192–93
        and 'family', 185–87, 190, 191–92
        land left behind, 182–84
        land and rehabilitation, 190
        'mobile' citizens, 193
    'right to choose citizenship', 166–68
    section 7 of Citizenship Act 1955, 167–68, 192
    state assembly elections, 189–90, 191–92, 197
law
    anthropological *effect*, 6–8
    anthropological function of, Alain Supiot, 7n.7
    anthropological scrutiny, 4–5
    anthropological subject, Laura Nader, 7n.7
    Article 13 of the Indian Constitution, 22–23
    authorial power of state, 9–10
    Bare Act, 4–5
    coalescent present, 4–5
    constitutional standards, 23–24
    deliberative content, 31–32
    enforceability of, 22–23, 24
    field of, 23–24
    force of, 2–3, 23, 25–26
    in force, 22–23
    foundational violence, 25–26
    ideological embeddedness, 4–5
    imperative of command, 23–24
    iterations of, 8–9
    juridical person, 6–8, 7n.7
    justice as legal virtue, 23–24, 26
    just law and morality, 25–26
    law-making, limits of, 28
    legal subject, 6–8, 22–23
    limits of, 22–23
    'moral order', 23–24
    normative claim, 23, 28–29, 120–21
    originary violence, 25–26
    question of authority, 23, 120–21

rules of recognition, 25–26
standards of validation, 23–24
temporalities of, 4–5
test of validity, 23
vertical structure, obedience, 22–23
violence of, 9–10, 23–24, 25–26

Manto, Saadat Hassan, 1, 2–3
Singh, Toba Tek, 1
Marshall, T.H., 5–6, 240–41
migrant
  ambivalent location, 9–10
  disruptive figure, 9–10
  'illegal'
    act of aggression, 15–16, 37–38, 46–47
    and Assam Accord 1985, 18–19
    and CAA 2019, 21, 28–29
    Citizenship Rules 4A, 51
    and elections, 15–16
    Foreigners Act 1946, 14–15
    and the IMDT Act 1983, 15–18
    national security, 9–10
    section 6A, constitutionality, 43, 46–47

National Identity Cards, 6, 20–21, 26–27, 33–34, 38–39, 91t, 160–62
national identity systems, 59–60
National Register of Citizens (NRC)
  adjudicating citizenship, 34, 42–43
  All Assam Ahom Association, 42–49
  Assam exception, 34–36, 37–40, 46–47, 56–57, 90t, 158–59
  Assam Public Works, petition, 42–49
  Assam Sanmilita Mahasangha, petititon, 42–49
    challenging 6A, 43–44
    challenging Rule 4A, 51
    judgement in, 43–49
  bureaucratic rationality, 61–62
  children of 'illegal migrants', 51–56
  'detectability', 68n.30
  detection and expulsion, 28–29
  documentary practices, 26–27
  documentary regimes, 6, 57–76
  emotive appeal, 60–61

hyphenated citizenship (*see under* citizenship)
  identification regimes, 29–30, 59–60, 68, 247
  ideological alignment with CAA, 28–29
  JACBR, 50
  legacy, 21, 26–27, 33–34, 55, 58, 243–47
    constitutive belonging, 247
    legacy data, 33–34, 63–64, 65, 68, 246–47
    legacy document, 67–68, 69–72
    and electoral rolls, 63–64, 69–70, 246–47
    evidentiary paradigm, 68–69
    and 'family tree', 65–66
    and linkage documents, 63–64, 67–68
    panchayat certificate AND 'migrated married women', 71–75
    'public document', 67–68, 243–44, 246–47
    legacy person, 65–66, 72, 74–75, 246–47
    legacy trace, 68–70
  legal myth, 247
  lists/drafts, 33–34, 41–42
    unique legacy data code, 63–64, 68
  'Miya poetry', 79–80
  National Registration Authority, 33
  NRC 1951, 40–41, 58–59, 68
  NRC Ulaigol, 66
  NRIC, 6, 20–21, 38–39, 53–54, 244–45
  pilot project, 40–41
  Protests against
    anti-NRC anthem, 203
  responsible participation, 62–63
  re-verification of final list, 80–81
  statelessness, 29–30, 200–1
  section 14A CAA 2003, 38–39
  section 4A Citizenship Rules 2003, 38–39
  Swajan and Bimalangshu Roy Foundation petition, 50
    challenging section 6A CAA, 50

Nehru, Jawaharlal, 10–11, 205–6
  and Constituent Assembly Debates, 14–15, 102–3, 117–18

Overseas Citizens of India (OCI), 19–20, 86–87, 91*t*, 136–37
  affective belonging, 19–20, 165–66, 247–48
  and CAA 2003, 89, 91*t*
  and foreigners, 90*t*
  section 7A, 91*t*

Partition, 1
  and belonging, 12–13
  and debates on citizenship in CA, 97–119
  and historical injustices, 3–4
  and OCI, 19–20
  and Part II of the Constitution, 10–11
Protests against CAA 2019, 4, 22–23, 26, 30–31, 83, 85–87, 88, 146, 157–58, 160–62
  alliances and solidarities, 215–16
  city as a critical space, 212–13
  constitutional citizenship, 30–31, 102
  Constitution-claiming as a moral experience, 212–13
  constitutional ethics, 130–31, 215–16
  constitutional morality and public conscience, 212–13
  courts and anti-CAA protests
    Bombay High Court, Aurangabad Bench, 217–22
    dharna at Idgah maidan, 217
    dissent of the people and sensitive government, 221–22
    'history of the constitution', 219–20
    'rule of law', 219–20
    sense of fraternity and the freedom struggle, 219–20
    Rajasthan High Court, 222
  dissidence, 30–31
  domestication of the 'public', 240
  empathy, 203–4, 207–8, 212–13, 215–16
  ethic of public action, 212–13
  fraternity, 31–32
  'irruptions', 215–16, 249–50
  and making spaces public, 213–14
  pandemic effect, 203–4
  petitions against CAA before the Supreme Court, 227–33 (*see also under* Supreme Court of India)
    Article 14 jurisprudence enhanced, 232–33
    'Assam perspective' in petitions, 228–30
    'civic nationalism', 231–32
    'founding principles' of the Republic in India, 231–32
    'illegal classification based on religion', 227–28
    'individual autonomy and personal self-determination', 232–33
    'religious segregation and 'reasonable differentiation', 227–28
  politics of democratic iterations, 223–25
  Preliminary counter-affidavit by the MHA, 233–36
    'indisputability of the power of Parliament', 232–33
    'legislative policy' and judicial scrutiny, 235–36
    'plenary domain of competent legislature', 235–36
  proliferation of, 215–16
  public conscience, 30–31, 207–8, 212–13, 240
  public interest petition, 235–36
  Shaheen Bagh, 210–11, 212–14, 215–17, 219–20, 221, 239
    Dhamma-Swaraj invocation, 215–16
    emotional citizenship and performance of affect, 214–16
    the sit-in, 214
    Supreme Court decisions
      'blockage of public way', 239
      dissent and democracy, 237–38
      'social interest', 237–39
      trope of motherhood, 214–15
  state assembly resolutions against, 222–27

INDEX

refugees
   and JPC, 85–86
   Long Term Visa (LTV), 83–85, 89
   rehabilitation of, 87
   Sodha community, 83–85
   SOP for citizenship certificates, 83–85
   SOP 2004 and 2011 and minority communities, 83–85
Registration Act of Transvaal 1906, 1–2
religious minorities, 21–22, 83, 122–23, 231–32, 234–35
religious persecution, 27–28, 50, 76–77, 83–86, 89–96, 122–24, 125, 136–38, 143–45, 148–49, 157–58, 228n.39, 231–32, 234–35
Resolution IV, jail going, 1–2

Sarbananda Sonowal case and judgement (2005), 16–18, 22–23, 37–38, 44–45, 47–48, 49, 56–57, 73–74, 76–77
   illegal migration
      act of aggression, 37–38, 47–48, 245
   and JPC, 159–60, 228–30, 245
   and state sovereignty, 22–23, 37–38
secularism
   basic structure of the Constitution, 228–30
   basis of republican citizenship, 14–15
   constitutional secularism, 137–38, 150–51
   constitutional value, 133
   debate on CAA, 109, 138–39, 159–60, 245
   democratic ideal, 14–15, 101
sovereignty
   parliamentary, 27–28, 117–18
   popular, 28, 69, 117–18, 129, 140–41, 205–6, 212–13
   state, 16–18, 37–38, 106, 243
   territorial, 10–11, 29–30, 163–66, 168–70
   'the people', 149–50
state
   as association of citizens, 106
   field of power, 4–5

governmental power, 69
   and legibility of citizens, 9–10, 29–30, 59–60, 244–45
   and policing activities, 12–13, 16–18, 59–60, 239, 240
   process of structuration, 5–6, 206–7
   structural effects of, 4–5, 59–60, 244–45
   tangible apparatus, 4–5
Supreme Court of India
   anti-CAA petitions, 227–28
   anti-CAA affidavit, Kerala, 222–23
   anti-CAA petitions, AASU and Assam Congress, 228–30
   anti-CAA petition by 'public servants', 231–33
   anti-CAA petitions, IUML, 227–28
   'legal dispute between the state and Centre', 222–23
   and Berubari Union, 169–70
   constitutional validity of rule 4A of Citizenship Rules 2003, 51
   constitutional validity of section 6A, 45–46, 50, 51–52, 63–64
   and the IMDT Act, 15–18
   modalities and schedule for updating the NRC, 26–27, 33–34, 37–38, 40–46, 47–50, 51–54, 56–57, 64–65, 76–78, 80, 245
   children of 'illegal migrants', 54–56
   gram panchayat certificate, 71–75
   'originally inhabitants' of Assam, 76
   ordinary people as rights-bearing citizens, 206–7
   preliminary counter-affidavit, MHA, 233–36
   section 144 Cr.PC, 216–17
   Shaheen Bagh sit-in, 219–20, 237–39
   state of West Bengal v. Anwar Ali Sarkar (1952) 123–26

'territorialized assemblage', 6–8
Transformative Constitutionalism, 11–12, 149–50, 211–13
   'affective appeal', 11–12
   democratic future, 211–12

Transformative Constitutionalism (*cont.*)
'magnificent goal of democracy', 11–12, 211–12, 249–50
notion of past and future, 10–12
Pius Langa, 'metaphor of a bridge', 11–12, 211–12, 249–50

South African Constitution, 211–12
sovereign people, 149–50

'urban street', 8–9, 26, 130–31, 223–25

'walls of separation', 27–28, 122

Lightning Source UK Ltd.
Milton Keynes UK
UKHW021002260822
407848UK00004B/373